OXFORD MEDIEVAL TEXTS

General Editors

C. N. L. BROOKE   D. E. GREENWAY

M. WINTERBOTTOM

THE LETTERS OF
LANFRANC
ARCHBISHOP OF
CANTERBURY

recedire delocif qub; psunt f; sup cathedra mossi sedere
scribe & pharisei· que dicunt facere· que aut faciunt facere
nolite; Et beat benedictus in regla monachor; preceptis inqt
abbatis in omnib; obedire· etia si ipse qd absit alr agat; De
monacho fulgure infecto· uir sapiens aptissima sententia
omne ambiguitatem nodu soluit dicens; Iustus qcuq; morte
p occupatus fuerit· anima ei in refrigerio erit; Deniq;
ecclia xpi alios mortuos a sua comunionis consortio non
repellit n eos tantu qb; uiuentib; canonica censura co-
municare contempsit; O mps dns uita uram custodiat·
qa multu utilis est in terra ad confutandas garrulor
in eptias;

Domino patri fri amico ans l peccator ppetua a do
salute; Quid in expediat beatitudo ura optime nouit
in anglor eni tra ueniens siue roma pficiscens omnia scata
ure reseruaui que reseranda esse tunc teporis p mearu
reru necessitate iudicaui; Sic g orate· sic ab amicis ac
familiarib; uris oratu in deposcere· quatin omps ds
aut ad meliore fructu me pducat· aut ergastulo hui
carnis anima mea in sui sci nominis confessione educat;
Tot eni tantisq; tribulationib; tra ista in qua sunt cotidie qrit· tot adulteriis aliisq; spurcitiis in quar ure

[marginal note:] queritur si ualde tribulatum ee·

MS. London B.L. Cotton Nero A. VII, f. 19ᵛ (N), showing letters 17–18:
actual size

THE LETTERS OF LANFRANC ARCHBISHOP OF CANTERBURY

EDITED AND TRANSLATED
BY

THE LATE HELEN CLOVER
Fellow of New Hall, Cambridge

AND

MARGARET GIBSON
*Senior Lecturer in Medieval History
the University of Liverpool*

OXFORD
AT THE CLARENDON PRESS
1979

Oxford University Press, Walton Street, Oxford OX2 6DP

OXFORD LONDON GLASGOW
NEW YORK TORONTO MELBOURNE WELLINGTON
KUALA LUMPUR SINGAPORE HONG KONG TOKYO
DELHI BOMBAY CALCUTTA MADRAS KARACHI
NAIROBI DAR ES SALAAM CAPE TOWN

Published in the United States by
Oxford University Press, New York

© *Oxford University Press 1979*

British Library Cataloguing in Publication Data
Lanfranc
    The letters of Lanfranc, Archbishop of
    Canterbury – (Oxford medieval texts)
    1. Lanfranc   2. Great Britain – History –
    William 1, 1066–1087 – Sources
    I. Title   II. Clover, Helen   III. Gibson,
    Margaret Templeton
    942.02′1   DA199.L2   78–40748
    ISBN 0–19–822235–1

Printed in Great Britain
at the University Press, Oxford
by Eric Buckley
Printer to the University

PREFACE

HELEN CLOVER presented a critical edition of Lanfranc's Letters, together with cognate material, in fulfilment of the degree of Ph.D. at Cambridge in 1961. At the time of her death the Latin text had been revised, with the punctuation modernized. In the present edition this text has been retained without substantial alteration; the *order* of the letters however is that of the two principal manuscripts (NV), and I have ventured to divide no. 33. The introduction, translation, and notes are mine.

I am indebted to many friends for information and advice, especially to Martin Brett, Christopher Brooke, Marjorie Chibnall, and Michael Winterbottom. Anthony Clover has taken a close interest in the preparation of the work and given every assistance. Above all I remember the excitement of arguing about Lanfranc with Helen Clover herself in the hospitable courts of New Hall. It is a grief to all of us that her work should have had to be finished by another hand.

MARGARET GIBSON

CONTENTS

ABBREVIATIONS

A.L.   *Acta Lanfranci* in *Two of the Saxon Chronicles Parallel*, ed. C. Plummer and J. Earle (Oxford, 1892–9), i. 287–92

Anselmi Epp.   *S. Anselmi Cantuariensis Archiepiscopi Opera Omnia* ii–v, ed. F. S. Schmitt (Edinburgh, 1946–51), cited by number

A.S. Chron.   *The Anglo-Saxon Chronicle*, ed. D. Whitelock et al. (London, 1961)

Barlow, *English Church*   F. Barlow, *The English Church 1000–1066* (London, 1963)

Bede, *H.E.*   *Bede's Ecclesiastical History of the English People*, ed. B. Colgrave and R. A. B. Mynors (O.M.T., 1969)

Brooke, *English Church*   Z. N. Brooke, *The English Church and the Papacy* (Cambridge, 1931)

C.C.S.L.   *Corpus Christianorum Series Latina* (Turnhout, 1954–)

Clover, 'Correspondence'   V. H. Clover, 'The Correspondence of Archbishop Lanfranc' (unpublished Ph.D. thesis: Cambridge, 1961)

Constitutions   *Decreta Lanfranci Monachis Cantuariensibus Transmissa*, ed. D. Knowles (revised edn., Siegburg, 1967: *Corpus Consuetudinum Monasticarum* iii; 1st edn., with English trans., N. M. T., 1959)

Councils and Synods   *Councils and Synods* i, ed. D. Whitelock, C. N. L. Brooke and M. Brett (Oxford, forthcoming)

Cowdrey, *Epistolae Vagantes*   *The Epistolae Vagantes of Pope Gregory VII*, ed. H. E. J. Cowdrey (O.M.T., 1972)

C.S.E.L.   *Corpus Scriptorum Ecclesiasticorum Latinorum* (Vienna, 1866–)

D'Achery   *Beati Lanfranci Opera Omnia*, ed. L. D'Achery (Paris, 1648)

Eadmer, *H.N.*   *Eadmeri Historia Novorum in Anglia*, ed. M. Rule (R.S., 1884)

E.H.R.   *English Historical Review*

Fauroux   *Recueil des actes des ducs de Normandie (911–1066)*, ed. M. Fauroux (Caen, 1961: Mémoires de la Société des Antiquaires de Normandie xxxvi)

Flor. Wig.   *Florentii Wigorniensis Monachi Chronicon ex Chronicis*, ed. B. Thorpe, 2 vols, English Historical Society (London, 1848–9)

Fulbert, *Letters*   *The Letters and Poems of Fulbert of Chartres*, ed. F. Behrends (O.M.T., 1976)

Gesta Pontificum   *Willelmi Malmesbiriensis de Gestis Pontificum*, ed. N. E. S. A. Hamilton (R.S., 1870)

Gesta Regum   *Willelmi Malmesbiriensis de Gestis Regum*, ed. W. Stubbs, 2 vols. (R.S., 1887–9)

Gibson   M. T. Gibson, *Lanfranc of Bec* (Oxford, 1978)

Giles   *Beati Lanfranci Archiepiscopi Cantuariensis opera quae supersunt omnia*, ed. J. A. Giles, 2 vols. (Oxford and Paris, 1844)

G.VII, *Reg.*   *Gregorii VII Registrum*, ed. E. Caspar, 2 vols. (Berlin, 1920–3: *MGH Epistolae Selectae* II. i–ii)

Hinschius   P. Hinschius, *Decretales Pseudo-Isidorianae* (Leipzig, 1863)

J.L.   P. Jaffé, *Regesta Pontificum Romanorum*, 2 edn., ed. G. Wattenbach, S. Loewenfeld, F. Kaltenbrunner, P. Ewald, 2 vols. (Leipzig, 1885–7)

Knowles, Brooke,   *The Heads of Religious Houses, England and Wales: 940–1216*, ed. D. Knowles, C. N. L. Brooke, V.C.M. London (Cambridge, 1972)
    London

L.D.C.S.D.   *Lanfranci Liber de Corpore et Sanguine Domini*, in D'Achery, pp. 230–51 (= *PL* cl. 407–42)

Lemarignier, *Privi-*   J.-F. Lemarignier, *Étude sur les privilèges d'exemption et de juridiction ecclésiastique des abbayes normandes depuis les origines jusqu'en 1140* (Paris, 1937: Archives de la France Monastique xliv)
    lèges

Le Neve/Greenway   *John Le Neve, 'Fasti Ecclesiae Anglicanae 1066–1300'*, ed. D. E. Greenway (London, 1968–)

London, B.L.   London, British Library

MGH   *Monumenta Germaniae Historica*

N.M.T.   Nelson's Medieval Texts (London–Edinburgh, 1950–65)

O.M.T.   Oxford Medieval Texts (Oxford, 1965–)

Orderic, *Hist.*   *The Ecclesiastical History of Orderic Vitalis*, books III–XIII, ed. M. M. Chibnall, vols. ii–vi (O.M.T., 1969–78)
    Eccles.

Paris, B.N.   Paris, Bibliothèque Nationale

PL   *Patrologiae cursus completus: series latina*, 221 vols., ed. J.-P. Migne (Paris, 1844–64)

PRG	*Le Pontifical Romano-Germanique du dixième siècle*, ed. C. Vogel and R. Elze, 2 vols. (Vatican, 1963: *Studi e Testi* 226–7)
Regesta	*Regesta Regum Anglo-Normannorum*, i, ed. H.W.C. Davis and R. J. Whitwell (Oxford, 1913)
Richter	M. Richter, *Canterbury Professions*, Canterbury and York Society lxvii (London, 1973)
R.S.	Rolls Series (Chronicles and Memorials etc.)
Schmitt	*S. Anselmi Cantuariensis Archiepiscopi Opera Omnia* 6 vols., ed. F. S. Schmitt (Edinburgh, 1946–61)
Southern, *Anselm*	R. W. Southern, *St Anselm and his Biographer* (Cambridge, 1963)
Southern, 'Canterbury Forgeries'	R. W. Southern, 'The Canterbury Forgeries', *E.H.R.* lxxiii (1958), 193–226
V.L.	*Vita Lanfranci*, in D'Achery, pp. 1–42 (= *PL* cl. 29–98)
Williams, *Codices*	S. Williams, *Codices Pseudo-Isidoriani*, Mon. Iur. Canon. ser. C, subsid. 3 (New York, 1971)

The reader is referred at all times to Knowles, Brooke, London for heads of houses, to Le Neve/Greenway for bishops and major cathedral dignitaries, and to F. M. Powicke and E. B. Fryde, *Handbook of British Chronology*, edn. 2 (London, 1961) for cathedrals not yet covered by Le Neve/Greenway.

MANUSCRIPTS CITED BY INITIALS

CONCORDANCES WITH EARLIER EDITIONS

THE present edition follows the order of NV. D'Achery (1648) revised the order, as did Giles (1844). Migne, *PL* cl (1854), followed D'Achery's order, appending the two missing letters (our nos. 50–1), which he found in Giles.

i. *Concordance of the present edition with D'Achery/PL and Giles*

The present edition	D'Achery/ PL	Giles	The present edition	D'Achery/ PL	Giles
1	1	3	32	40	46
2	2	4	33	41	47
3	—	—	34	34	37
4	3	5	35	35	38
5	5	7	36	25	28
6	6	8	37	58	64
7	—	9	38	8	11
8	—	40	39	7	10
9	37	43	40	24	27
10	38	44	41	17	20
11	—	—	42	19	22
12	11	14	43	21	24
13	12	15	44	18	21
14	13	16	45	26	29
15	16	19	46	50	56
16	14	17	47	23	26
17	15	18	48	57	63
18	43	49	49	33	36
19	47	53	50	61	41
20	45	51	51	62	42
21	46	52	52	59	65
22	42	48	53	32	35
23	10	13	54	56	62
24	22	25	55	55	61
25	30	33	56	54	60
26	9	12	57	53	59
27	29	32	58	52	58
28	49	55	59	31	34
29	28	31	60	51	57
30	27	30	61	48	54
31	39	45			

Additional letters in D'Achery's edition (his numbering):

4 Accepimus a quibusdam   J.L. 4761

20	Non minima ammiratione	J.L. 4803
36	Vestrae paternitati est cognitum	letter from the clergy and people of Dublin
44	Quotiens uobis	*Anselmi Epp.* 32
60	Indicatum est mihi	Spuria (see p. 185)
—	Mittimus uobis nostri ordinis	Lanfranc to Prior Henry (*Constitutions*, pp. 3–4)

D'Achery omits nos. 3, 7, 8, 11, 50, 51 (our numbering).

Giles adds (coincidence with D'Achery starred):

1	Peruenit ad me frater Lanfrance	Berengar to Lanfranc
2	Quia facile uobis factum esse	Berengar to Richard
*6	Accepimus a quibusdam	J.L. 4761
*23	Non minima ammiratione	J.L. 4803
*39	Vestrae paternitati est cognitum	letter from the clergy and people of Dublin
*50	Quotiens uobis	*Anselmi Epp.* 32
*66	Indicatum est mihi	Spuria
67	Concedimus et presentis carte pagina confirmamus	Spuria (see p. 185)
*—	Mittimus uobis nostri ordinis	Lanfranc to Prior Henry

Giles omits 3, 11 (our numbering).

PL adds *4, *20, *36, *44, *60, *Mittimus uobis nostri ordinis, 63 (= Giles 67).

PL omits 3, 7, 8, 11. Nos. 7 and 8 are printed among the letters of Alexander II (*PL* cxlvi. 1365B–6B: no. 7) and Gregory VII (*PL* cxlviii. 643B–4C: no. 8).

ii. *Concordance of D'Achery/PL with the present edition.*

D'Achery/*PL*	The present edition	D'Achery/*PL*	The present edition
1	1	16	15
2	2	17	41
3	4	18	44
4	omitted	19	42
5	5	20	omitted
6	6	21	43
7	39	22	24
8	38	23	47
9	26	24	40
10	23	25	36
11	12	26	45
12	13	27	30
13	14	28	29
14	16	29	27
15	17	30	25

D'Achery/*PL*	The present edition	D'Achery/*PL*	The present edition
31	59	48	61
32	53	49	28
33	49	50	46
34	34	51	60
35	35	52	58
36	omitted	53	57
37	9	54	56
38	10	55	55
39	31	56	54
40	32	57	48
41	33	58	37
42	22	59	52
43	18	60	omitted
44	omitted	61 (*PL* only)	50
45	20	62 (*PL* only)	51
46	21	63 (*PL* only)	omitted
47	19		

iii. *Concordance of Giles with the present edition*

Giles	The present edition	Giles	The present edition
1	omitted	24	43
2	omitted	25	24
3	1	26	47
4	2	27	40
5	4	28	36
6	omitted	29	45
7	5	30	30
8	6	31	29
9	7	32	27
10	39	33	25
11	38	34	59
12	26	35	53
13	23	36	49
14	12	37	34
15	13	38	35
16	14	39	omitted
17	16	40	8
18	17	41	50
19	15	42	51
20	41	43	9
21	44	44	10
22	42	45	31
23	omitted	46	32

Giles	The present edition	Giles	The present edition
47	33	58	58
48	22	59	57
49	18	60	56
50	omitted	61	55
51	20	62	54
52	21	63	48
53	19	64	37
54	61	65	52
55	28	66	omitted
56	46	67	omitted
57	60		

INTRODUCTION

I. ARCHBISHOP LANFRANC: 1070–89

I pleaded that the language was unknown to me and the native races barbarous, but to no avail . . . I accepted the appointment, I arrived, I took office. Now I endure so many troubles and vexations every day—such hardness of heart, greed and dishonesty—that 'I am weary of my life'.[1]

LANFRANC's initial assessment of England was less than enthusiastic. Be it on your conscience, he wrote to Alexander II, if you do not release me from an office in which I achieve nothing for others and only spiritual deprivation for myself.[2] In due course he accepted his fate,[3] but he remained an alien. This was Lanfranc's strength. Like Theodore of Tarsus (whose career he had studied in Bede) he was the outsider; and like him too he was 'the first archbishop whom the whole English Church consented to obey'.[4]

i. *The chronology of Lanfranc's life*[5]

Lanfranc was born in Pavia *c.* 1010 and educated in northern Italy. After ten or fifteen years spent as an itinerant master there and in France, he came to Normandy where, it is said, he taught in Avranches and where *c.* 1042 he entered the newly founded ascetic community of Bec (dioc. Rouen). By *c.* 1045 he was prior and by the later 1050s he had returned to teaching; for a few years Bec had one of the outstanding schools in northern Europe. Lanfranc's students included both Norman aristocrats and men from further afield, notably St. Anselm, who was to succeed him as prior of Bec. In 1063 William the Conqueror made Lanfranc abbot of his new foundation of S. Étienne, Caen. There, or possibly in his last years at Bec, he wrote in defence of the eucharistic confession imposed by Nicholas II on Berengar of Tours; this

---

[1] No. 1, lines 19–27.

[2] Ibid., lines 53–5.

[3] Cf. the phrase in his letter to the bishop of Munster: 'neque transmarinas ecclesias neque *nos* Anglos' (no. 49, lines 13–14).

[4] Bede, *H.E.* iv. 2, p. 332; cf. no. 4, lines 26–42.

[5] See further Gibson, cap. 1–5.

Liber de corpore et sanguine Domini was the work that established Lanfranc's reputation as a theologian.[1] In 1070 William the Conqueror transferred him, in due form and with papal approval, to the see of Canterbury. Lanfranc did homage to the king on 15 August; he was consecrated on 29 August (the date from which the years of his archiepiscopate are reckoned);[2] he died in office on 28 May 1089.

Lanfranc was well over fifty when he came to England. His knowledge of the higher reaches of ecclesiastical government was limited to seven years at S. Étienne, Caen; but he had previously acquired a solid and varied scholarly expertise, and as prior of Bec he had thought through the principles of monasticism and helped to raise money for a struggling community. Even the prose style of Lanfranc's surviving letters, which were all written in England, reflects his long experience elsewhere: as a recent study has shown, his use of the 'cursus' follows the practice of northern Italy in the later tenth century.[3] As archbishop, Lanfranc was drawing on the resources of a lifetime. His letters concern a few great issues and many small cases of an abbot here or a deacon there, but essentially they relate to either the business of the realm or the internal affairs of the English Church.

ii. *The business of the realm*

Half the letter-collection (nos. 1–17: N, ff. 1–19ᵛ) shows Lanfranc acting as archbishop in the province of Canterbury and— rather more tentatively—as primate of the British Isles. It was he who maintained contact with Rome and acted as Alexander II's representative in England; in contrast with the flurry of papal legates in the months before his arrival, subsequent papal business was conducted by Lanfranc himself.[4] He asked for authorization to replace two bishops: Hermann of Sherborne, who wished to retire (although in the event he stayed on) and Leofwine of Lichfield, who had been deposed.[5] The pope in turn delegated

---

[1] *PL* cl. 407A–42D; cf. Gibson, cap. 4.

[2] See Appendix C.

[3] T. Janson, *Prose Rhythm in Medieval Latin from the ninth to the thirteenth century* (*Studia Latina Stockholmiensia* xx, Stockholm, 1975) p. 42, cf. p. 109.

[4] The only papal legate to visit England after Lanfranc's consecration was Hubert the subdeacon, who took part in the primatial settlement of 1072: no. 3, lines 136–8. He returned in 1080: nos. 38–9.

[5] No. 2.

similar questions to Lanfranc. Archbishop Thomas's claims to primacy and to jurisdiction over the border sees of Worcester, Lichfield and Dorchester were referred to an English council, for which Lanfranc prepared the ground and on which he sent Alexander a detailed report.[1] Again Lanfranc was directed to inquire into the deposition of Ailric of Chichester.[2] Such exchanges continued under Gregory VII, though sporadically. Lanfranc was obliquely involved in two appeals to Rome: a claim against Archbishop Manasses of Rheims and a dispute between Bishop Stigand of Chichester and an unnamed woman in his diocese.[3] But as early as 1075 the transfer of three episcopal sees was effected by a provincial council on the authority of the king and canon law, without reference to the pope;[4] and five years later, when Gregory VII demanded fealty from the king and the payment of Peter's Pence, disengagement had gone further still. 'Were I to have the opportunity to discuss the matter,' Lanfranc wrote, 'I might show that it is your cordiality that has grown cold rather than my devotion.'[5] It was not a moment for Gregory to be losing friends, for he seems to have dispatched the letters to which nos. 38–9 are the reply in the weeks between the definitive excommunication of Henry IV and the election of Clement III as antipope.[6] The final stage of papal relations is reached in Lanfranc's temporizing reply to an emissary of Clement III himself.[7] The tone is chill, yet a reply is indeed being sent: communication is to be kept open with both sides.

Lanfranc's title of 'primate of Britain'[8] was the ecclesiastical

[1] See no. 3 (circumstances and text of the council); no. 7, p. 63 n. 8 (preparatory discussion of a territorial dispute between York and Dorchester); no. 4 (report to Alexander II).

[2] No. 7.

[3] Nos. 25 (Rheims) and 29 (Chichester).

[4] No. 11, *can.* iii. The transfer of the see of Crediton to Exeter twenty years before had been expressly authorized by Leo IX (J.L. 4208).

[5] No. 38, lines 17–20.

[6] Henry IV was excommunicated at the Easter synod of 1080 (7 Mar.: G.VII, *Reg.* vii. 14a). Gregory refers to Hubert's legation in his letter of 24 April to William the Conqueror (ibid., vii. 23). Two months later Gregory himself was deposed by the synod of Brixen (25 June: *MGH Leges* IV. i. 118–19); cf. Ekkehard of Aura, *Chronicon Vniversale* s.a. 1080 (*MGH Scriptores* vi. 203–4).

[7] No. 52.

[8] The most convincing evidence for the currency of this and similar titles is to be found in the professions of obedience made by bishops of the province of Canterbury: Richter, nos. 35–41, 44, 46–7; cf. Gibson, p. 121. Within the letter-collection see William the Conqueror's writ of 1072 (no. 3, line 109)

complement of William the Conqueror's dominion over the British Isles; still further afield Canterbury had historic links with the kings of Dublin, which again William or his successors might exploit. In 1074 Lanfranc commended Bishop Patrick to Guthric of Dublin and to his overlord, Toirrdelbach Ua Briain (nos. 9–10); six or seven years later he was writing to Domnall Ua h-Énna, bishop of Munster, 'as a father to his beloved son' (no. 49). But the practical implication of Lanfranc's primacy was jurisdiction over York. The letter-collection includes all the documents of his archiepiscopate that are relevant to this issue: the Canterbury version of Lanfranc's dispute with Archbishop Thomas and its resolution (no. 3), the crucial royal writ of Easter 1072 (no. 3, lines 97–138), Thomas's profession of obedience (no. 3, lines 83–96) and Lanfranc's report to Alexander II, in which he asked that the royal judgement be confirmed in a papal privilege (no. 4). Although such confirmation was never secured, Gregory VII wrote one letter (no. 8) that might imply Lanfranc's jurisdiction over Ireland, a jurisdiction that could only be primatial. Again, the council of London, 1075 (no. 11), in clarifying the order in which the senior bishops should be seated in council, reinforced the precedence of Canterbury over York. All this material might well assist some future archbishop to assert his primacy; ancient privileges were substantiated by recent practice.[1]

Archbishop Thomas himself remained on good terms with Lanfranc, in spite of all he had lost by the settlement of 1072. Having studied under Lanfranc in Normandy,[2] he looked to him now for guidance and support in a position that was even more isolated than Lanfranc's own: the church of York appeals to you, he wrote, from her outpost among a barbarous people.[3] Thomas had only one effective suffragan, Durham, for whose consecration,

and Lanfranc's somewhat curious language to Herfast of Thetford, a bishop of his own province: 'Nec sobrius quisque putauerit hoc esse in aliena parrochia aliquid temere presumere, cum per misericordiam Dei totam hanc quam uocant Britannicam insulam unam unius nostrae aecclesiae constet esse parrochiam' (no. 47, lines 41–4; cf. Gibson, pp. 148–50).

[1] The primatial controversy was renewed briefly in 1086 and at Anselm's consecration, but it did not become a major political issue until the reign of Henry I. See further Southern, 'Canterbury Forgeries', pp. 206–8 et passim.

[2] Hugh the Chanter, *History of the Church of York 1066–1127* s.a. 1070, ed. C. Johnson (N.M.T., 1961), p. 2.

[3] No. 12, lines 6–11.

as for his own, he had to travel south.[1] But he did in one instance act as metropolitan in his own city. When Earl Paul of the Orkneys sent him a bishop for consecration, Thomas performed the ceremony in York itself, with the help of two of Lanfranc's suffragans, who were sent north for the purpose.[2] Bishop Ralph's jurisdiction no doubt coincided with that of his patron, Earl Paul. Twenty years later, when the Isles were divided between Paul's son, Hákon, and his nephew, Magnus,[3] we may assume that each area had its own bishop. Hákon's bishop was presumably of the line that recognised the metropolitan authority of York. Magnus's first known bishop was William 'the Elder', who had his see at Birsay on the north-west coast of the main island and then moved to Kirkwall;[4] he recognized Nidaros (Trondheim) as his metropolitan see. It was William's line that became established as the sole bishops of Orkney,[5] and his eleventh-century predecessors were forgotten. But that is history as seen from Kirkwall.

Lanfranc's fundamental virtue in public life was an unquestioned loyalty to William the Conqueror and a readiness to commend such loyalty to wavering magnates. The reiterated 'fidelis', which forces itself on the attention in no. 34—'Domino suo Anglorum regi Willelmo fidelis suus Lanfrancus fidele seruitium et fideles orationes'—is a continuing undertone throughout the letters on the crisis of 1075 (nos. 31–5). William fitzOsbern 'fideliter domino

---

[1] William of St. Carilef was consecrated in Gloucester (3 Jan. 1081) by Archbishop Thomas with the assistance of the bishops of Worcester, Exeter, Wells, and Hereford, 'Lanfranco praecipiente': A.L., pp. 289–90; cf. Appendix C ad loc.

[2] Nos. 12–13.

[3] *Orkneyinga Saga* xxxiv–xxxv, trans. A. B. Taylor (Edinburgh, 1938), pp. 192–3.

[4] Ibid., cap. lii, p. 213; cf. D. E. R. Watt, *Fasti Ecclesiae Scoticanae Medii Aevi ad annum 1638*, edn. 2 (*Scottish Record Society* N.S. i, Edinburgh, 1969), pp. 248–9.

[5] William was bishop *c.* 1112–1168. He is called 'first bishop' of the Orkneys in *Orkneyinga Saga* lii, ed. cit., p. 213: i.e. in the late twelfth century or the early thirteenth. The title is corroborated by the incised lead plate found when his tomb in Kirkwall was opened in 1848. It reads (obverse) 'Hic requiescit Wiliamus Senex felicis memorie' and (reverse) 'Primus episcopus'. This inscription must date either from William's burial in 1168 or from his reinterment when the choir of Kirkwall cathedral was extended in the mid thirteenth century. On palaeographical grounds the later date is more likely; obverse and reverse may be in the same hand—it is difficult to be certain. See further J. Mooney, 'Notes on discoveries in St Magnus cathedral, Kirkwall', *Proceedings of the Society of Antiquaries of Scotland* lix (1925), 243, with references.

suo seruiuit' (no. 31 and cf. no. 32); his son must be an 'exemplum fidelitatis' (no. 32); even the monk bringing Lanfranc's letter to the king 'fidelitatem michi fecit' (no. 34). It is a new use for an old stylistic conceit. These letters are the only absolutely contemporary record of the revolt,[1] and they do indeed show Lanfranc as 'guardian of England'.[2] But 1075 was an exceptional year. Lanfranc's normal role was not as one of the great magnates continually at court, a 'primas Angliae' such as Geoffrey of Coutances,[3] but as an advisor in the background. He was one of the few men whom William the Conqueror trusted, and for whom he seems even to have shown personal solicitude.[4] So Lanfranc could negotiate on behalf of his colleagues and occasionally put in a word at the right moment.[5] Not that he invariably prevailed: his advice that the rebel earls should throw themselves on the king's mercy led to the life-imprisonment of Roger and the execution of Waltheof.[6] Yet Lanfranc could have proposed no other course of action; his own words to Abbot G. apply to all his participation in affairs of state: 'contra preceptum regis nil rogare et nil iubere praesumo.'[7]

iii. *The English Church*

The letter-collection includes two of Lanfranc's councils: the primacy agreement of 1072 (no. 3) and the council of London, 1075 (no. 11). The former is as much a royal council as an ecclesiastical, but in the latter the higher clergy of England are acting on their own in the king's absence overseas. They are concerned with diocesan organization and pastoral care: the discipline of the clergy, the marriage customs of the laity, and good order within

---

[1] *A.S. Chron.* DE 1075 may have been written in the same year, but nos. 31–6 are part of the very sequence of events.

[2] 'Quando gloriosus rex Willelmus morabatur in Normannia, Lanfrancus erat princeps et custos Angliae, subiectis sibi omnibus principibus et iuuantibus in his quae ad defensionem et dispositionem uel pacem pertinebant regni, secundum leges patriae': V.L., cap. 15 (*PL* cl. 55B).

[3] Cf. no. 11, lines 9–11.

[4] No. 44.

[5] Lanfranc speaks for example on behalf of Archbishop John (no. 16, lines 22–3: concerning the S. Ouen riot), Bishop Remigius (no. 37: perhaps concerning the revolt of 1075), Hugh, bishop-elect of London (no. 41: concerning his lands) and Abbot Thurstan (no. 57: to mitigate the king's displeasure).

[6] No. 33; cf. *Flor. Wig.* ii. 12 and *Gesta Regum* iii. 255.

[7] No. 58.

the monasteries—which the Conquest had put under greater stress than any other part of the English Church. These are issues that recur throughout Lanfranc's letters. He gives directives and offers advice: that Bishop Herfast should show him a proper obedience as metropolitan (no. 47); that Archbishop Thomas should enforce the canonical prohibition of divorce and remarriage (no. 23); that the bishop of London should endeavour to calm the public dispute between the abbess and the prioress of Barking (no. 59); that a monk who has been killed by lightning (and so died without absolution) is not thereby cut off from the Church (no. 17). In the letter to Herfast Lanfranc quotes canon law, which he could find in his own abridged Pseudo-Isidore.[1] But that is the exception; normally he had to reach his decision without the support of specific texts.[2] His rulings were a compromise between Pseudo-Isidore and new situations that were not quite covered by the available written texts. Like any metropolitan in the era before the *Decretum* Lanfranc was the final court of legal appeal and the source of new law.[3] He could also initiate new procedure. Here his letters on the 1075 revolt are doubly illuminating. The first letter to Roger of Hereford (no. 31) includes the proposal that the earl come in person to discuss the matters in dispute; in the second (no. 32) the invitation is repeated more urgently: Lanfranc will come to any meeting-place that Roger chooses to name. In the third (no. 33A) Roger is excommunicated, not for offences committed but for his failure to answer the summons made 'legatis . . . et litteris semel et iterum'.[4] Clearly ecclesiastical censure is being used here to restrain Roger from a feudal misdemeanour; yet the grounds of his excommunication are technically correct. Lanfranc achieves a similar balance in defining the authority of the council of Winchester: it derives from Alexander II's injunction to the two archbishops and from the feudal duty of 'counsel' that both lay and clerical members owe to the king.[5] Even canon law naturally ministers to the king's needs,

---

[1] No. 47: see further Brooke, *English Church*, pp. 68–9.

[2] See for instance no. 23, lines 24–7; no. 40, lines 7–11; no. 43, lines 5–16.

[3] Fulbert of Chartres had a similar role half a century before: Fulbert, *Letters, passim*; cf. p. 13 below. Several of Lanfranc's own letters survive in association with collections of canon law: see MSS CcCdCpHLcLz, pp. 17–19 below. For advice on legal procedure at this time I am greatly indebted to Professor Colin Morris.

[4] No. 33, lines 9–13; cf. also no. 2, lines 34–5.   [5] No. 4, lines 20–4.

as the king himself must offer to God the gift of good laws and equitable judgement.[1]

Lanfranc's only sustained correspondence with a colleague is the four letters to Archbishop John of Rouen (nos. 14–17) and the fifth (no. 41) that follows some years later. They illustrate the common anxieties of archbishops. The archdeacon was an official of growing importance, whose role was in certain respects still undefined.[2] Thus the liturgical minutiae of the vestments appropriate to a subdeacon (no. 14) concern not only the status of the subdeacon himself but also the part played by the archdeacon in conferring his orders. In what ways could the archdeacon act on behalf of his bishop? Did he for instance control a particular area within a diocese? If so, should he hold that land by an oath of fealty?[3] Again it was essential that the subdeacon's vestments should in no way imply that he could celebrate Mass; for subdeacons were still permitted to marry. Lanfranc's determination to enforce clerical celibacy is evident time and again: the priest who is doing penance for manslaughter may have his priestly functions restored if he performs his penance wholeheartedly, 'and above all if he observes physical chastity and will promise to do so until the end of his life';[4] the diaconate and the priesthood may be conferred only on men willing to promise celibacy, and in the restoration of suspended orders the same applies.[5] On the issue of celibacy Archbishop John provoked a violent reaction from his clergy which Lanfranc was apparently able to avoid;[6] what neither archbishop could escape was a violent confrontation with his local monastery. John's efforts to assert his diocesan rights over S. Ouen, which have Lanfranc's ready

---

[1] See notably no. 10, lines 4–17, 35–48.

[2] On the subject as a whole see M. Brett, *The English Church under Henry I* (Oxford, 1975), pp. 199–211, with references. Lanfranc's own archdeacon, Ansketil, is among the witnesses to the council of London, 1075 (no. 11, p. 79 n. 16). Where diocesan synods were held (e.g. nos. 30, 43, 45), the archdeacon would play a significant part.

[3] For an archdeaconry held (by a layman) 'in feodo' from the archbishop of Rouen see Orderic, *Hist Eccles.* ii. 152, 153 n., with references. It may well be that the 'fides' professed by the archdeacons to the bishops of Bayeux and Coutances (no. 41, lines 40–4) is a feudal oath of this kind; see alternatively no. 41, p. 137 n. 6.

[4] No. 51, lines 14–16.

[5] No. 43; cf. no. 19, line 12: 'parentes, possessiones, carnalia oblectamenta', in ascending order of renunciation.

[6] Orderic, *Hist. Eccles.* ii. 200–1 (council of Rouen, 1072).

approval (nos. 16–17), are matched by Lanfranc's equally unhappy attempt to impose the abbot of his choice on St. Augustine's,
Canterbury.[1] S. Étienne, Caen had been exempt from within a
few years of its foundation; but now that Lanfranc was himself a
diocesan, he saw episcopal jurisdiction as far more important than
monastic autonomy.[2]

The monastic virtues that Lanfranc valued, and which he tried
to promote within his province, did not require legal independence.
'I am sending you,' he wrote to prior Henry, 'the customs of our
order' (App. B); Lanfranc's nephew is directed as his first duty at
Bec to gain a thorough knowledge of his order (no. 18); again in the
same phrase Abbot Odo of Chertsey is urged to live up to his
monastic profession (no. 48). In all these cases, and in others
throughout the collection, 'noster ordo' is the way of life accepted
(or believed to have been accepted) by monks *semper ubique*:
the norm of stability, austerity of life and regular worship to
which any monk might reasonably be recalled.[3] Where a community
was failing in these respects, the local bishop had a duty to intervene; conversely a house could appeal directly to Canterbury.[4]
The latter part of the collection (nos. 42–61) contains a number of
such letters—fragments of negotiations for which no other scrap
of evidence survives. The extreme example is no. 60, to Abbot
T.; among the most interesting is the letter to Abbot Riwallon
(no. 55), concerning a monk whom Lanfranc had been ill-advised
in sending to New Minster, as he now freely admits.

Throughout his letters Lanfranc appears as the defender of the
rights of Canterbury, the canonist giving advice, the archbishop
imposing discipline on the English Church. In all this he had the
approval, and even the practical support, of his community at

---

[1] A.L., pp. 290–2: cf. Appendix C.
[2] S. Étienne received an exemption privilege from Alexander II in 1068
(J. L. 4644). Three years later Bury St. Edmunds obtained a similar exemption
from the jurisdiction of the bishop of Elmham/Thetford (J.L. 4692); but
although Lanfranc's personal sympathy lay with Abbot Baldwin, he never
countenanced the use of that privilege against the bishop. See Gibson,
pp. 148–50, with references.
[3] Lanfranc uses the same term of the parish clergy in the discharge of their
duties (no. 30, line 20) and again, most strikingly, when he deplores the social
and political ills of England: 'nullus fere hominum ordo sit qui uel animae
suae consulat, uel proficiendi in Deum salutarem doctrinam saltem audire
concupiscat' (no. 18, lines 11–13).
[4] See no. 27 (Coventry) and perhaps also no. 59 (Barking).

Christ Church; yet it is clear that as a monk he relied primarily on the men whom he had known for so long at Bec. He writes to Anselm in the style that they both knew;[1] he rebukes his nephew Lanfranc in accents that we now regard as typically Anselmian: 'the more dearly I love a friend, the greater my anger against him for even a trivial fault' (no. 19). In Canterbury he was trapped by affairs of state;[2] Bec was home. 'Take my advice,' he wrote to William Bona Anima, his successor as abbot of S. Étienne, Caen, 'if you think it sound. But if you are in any doubt . . . act according to the advice given you by the lord abbot Herluin and Dom Anselm. For I am a sinful man who has no understanding of God's counsel, whereas both of them are, we believe, filled with the Holy Spirit, and have men with them to give support in such matters by their prayers to God.'[3]

II. THE LETTER-COLLECTION

i. *The structure of the collection*

Lanfranc's surviving letters (with the exception of the letter to Prior Henry that prefaces the *Constitutions*)[4] are all contained in a single collection consisting of sixty-one items: fifty-nine letters (nos. 1–2, 4–10, 12–61), a memorandum on the primacy of Canterbury (no. 3), and the *acta* of the council of London, 1075 (no. 11). All these items date from Lanfranc's archiepiscopate (1070–89); all the letters except nos. 6, 8 and 12 are of his own composition: he no doubt scrutinized, and could well be responsible for, nos. 3 and 11 as well. Of the letters that Lanfranc received a few are included (nos. 6, 8, 12), but most are not: these 'epistolae vagantes' are listed in Appendix B. Although neither of the principal manuscripts now surviving was written in Canterbury, the collection so combines archiepiscopal business with Lanfranc's private correspondence as to make it clear that the materials originated in Christ Church, wherever they may have been assembled. So much is clear. But other questions are still open to

[1] No. 18, p. 97 n. 5.
[2] See for instance his opening words to Reginald of Poitiers: 'ego tot tantisque huius mundi negotiis obuolutus sum' (no. 46, lines 7–8).
[3] No. 61, lines 14–20.
[4] *Constitutions*, pp. 3–4.

debate. When and by whom was the collection compiled? On what principle (if any) was it arranged?

The oldest manuscript (N) was written c. 1100.[1] Evidence that the collection was in existence in the late eleventh century is provided by the *Acta Lanfranci*, the memorandum of archiepiscopal business written at Christ Church c. 1090. The chronology of these *Acta* is in the main accurate, but the consecration of Ralph, bishop of the Orkneys, has been displaced from 1073 to 1077; this error no doubt derives from the letter-collection, in which the 1075 council (no. 11) precedes the Orkney letters (nos. 12–13).[2] Another pointer is the letter to the envoy of Clement III (no. 52), a document highly relevant in 1092–3 and of no interest thereafter. All these considerations suggest that the collection as we have it was in existence by 1100, at the very latest. A much earlier date is implied by the suggestion that the collection is in some sense a register: throughout his archiepiscopate, Lanfranc entered up copies of his correspondence in a single book. This position is fatally undermined by the dating of individual letters; the collection is not in chronological order. The same objection applies to a selective register (omitting most of the papal correspondence); but the argument may be restated in terms of an unbound register (in which the order is liable to be disturbed) or of a collection based on a register (rather than the register itself). There is the further difficulty that the only known contemporary registers are papal. Certainly the lack of material at provincial level does not prove that archiepiscopal registers never existed; papal registers of the time would look slight indeed if some careless official had mislaid *Registrum Vaticanum 2*. Nevertheless on internal evidence papal letters manifestly emanate from an organized chancery, as episcopal letters of the period do not. Here Lanfranc is no exception: his letters do not imply a systematic secretariat such as Christ Church eventually acquired under Archbishop Theobald (1139–61).[3] Again it is noticeable that in the

---

[1] See below, p. 16.

[2] A.L., p. 289. Exactly the same mistake (1077 for 1073) is made in V.L., cap. 13.

[3] A. Saltman, *Theobald, Archbishop of Canterbury* (London, 1956), pp. 181–534. The number and regularity of Theobald's charters is in sharp contrast to the handful of documents surviving from even his immediate predecessor, William of Corbeil: C. R. Cheney, *English Bishops' Chanceries 1100–1250* (Manchester, 1950), pp. 52–4 *et passim*.

manuscript tradition few items in the letter-collection are associated
with documentary material from Christ Church: *Domesday Monachorum*, charters, episcopal professions, forged privileges. In short,
it may be well to abandon the hypothesis of a formal Register.
We are then free to assume that the collection was assembled
after most of the letters had been written; so the *terminus a quo* is
moved to *c.* 1086.[1]

It may be thought that Lanfranc chose, arranged and perhaps
polished his own letters, as Anselm did in 1092–3. But Anselm saw
himself as an author, while Lanfranc (although he must have
known that he wrote good Latin) cultivated anonymity on principle. On the other hand, just as it was probably Lanfranc who
collected the administrative documents that now survive as
Domesday Monachorum, so he might have preserved his letters as
evidence of the rights of Canterbury on a wider stage. But only the
first half of the collection (nos. 1–17) can be called 'primatial':
the 'monastic' letters (nos. 18–21, 61), the lengthy memoranda on
the Eucharist (nos. 46, 49) and a number of others are very marginal to the rights of Canterbury, however interpreted. What is
more, no one at Christ Church did subsequently see the collection
as useful in practical politics. The relevant letters were quoted,
the collection as a whole was ignored.[2] As there is no external
evidence (for example in the historical notices of Eadmer or
Sigebert of Gembloux) that Lanfranc collected his own letters,
we should perhaps not assume an activity that would have been
uncharacteristic, though not of course impossible. We thus reach
the interregnum after Lanfranc's death: 1089–93. It is in these
years that the community at Christ Church, possibly led by
Osbern the precentor, might be expected to review Lanfranc's
work and preserve his literary remains. Another line of thought,
and an attractive one, is suggested by the link with Anselm's
letters in the earliest manuscript (N). When Anselm made that
collection, he was staying with Gilbert Crispin[3]; and it is likely

[1] Lanfranc's letter concerning the Domesday Inquest (no. 56) is the latest
that can be dated precisely.
[2] The makers of the privilege-register at Christ Church (Le), who searched
very diligently for their material, used nos. 3, 4, 7, 11 and no others. Eadmer
quotes the one letter (no. 30) that relates to the archbishop's spiritual jurisdiction in south-east England.
[3] R. W. Southern, 'St. Anselm and Gilbert Crispin, Abbot of Westminster',
Mediaeval and Renaissance Studies iii (1954), 87–8.

enough that the search for Anselm's letters at the same time drew attention to Lanfranc's. On that hypothesis a possible compiler of our letter-collection is someone in Anselm's personal circle rather than within the community at Canterbury. One name that comes to mind is Bishop Gundulf of Rochester, Lanfranc's old lieutenant in S. Étienne and Christ Church.

Finally, how was the collection arranged? As a literary form the letter-collection in this period ranges from the copy-book models of the cathedral schools to the personal letters of Anselm and the mixture of politics, diocesan business, and letters of friendship in the correspondence of Fulbert of Chartres.[1] Among these varying types it is the collection of Fulbert's letters that offers the obvious precedent for Lanfranc's, a precedent which the compiler may well have recognized.[2] Now in the case of Fulbert it can be shown that the letters were originally preserved in fairly small groups.[3] When the collection was copied out formally, the order of the groups might be changed, but within each group the order of individual letters remained intact. This phenomenon reflects the physical state of the letters in Fulbert's time: originally each group filled a separate bifolium or even a single leaf. Such loose schedules of material were likely to be in chronological order internally; but externally they had little chance of being so. If the principles exemplified in Fulbert's letter-collection are applied to Lanfranc's, the overall pattern is as follows:

PAPAL AND PRIMATIAL

These seventeen letters account for half the total bulk of the collection (ff. 1–19^v).

nos. 1–8	papal correspondence; primacy	1071–5
9–10	Irish kings	1073–4
11	council of London	1075
12–13	Orkney bishopric	1072–3
14–17	John, archbishop of Rouen	1070–7

[1] For eleventh-century letter-collections see C. Erdmann, *Studien zur Briefliteratur Deutschlands im elften Jahrhundert* (Leipzig, 1938: *MGH Schriften* i) and for the genre as a whole G. Constable, 'Letters and letter-collections', in *Typologie des Sources du Moyen Âge Occidental*, fasc. 17 A. ii, ed. L. Genicot (Turnhout, 1976).

[2] A considerable collection of Fulbert's letters was available in Bec by the mid twelfth century and smaller groups circulated in England: see for instance HLz below.

[3] Fulbert, *Letters*, pp. xlii–lx.

PERSONAL

no.	55	Riwallon, abbot of New Minster	1082–8
	56	S.	1086

ENGLISH MONASTIC AFFAIRS

no.	57	Abbot Thurstan	1070–3 or 1083
	58	Abbot G.	1070–89
	59	Maurice, bishop of London	1086–9
	60	Abbot T.	1070–89

BEC/CAEN

no.	61	William, abbot of S. Étienne, Caen	?1070

As in Fulbert's case there are anomalies; but it is certainly easier to distinguish small coherent groups (e.g. nos. 31–9) than to establish a convincing chronological sequence (or any other principle of organization) for the collection as a whole. Wherever the truth lies, it is right to preserve the manuscript order of the collection; astonishingly, this is the first edition to do so.

ii. *The manuscripts*

THE ENGLISH TRADITION

The fundamental manuscript for the whole collection is London B.L. Cotton Nero A. VII, ff. 1–39ᵛ (N). Given its association with the first collection of Anselm's letters and its textual agreement with the conciliar documents from Canterbury (Cantaβ and J) and the minor English manuscripts described below, we may reasonably assert that N itself was transcribed in England, though not necessarily in Canterbury.[1] Further, if we think that the Anselm collection (Nero A. VII, ff. 41–112ᵛ) was copied directly from unbound letters that Anselm assembled for the purpose, then it may well be proposed that the history of the Lanfranc collection is parallel: N is a direct transcript of the comparable *schedulae* that have just been postulated. We may if we wish insert a lost exemplar, but there is no logical or textual necessity

---

[1] Southern, *Anselm*, pp. 67–8. The only manuscript of Lanfranc's letters that is recorded at Christ Church cannot be identified with N, but a manuscript very similar to N had reached Rochester by *c.* 1120: see pp. 21–2 below.

to do so. The other English manuscripts contain either single letters or small groups incorporated in other material; with the possible exception of Lv, they do not point to other manuscripts, now lost, of the collection as a whole.

N *London, B.L., Cotton Nero A. VII ff. 1–39^v*   *c.* 1100: English

The book now contains three separate manuscripts, that were probably bound together for Sir Robert Cotton. We are concerned only with the first: ff. 1–112^v (quires i–xiv). This in turn is in two parts, whose alliance is much older. The first (ff. 1–40^v: quires i–v) contains Lanfranc's letters, followed (f. 40) by his epitaph, *Hic tumulus claudit . . .*[1] and (f. 40^v, in another hand) by miscellaneous recipes. The second (ff. 41–112^v: quires vi–xiv), which is in a similar format and script, contains the earliest collection of Anselm's letters.[2] In both parts the text is in long lines, ruled with a stylus; the first part measures 116 × 152 mm. (page), 90 × 122 mm. (text), 22 lines per page. The text opens with a small red capital touched with yellow, green and silver; subsequent initials are red, touched occasionally with green or silver: they are always very simple. In the early seventeenth century N reached the Cottonian library; in the eighteenth it passed to the King's Library and thence to the British Museum, where in the nineteenth century it was rebound.

N has four categories of annotation: (i) scribal omissions supplied in the margin by the scribe himself or his contemporary and marked with a reference-sign such as .c. or .x.; (ii) words and phrases repeated by a fourteenth-century annotator; (iii) notes on the content or type of individual letters—e.g. 'gratulatoria', 'suasoria'—added in the seventeenth century; (iv) a late copy, possibly contemporary with (iii), of a scribal omission on fol. 7 which was at risk from the binder's shears. This annotation, the phrase 'Eboracenses antistites ad ipsa concilia uocasse' (no. 4, lines 36–7), essentially belongs to category (i); it does not affect the relation of N to the other manuscripts.

The other English manuscripts are mainly of the first half of the twelfth century: CcCdCpHLcLdLeLvLzCantaβJ. They may be described more summarily.

---

[1] Giles, i. 313: perhaps the epitaph on Lanfranc's original tombstone (Clover, 'Correspondence', p. vii *app.*).

[2] Schmitt, iii. 93–294; ff. 93^v–4 are reproduced as the frontispiece.

Cambridge, Corpus Christi Coll., 130 f. 218^{r–v}   s. xi/xii: English   Cc

The complete text (ff. 1–218) of Lanfranc's canon law collection—
the abridged Pseudo-Isidore which he used and distributed in
England—is followed by his letter to Domnall Ua h-Énna.

Brooke, *English Church*, pp. 231–5; Williams, *Codices*, p. 80.
No. 49 of the present edition.

Cambridge, Univ. Lib., Dd.1.11 ff. 203va–5ra   s. xv: Christ   Cd
Church, Canterbury

C.U.L., Dd. 1. 10–11 are companion volumes containing the
complete Pseudo-Isidore, with additional material relating to
Christ Church, Canterbury; the last section of Dd. 1. 11 (ff. 233
ff.) is a fourteenth-century text of Nicholas Trivet that was
originally a separate manuscript. In other respects the two volumes
may well be a direct copy of Lc (see below); the text breaks off
incomplete during Honorius II's confirmation of William of
Corbeil as papal legate (J.L. 7284: f. 232^v). The manuscript was
presented to the University by Archbishop Parker in 1574.

Hinschius, pp. xxxvi–xxxvii; M. R. James, *A Descriptive
Catalogue of the Manuscripts in the Library of Corpus Christi
College* (Cambridge, 1912), p. xxiii; Brooke, *English Church*,
pp. 85–6, 236; Williams, *Codices*, p. 16; Cowdrey, *Epistolae
Vagantes*, no. 1.
Nos. 7–8.

Cambridge, Peterhouse, 74 ff. 217–18   1080–96: Durham   Cp
cathedral

The complete text of Lanfranc's canon law collection, in a form
very close to Cc, is followed by no. 49, again as in Cc.

Brooke, *English Church*, pp. 231–5; R. A. B. Mynors, *Durham
Cathedral Manuscripts* (Oxford, 1939), no. 50; Williams, *Codices*,
pp. 79–80.
No. 49.

Hereford, Cathedral Library, P. ii. 15 f. 161^{r–v}   s. xii^1: H
Cirencester

A major collection of the letters of Ivo of Chartres (ff. 1–146^v),
followed by a smaller collection of Fulbert's (ff. 147–61) and in

conclusion three of Lanfranc's letters and two of Anselm's
(ff. 161–2).

Fulbert, *Letters*, p. xlix; *Anselmi Epp.* v, nos. 434, 436.
Nos. 55–6, 59.

Lc *London, B.L., Cotton Claudius E. V f. 244^{ra–vb}*   *c.* 1125:
Christ Church, Canterbury

A grand folio volume of the complete Pseudo-Isidore (not
Lanfranc's abridgement), which ends with three quires in a
different hand containing further papal letters and synods. Most
of these relate to England; they include nos. 7 and 8 of the present
collection.

Brooke, *English Church*, pp. 85–8; Williams, *Codices*, pp. 29–30;
Cowdrey, *Epistolae Vagantes*, no. 1.
Nos. 7–8.

Ld *London, B.L., Cotton Domitian V ff. 13–14*   s. xii[1]: Christ
Church, Canterbury

Archbishop Ralph's letter of 1120 to Calixtus II arguing his case
for primacy over York (ff. 2–12^v) is followed by a number of
supporting documents (ff. 13–20), of which the first two are
relevant here: the 1072 council and Archbishop Thomas's profession.

Southern, 'Canterbury Forgeries', pp. 208–10, with references.
No. 3, lines 97–143 and 83–96.

Le *London, B.L., Cotton Cleopatra E. I ff. 47vb–54rb*   s. xii[1]:
Christ Church, Canterbury

A collection of Christ Church privileges which has been much
scrutinized as a witness to the origin and purpose of the so-called
Canterbury Forgeries. It includes the conciliar material in the
letter-collection (nos. 3, 11), with its implication of Lanfranc's
primacy: the 1075 council has the significant rubric, 'Concilium
totius Anglicę regionis'. The two letters chosen (nos. 4, surprisingly
omitting lines 104–21, and 7) again relate directly to Lanfranc's
primatial jurisdiction.[1]

---

[1] Le (no. 3, lines 83–96 only) is transcribed, without significant variants,
in Canterbury Dean and Chapter Reg. A, f. 6^v (s. xiv).

Southern, 'Canterbury Forgeries', pp. 193–226; H. Clover, 'Alexander II's letter *Accepimus a quibusdam* and its relationship with the Canterbury Forgeries', in *La Normandie Bénédictine*, ed. G.-U. Langé (Lille, 1967), pp. 417–42.

Nos. 3, 4, 7, 11.

London, B.L., Cotton Vespasian E. IV ff. 204–6   s. xii[1]: Lv
Worcester cathedral

A detached quaternion containing three of Lanfranc's letters (ff. 204–6) and a fragment *De malo et nihil* (f. 206^{r-v}) attributed to Anselm. The first letter (no. 49) reflects Worcester's interest in Ireland. The other two (nos. 13, 12) are letters concerning the bishop of the Orkneys. Wulfstan was instructed to preserve these in his archives (no. 13). Lv may well be a direct transcript of Lanfranc's originals; it alone dates no. 13.

Nos. 49, 13, 12.

London, Lambeth Palace Library, 363 ff. 110vb–11rb   s. xii: Lz
?Lanthony (Glos.), Canons Regular

Nine letters of Fulbert of Chartres, chosen principally for their canonistic decisions, are followed by excerpts from five of Lanfranc's letters, also embodying legal judgements. The scribe attributes the first of these (no. 23) to Fulbert.

Fulbert, *Letters*, p. lx.

Nos. 23, 43, 45, 51, 53.

The conciliar material (nos. 3, 11) exists in the contemporary documents described below, and in a number of later copies, for which see *Councils and Synods*, ad loc.

Canterbury, Dean and Chapter, Cart. Ant. A.2   1072: Christ Cant α
Church, Canterbury

Text of the agreement between Lanfranc and Archbishop Thomas of York reached at Winchester (Easter 1072): no. 3, lines 97–138. There are nine 'signa', all autograph.

Canterbury, Dean and Chapter, Cart. Ant. A.1   1072: Christ Cant β
Church, Canterbury

Text of the agreement between Lanfranc and Archbishop Thomas confirmed at Windsor (Whitsun 1072) and circulated throughout

England:[1] no. 3, lines 97–143. There are two 'signa' and 28 subscriptions, none of which is autograph. The text is slightly inferior to Cant α.

T. A. M. Bishop and P. Chaplais, *Facsimiles of English Royal Writs to A.D. 1100* (Oxford, 1957), pl. xxix, with bibliography; Southern, 'Canterbury Forgeries', pp. 198–200; Gibson, App. A. 14ᶜ; *Councils and Synods*, ad loc.

No. 3, lines 97–143.

J *Cambridge, St John's Coll., 236 (L.9)*   1075: Christ Church, Canterbury

The *acta* of the council of London, 1075: a single sheet (547 × 375 mm.). J ends with a list of 36 signatories; it is a direct copy, made by one of Lanfranc's scribes, of an original with autograph 'signa'. The text of the *acta*, but not the witness-list, constitutes the whole of no. 11.

C. N. L. Brooke, 'Archbishop Lanfranc, the English bishops and the council of London of 1075', *Studia Gratiana* xii (1967), 39–59, with a note by T. A. M. Bishop, pp. 57–8; Gibson, App. A. 14ᶜ; *Councils and Synods*, ad loc., with details of further manuscripts.

No. 11.

THE CONTINENTAL TRADITION

The only substantial continental manuscript is Vatican Reginensis lat. 285, ff. 1–18 (V), from Bec. A manuscript from S. Étienne, Caen, which may well have been related to V, survived into the seventeenth century; but it has since disappeared.[2] The transcript A however (see below) may preserve an independent text of no. 46.

V *Vatican, Biblioteca Apostolica Vaticana, Reginensis lat. 285 ff. 1–18*   s. xii ᵐᵉᵈ·: *Bec*[3]

The manuscript as a whole consists of four sections that were

---

[1] 'Facta est igitur communi omnium astipulatione de hac re quaedam scriptura, cuius exemplaria per principales Anglorum aecclesias distributa futuris semper temporibus testimonium ferant ad quem finem causa ista fuerit perducta': no. 4, lines 95–9; cf. Hugh the Chanter, *History of the Church of York 1066–1127* s.a. 1072, ed. C. Johnson (N.M.T., 1961), p. 5.

[2] See below, pp. 21–2.

[3] A. Wilmart, *Catalogus Codicum Reginensium* (Vatican, 1937–45), ii. 94–9. The manuscript is no. 1548 in the pre-Revolution Maurist catalogue later edited by B. de Montfaucon: *Les Manuscrits de la reine de Suède au Vatican* (Vatican, 1964: *Studi e Testi* 238), p. 88.

probably brought together in the sixteenth century: V is the first
(quires i–iii). Originally V contained the complete letter-collection,
and nothing else; but with the loss of a leaf between f. 16 and f. 17
(quire iii, f. 1) V now lacks nos. 49 ad fin., 50, 51. In format V is
distinctly larger than N: page 160 × 260 mm.; text 115 × 190 mm.;
36 lines per page, ruling part stylus, part pencil. The script is a
good continental minuscule, the decoration simple. Helen Clover
showed that V is almost certainly from Bec. Together with MS
Vat. Reg. lat. 278 it corresponds with an entry in the mid twelfth
century catalogue of the house:

> in alio epistole Lanfranci.
> in eodem epistole Fulberti Carnotensis
> et Hildeberti Cenomanensis episcopi.
> in eodem liber Ernulfi de incestis coniugiis
> item .iiii. questiones diuine solute ab eo.[1]

In the seventeenth century V passed to Queen Christina of Sweden,
and thence to the papal library.

THE LOST MANUSCRIPTS

The lost manuscripts that particularly claim our attention are
recorded at Christ Church, Canterbury, Rochester and S. Étienne,
Caen. The first is listed in the *Registrum Angliae*[2] and described
in detail in the catalogue of the Christ Church library that was
drawn up for Prior Eastry (died 1331).

Gesta Lanfranci. In hoc vol. cont.:
Epistola Lanfranci Cant. Archiep. de corpore et sanguine Domini contra
Berengarium hereticum.
Epistole et Gesta eiusdem.
Anselmus de ueritate.
Item Anselmus de libertate arbitrii.
Anselmus de casu diaboli.
etc. (works of Ralph d'Escures and Bernard of Clairvaux).[3]

As effectively the 'complete works' of Lanfranc, this book is

---

[1] G. Becker, *Catalogi Bibliothecarum Antiquarum* (Bonn, 1885), no. 127,
item 81; cf. Fulbert, *Letters*, pp. xlvii–xlviii.

[2] For the entry in the *Registrum Angliae* (1250+) see MS. Oxford Bodleian
Tanner 165, f. 117ᵛ: '*Opera Lanfranci*. Epistole eius'; cf. M. R. James, 'The
List of Libraries Prefixed to the Catalogue of John Boston and the Kindred
Documents' in *Collectanea Franciscana* ii, ed. C. L. Kingsford et al. (Man-
chester, 1922: British Society of Franciscan Studies x), 37–60.

[3] M. R. James, *The Ancient Libraries of Canterbury and Dover* (Cambridge,
1903), p. 33, no. 161.

more likely to depend on N than to be N's exemplar. It may well
have been the manuscript known to Eadmer and to William of
Malmesbury.[1] The Rochester manuscript is recorded *c.* 1120 as
'Epistolae domni Lanfranci archiepiscopi cum aliis minutis opus-
culis in uno uolumine', and in 1202 as 'Epistole Lanfranci et
Anselmi cum aliis in uno uolumine'; the later entry is close to
being a description of N.[2] The S. Étienne manuscript is known
only from D'Achery's introduction to his own edition of the letters.
D'Achery writes: 'Suppetias quoque attulit exemplum earumdem
literarum (e monasterio, ni fallor, sancti Stephani Cadomensis)
ab eruditissimo Ioanne le Preuost Rotomagensi Canonico trans-
missum.'[3] This ancillary manuscript did not provide D'Achery
with nos. 49–51, the letters lost by accident from V. Thus it was
either a transcript of V made after the disappearance of the leaf
between ff. 16 and 17, which is unlikely, or it was an abbreviated
collection. In certain letters—but which letters we have no means of
telling—readings that are peculiar to D'Achery's printed text may
reflect this lost manuscript from S. Étienne. Other manuscripts
containing an unspecified number of Lanfranc's letters are recorded
at Glastonbury[4] and (less certainly) at St. Mary's Abbey, Dublin.[5]

THE LATER TRANSCRIPTS

Lanfranc's letters had a limited circulation that depended largely
on Christ Church, Canterbury. The materials for N came from
Christ Church, as did CdLcLeCant$\alpha\beta$J; H (Cirencester), Lv
(Worcester) and perhaps Lz (? Lanthony) are a western group
in which at least Worcester had close ties with Christ Church;

---

[1] Eadmer quotes in full no. 30 and J.L. 4761 (App. B): Eadmer, *H.N.*,
pp. 19–22. William of Malmesbury quotes nos. 3, 4 and 11 and refers to no. 8:
Gesta Pontificum, pp. 39–46, 66–8. What is more, William specifically refers
to Lanfranc's letters as a collection: ibid, p. 66.

[2] R. P. Coates, 'Catalogue of the library of the priory of St. Andrew,
Rochester, from the *Textus Roffensis*', *Archaeologia Cantiana* vi (1886), 127,
with references.

[3] D'Achery, *Ad lectorem*, p. (5). The manuscript does not survive in the
present Fonds S. Germain, notwithstanding Delisle's description of MS.
Paris B.N. lat. 13575, ff. 44–58: *Inventaire des manuscrits de Saint-Germain-
des-Prés* (Paris, 1868), p. 105.

[4] J. Leland, *Collectanea* iii. 260, ed. Th. Hearne (Oxford, 1715), iv. 154:
'Liber epistolarum Fulberti, Epistolae Lanfranci'. Possibly this book was
related to the surviving manuscript from Cirencester (H).

[5] *Annals of St. Mary's, Dublin* s.a. 1120, in *Chartularies of St. Mary's
Abbey, Dublin*, ed. J. T. Gilbert (R.S., 1884), ii. 254.

Cp is one of several Durham books of this period known to have come from Canterbury; and even Cc, though of unknown provenance, is attached to a Christ Church collection of canon law. V (Bec) is the only surviving continental manuscript. Taken as a whole the letter-collection was probably not widely known, even in England and even while its author was still within living memory. With one readily explicable exception (Cd) the manuscript tradition is suspended from the later twelfth century until the later sixteenth. Then a transcript was made in France (P), which influenced all the printed editions until the present text. The other continental transcripts (AR), though brief, may preserve independent readings. The two English transcripts (CtO), were neither independent nor influential. As a group, however, these transcripts do testify to the interest shown in the letter-collection by both Catholic and Protestant historians *c.* 1600.

Paris, B.N., lat. 13412 ff. 7–36   s. xvi²: French **P**

P is a transcript of V, also lacking nos. 49 ad fin., 50, 51. It is first seen in the hands of the Parisian scholar Nicolas Le Fèvre (1544–1612), who lent it to Baronius for his *Annales Ecclesiastici*.[1] Fifty years later it was still circulating in the learned world: D'Achery used it for the *editio princeps* of the letters, completing no. 49 with the help of Jean Le Prevost but still unaware of the existence of nos. 50–1.[2] He noted the recent history of P: 'Epistolas Lanfranci mihi dono dedit R.P. Iacobus Sirmondus, qui easdem ab Eminentissimo Cardinali Baronio cum Roma deger(i)t accep(tat).'[3] Thereafter P passed into the Maurist library at Saint-Germain-des-Prés and so to the Bibliothèque Nationale.

[1] 'Hucusque Lanfranci epistola ad Alexandrum Romanum Pontificem quam accepi una cum aliis ab amico coniunctissimo mihi Christiana charitate Nicolao Fabro Parisiensi, cui rerum antiquarum studiosi hoc etiam nomine bene precentur': C. Baronius, *Annales Ecclesiastici* (Rome, 1605), xi. 1070, xxi. For Le Fèvre see *Biographie Universelle* (Paris–Leipzig, s.d.), xxiii. 585, and P. Gasnault, 'Baluze et les manuscrits du concile d'Éphèse', *Bulletin de la Bibliothèque Nationale* i (1976), 72, with references.

[2] D'Achery, *Ad lectorem*, p. (5); cf. his notes to his no. 33 (sic). Archbishop Ussher had published no. 49 (we assume from N) in his *Sylloge* of 1632.

[3] P, f. 6ᵛ (D'Achery's annotation); cf. *Ad lectorem*, p. (4). In regarding P as a transcript of a Cotton manuscript (ibid.) D'Achery was misled by Selden: 'Neque ex alio traduxit exemplar suum, ut audiui, Petriscius [sc. Le Fèvre] quam ex Cottoniano quod uetustissimum est' (*Eadmeri. . . . Historia Novorum* [London, 1623], p. viii).

A *Angers, Bibliothèque Municipale, 891 (803), ff. 68–70*   s. xvii[1]:
French[1]

No. 46 is here included in a collection of transcripts belonging to
Claude Ménard (1574–1652), editor of Augustine, *Contra Julianum*,
and Joinville, *Vie de St Louis*. Judging by the variants, Ménard's
source was a manuscript rather different from VP; perhaps indeed
the recipient's copy of this letter, which is addressed to the abbot
of S. Cyprien at Poitiers, survived independently in Poitiers
itself or in the Loire valley.

R *Rome, Biblioteca Vallicelliana, G. 94 ff. 141–2ᵛ*   *c.* 1600: Italian

No. 14 only, in a calligraphic hand of the late sixteenth or early
seventeenth century. The variants suggest that R is a transcript
of V.[2]

Ct *Cambridge, Trinity Coll., O. 10. 16 pp. 225–68*   *c.* 1613: English

Ct is a transcript of N. It contains all the letters, in the same
order, but omits the councils (nos. 3, 11) and adds (p. 268) the
letter to Prior Henry (App. B). Ct is one of a series of texts relating
to the history of the English Church that together make up MS
O. 10. 16. They were almost certainly transcribed for Patrick
Young, the royal librarian, who in 1613 wrote to a friend in
Heidelberg concerning a projected edition, perhaps to appear
in Germany;[3] but the enterprise came to nothing. Ct has an
unexplained interpolation in no. 7, remarked on by Archbishop
Ussher.[4] The manuscript was presented to Trinity College by
Roger Gale in 1738.

---

[1] *Catalogue général des manuscrits des bibliothèques publiques de France* (Paris,
1898), xxxi. 480: ff. 68–70ᵛ are indeed in Ménard's hand. I am much indebted
here to Mlle Isabelle Battez of the Bibliothèque Municipale, Angers, and to
M. Pierre Gasnault of the Bibliothèque Mazarine.

[2] *Inventarium omnium codicum Manuscriptorum Graecorum et Latinorum
Bibliothecae Vallicellianae* (Rome, 1749), ii.

[3] J. Kemke, 'Patricius Junius' in *Sammlung bibliothekswissensch. Arbeiten*
xii, ed. K. Dziatzko (Leipzig, 1898), pp. 18–19, letter 29 to Abraham Scultetus
of Heidelberg (12 April 1613): 'in descriptione epistolarum Alcuini et Anselmi
(quarum uarias habeo ἀνεκδότους) Lanfranci, Elmeri, Osberti, Giraldi Cam-
brensis, et Roberti Grosseteste, Lincolnensis Episcopi, assiduus pergo etc.'

[4] See apparatus ad loc. Ussher's notes on N (à propos of which he mentions
the interpolation in Ct) are preserved in MS Oxford Bodleian Rawl. C. 850,
f. 70.

Oxford, Bodleian, James 28 (S.C. 3865), pp. 107–10   *c.* 1628–38   O

O is a series of excerpts from N: nos. 4, 6, 8, 10, 31, 39, 38, 1, 46, 52, all abridged except nos. 39 and 52. It forms part of a commonplace book made by Richard James (1592–1638), assistant to John Selden and for the last ten years of his life librarian to Sir Robert Cotton.[1] James's transcripts reached the Bodleian in 1678.

iii. *The early editions*[2]

From the twelfth century to the seventeenth Lanfranc was remembered chiefly for his eucharistic disputation with Berengar of Tours. It was this treatise, *De corpore et sanguine Domini*, that first appeared in print (Basel 1528). Many reprints followed; but no letters were published until 1605, when Baronius included several in *Annales Ecclesiastici* vol. xi. A few years later Archbishop Ussher noticed this material and identified it in N;[3] and Patrick Young (possibly alerted by Ussher) considered publishing the whole collection. But the effective transition from manuscript to print was the Maurist *editio princeps* of 1648. D'Achery based his edition on P. He also used (to an unspecified extent) a manuscript from S. Étienne, Caen that has now disappeared; and he referred where possible to letters quoted in Eadmer's *Historia Novorum* (no. 30, J.L. 4761) and in the *Vita Lanfranci* (nos. 1, 3–6, 11, 30). He arranged the letters in a new sequence, which he does not explain, and provided extensive notes. D'Achery's text was reprinted in 1745 in Venice and again by J. A. Giles in 1844. Giles consulted N, from which he supplied nos. 50–1; he altered the sequence yet again.[4] Finally J.-P. Migne reprinted D'Achery's text in the *Patrologia Latina*, with the newly-discovered nos. 50–1 as an appendix. Thus no critical edition was attempted after the Maurist text of 1648.

---

[1] There is a good characterization of James in *A Summary Catalogue of Western Manuscripts in the Bodleian Library*, ed. F. Madan, H. H. E. Craster and N. Denholm-Young (Oxford, 1937), II. ii. 750–1.

[2] For bibliographical details see pp. 180–1.

[3] Ussher printed no. 39 in his *Grauissimae Quaestionis de Christianarum Ecclesiarum . . . Statu Historica Explanatio* (London, 1613), p. 182, with this note: 'Ex Lanfranci epistolis MS in biblioth. Cotton et Baron. ann. 1079 sec. 25' (Ussher, *Whole Works*, ii. 200 app.).

[4] Concordances of D'Achery/Giles/Migne with the present edition are given above, pp. xiii–xvi.

iv. *The present edition*

Allowing for the page that is missing from V, NV contain exactly the same letters, in the same order. Textually they are very close. Some of the variants are manifest errors in either N or V: for example *3j* ecclesiam *deleted* (V), *4g* boni boni facio (N), *7d* pertinatia (N; *corr.* N¹), *10a* humanum (V), *14d* quantum (N *corr.*N¹), *15a* suspicio (N), *15b* motus (V), *49b* ut (V; *corr.*V¹). Others are indifferent: for example *3b* conuenerant/aduenerant, *3c* enim/autem, *19a* Deo/Domino, *28a* illorum/eorum, *46r* Dei/Domini, *53d* Dominus/Deus. The substantial variants are:

Letter	N	V
3e	rege	*omit*
17a	cum orationibus	et orationes
17b	coenobii	ecclesie
46k	pernicie	pertinacia
	pertinacia N¹	
49b	ne	ut
		ut . . . non V¹

In *3e* N has the better reading; in *49b* I have preferred V. The other variants are either stylistic improvements[1] or scribal inadvertence. As for the minor manuscripts, Lz identifies the recipient of no. 53; but generally CcCdHLcLeLvLz either support N or (nos. 3 and 11) reflect the superior readings of Cantaβ J. Of the late transcripts P and probably R depend on V and CtO depend on N; only A (no. 46) may be independent. Thus V is an isolated witness to the continental tradition, whereas N has solid support within England. It may be argued that NV have a common archetype, thus:

But it could well be that V depends on N, the variants being either independent emendations or made in the light of another manuscript. In that case there is no obstacle to regarding N as the original manuscript of the collection or a direct copy of that original.

The present edition is based on N. The scribe had a good clear

---

[1] The Bec monks of the mid twelfth century were, we know, very conscious of literary style: Gibson, App. A, nos. 1–4, with references.

hand, but he was unskilled in the steady transcription of long passages; N is an amateurish piece of work compared with V. The scribe of N omitted letters and syllables, substituted one letter for another and occasionally missed entire phrases. Nearly all such mistakes are corrected in his own hand or that of a contemporary;[1] these corrections, whether interlinear or marginal, have been absorbed in our text without comment. The errors that remain are noted in the apparatus, unless they are quite meaningless: for instance eō (no. 19, line 20). The scribe used medial 'c' and 't' indifferently, and he knew no standard—nor indeed correct—use of 'ae', 'ę' and 'e'. These idiosyncrasies and some bizarre spellings have been preserved.[2] For typographical reasons however 'ae' and 'ę' are both rendered as 'ae'. The punctuation has been modernized.[3] V was an orthodox scribe writing at least half a century later; his corrections (V[1]) have normally been absorbed without comment. V's variants of spelling and word-order have not been noted, except in the one case (9a) which might affect the sense. Biblical references are to the Vulgate; the English translation follows the Authorized Version as closely as is feasible.

---

[1] They form category (i) of the annotations: see p. 16 above.

[2] See for instance no. 42, line 13 (legittimum); no. 47, line 12 (quiaetum).

[3] N uses predominantly the *punctus elevatus* (⁏) and the *punctus* (.) for longer and shorter pauses respectively. This system bears little relation to syntactical punctuation, yet it is often more suited to the sentence-structure than the full panoply of commas at the end of every clause. Eadmer's system of punctuation, which is a little more sophisticated than N but essentially similar, is discussed by R. W. Southern, *Life of St. Anselm by Eadmer* (N.M.T., 1962), pp. xxviii–xxxiv.

THE LETTERS OF
LANFRANC
ARCHBISHOP OF
CANTERBURY

INCIPIVNT EPISTOLAE VENERABILIS[a] ARCHIEPISCOPI LANFRANCI[b] AD DIVERSOS MISSAE

1

Lanfranc to Pope Alexander II
25 Dec. 1072–21 Apr. 1073

Although placed first in order—no doubt as describing the circumstances of Lanfranc's election—this letter cannot be dated before his visit to Rome in Oct. 1071 (lines 57–63); thus it is unlikely to be prior to the council of Windsor (May 1072: no. 3, lines 141–3). If the phrase 'me facere non potu*isse*' (line 62) is taken literally, no. 1 is later than Christmas 1072. See further Introduction, pp. 3–4.

Summo sanctae aecclesiae pastori Alexandro papae Lanfrancus[c] indignus antistes canonicam oboedientiam.

Nescio cui aptius calamitates meas explicem quam tibi pater qui ipsarum michi calamitatum causa existis. Nam cum de Beccensi
5 congregatione in qua habitum religionis assumpsi a principe Normannorum Willelmo abstractus Cadomensi praeessem coenobio, imparque existerem paucorum regimini monachorum, incertum habeo quo iudicio omnipotentis Dei factus sum te cogente speculator multorum numeroque carentium populorum. Quod
10 cum prefatus princeps iam rex Anglorum factus multis uariisque modis laboraret efficere, cassatis tamen laboribus suis a me nullo modo potuit impetrare quoadusque legati tui Hermenfredus uidelicet Sedunensis episcopus atque Hubertus sanctae Romanae aecclesiae cardinalis in Normanniam uenerunt, episcopos abbates
15 eiusdemque patriae nobiles conuenire fecerunt, atque in eorum presentia ut Cantuariensem aecclesiam regendam susciperem ex apostolicae sedis auctoritate preceperunt.[1] Aduersus hoc imbecillitas mearum uirium morumque indignitas prolata in medium nichil profuit, excusatio incognitae linguae gentiumque barba-
20 rarum nullum apud eos locum inuenire praeualuit. Quid plura?

---

1 NV
   [a] *om.* V   [b] N[1] *adds* CANTVARIENSIS; V *adds* PRO DIVERSIS
NEGOTIIS   [c] L. N

THE LETTERS THAT THE VENERABLE ARCHBISHOP LANFRANC SENT TO VARIOUS PEOPLE BEGIN HERE

1

Lanfranc to Pope Alexander II

25 Dec. 1072–21 Apr. 1073

To Pope Alexander, the highest pastor of the holy Church, Lanfranc, an unworthy bishop, offers canonical obedience.

I do not know to whom I may more appropriately unfold my misfortunes than to you, father, who have brought these misfortunes upon me. When William duke of the Normans had removed me from the community at Bec, where I took the religious habit, and I was in charge of the monastery at Caen, I was unequal to ruling a few monks; so I cannot conceive by what judgement of almighty God I have at your insistence been made the overseer of many and numberless peoples. Although that duke, now king of the English, endeavoured in many different ways to bring this about, his labours were in vain. He could not win his point from me until finally your own legates came to Normandy, Ermenfrid, bishop of Sion, and Hubert, cardinal of the holy Roman Church; they assembled the bishops, abbots and magnates of that country and in their presence commanded me by the authority of the apostolic see to assume the government of the church of Canterbury.[1] I pleaded failing strength and personal unworthiness, but to no purpose; the excuse that the language was unknown and the native races barbarous weighed nothing with them either. In a word: I assented, I came, I took

---

1 ¹ Ermenfrid, bishop of Sion, was a papal legate with long experience of Norman and English affairs; he had just held councils at Winchester (Easter 1070) and Windsor (Whitsun 1070): see further H. E. J. Cowdrey, 'Bishop Ermenfrid of Sion and the penitential ordinance following the battle of Hastings', *Journal of Ecclesiastical History* xx (1969), 225–42, with references. This is Ermenfrid's last intervention: his authority passed effectively (if not formally) to Hubert, who continued as legate to Normandy and England until 1080 (no. 3, lines 136–8; nos. 38–9). Having deposed Archbishop Stigand at Easter 1070, the legates crossed over to Normandy after Whitsun (23 May) to confirm his successor; by mid August Lanfranc had arrived in England.

f 1ᵛ   Assensum prebui, ueni, suscepi. In qua tot molestias / tot tedia tantumque ab omni fere bono defectum mentis cotidie sustineo; tot aliorum in diuersis personis perturbationes, tribulationes, damna, obdurationes, cupiditates, spurcicias, tantumque sanctae
25 aecclesiae casum incessanter audio, uideo, sentio ut tedeat me uitae meae,[2] doleamque plurimum me usque ad haec tempora peruenisse. Mala siquidem sunt quae in praesenti cernuntur, multo uero deteriora ex istorum consideratione in futuro coniciuntur. Et ne diu celsitudinem uestram multis magnisque negotiis
30 occupatam prolixae orationis ambitu protraham, rogo quatinus propter Deum et animam uestram sicut uestra cui contradici fas non fuit auctoritate me alligastis, sic quoque alligatum abrupto per eandem auctoritatem huius necessitatis uinculo absoluatis, uitamque coenobialem quam pre omnibus rebus diligo repetendi
35 licentiam concedatis. Nec in huius rei sperni petitione debeo, quam tam pie tam necessarie tam iustis ex causis concedi michi a uobis deposco. Meminisse siquidem debetis, nec tradi obliuioni oportet, quam benigne consanguineos uestros aliosque a Roma scripta deferentes in prefatis adhuc coenobiis constitutus sepe
40 recepi, quam studiose eos pro captu meo ingeniique ipsorum tam in sacris quam in secularibus litteris erudiui,[3] ut taceam multa alia in quibus uobis uestrisque antecessoribus pro rerum ac temporum qualitate nonnunquam seruiui. Nec hoc iactando aut improperando teste conscientia dico, nec fauorem gratiae uestrae
45 quasi prolatis oboedientiae meae obsequiis solito maiorem captare
f. 2   requiro. Hoc tantum studeo harumque / litterarum[d] is solummodo finis est, ut congruam rationem iustamque causam possim ostendere, qua id quod peto a uestra munificentia Christo aspirante ualeam obtinere. Quod si fortasse considerata aliorum utilitate
50 secus agendum michique id denegandum esse decernitis, ualde uobis cauendum atque timendum est ne unde uos mercedem habere apud Deum existimatis inde—quod a uestris actibus semper procul sit—peccati periculum incurratis. Nullus est enim a me aut per me in hac terra animarum profectus; aut si ullus
55 existit, tam paruus est ut detrimentis meis comparari non possit. De his hactenus.

    Ceterum quando Rome fui, uestramque faciem uidere uestroque colloquio frui diuina gratia concedente promerui, rogastis me quatinus in sequenti anno circa natiuitatem Christi ad uos uenirem

    ᵈ litterum N

office. Now I endure daily so many troubles and vexations and such spiritual starvation of nearly anything that is good; I am continually hearing, seeing and experiencing so much unrest among different people, such distress and injuries, such hardness of heart, greed and dishonesty, such a decline in holy Church, that I am weary of my life[2] and grieve exceedingly to have lived into times like these. What can be discerned in the present is evil indeed; but it forbodes far worse evil to come. I do not wish to weary your highness with an elaborate and lengthy speech, for you have many great affairs to take up your time; but I implore you for God's sake and your own soul's, as you bound me by your own authority that could not lawfully be disputed, to free me from bondage, using that same authority to break the shackle of this duty and giving me leave to return to the monastic life, which I love more than anything else. I do not deserve to have a petition rejected which I implore you to grant me so devoutly, so urgently and for such excellent reasons. You may well recall—it is not right that it should pass from memory—what a friendly welcome I often extended to your kinsmen and others who brought an introduction from Rome when I was still in those monasteries, and how conscientiously I instructed them, according to my ability and their intelligence, in both sacred and profane learning.[3] I say nothing of the many other ways in which I have from time to time been of service to you and your predecessors as the need and opportunity arose. I say this neither boastfully nor in reproach—my conscience is witness; I am not trying to gain greater indulgence from your grace than normal by reminding you of faithful service in the past. My sole concern and the exclusive purpose of this letter is to show due reason and just cause why with Christ's blessing I should obtain from your generosity what I ask. Should you decide to do otherwise out of regard to other men's advantage, and refuse my request, think of the fearful risk that, just where you expect God to reward you, by that very act you may be falling into the danger of sin. May you always escape that danger! No spiritual progress has been achieved in this country by my act or agency: or if any has, it is too slight to bear comparison with the disadvantages to me. And that concludes the matter.

On another point, when I was in Rome and by God's grace had the privilege to see and talk with you in person, you asked me to visit you the following year about Christmas and stay in the palace

---

[2] Eccles. 2: 17.
[3] J.L. 4669 (App. B. ii; cf. Gibson, p. 103).

60 uobiscum in palatio uestris stipendiis tribus aut eo amplius
mensibus moraturus.⁴ Verum hoc sine magna rerum corporisque
incommoditate me facere non potuisse testis michi est Deus,
testes angeli eius. Cur autem non potuerim plures uariaeque
causae effecerunt, quae epistolari breuitate pro sui prolixitate
65 comprehendi non possunt. Sed si superna maiestas uitam michi
atque incolumitatem cum rerum commoditate concesserit, sanctos
apostolos et uos sanctamque Romanam aecclesiam uisitare desidero. Quod ut fiat, rogate obsecro diuinam clementiam quatinus
domino meo regi Anglorum longam uitam concedat, pacemque ei
70 de omnibus sibi aduersantibus faciat, cor eius ad amorem suum
sanctaeque^e aecclesiae suae spirituali semper deuotione com-
f. 2ᵛ pungat. / Eo enim uiuente pacem qualemcunque habemus; post
mortem uero eius nec pacem nec aliquod bonum nos habituros
speramus.

2

Lanfranc to Pope Alexander II   *24 Apr.–Oct. 1071*

The bishop of Lichfield was deposed by the papal legates at Easter 1070 (lines
32–7); he resigned his see the following Easter (24 Apr. 1071). Lanfranc
presumably wrote as soon as the see was vacant and at all events before he
himself went to Rome in the autumn of the same year. The bishops of Sherborne
and Lichfield were both men of the old regime, whose resignations invited the
charge that William the Conqueror and Lanfranc were removing bishops as they
pleased: Sherborne eased out by harassment and punitive taxation (lines 15–17)
and Lichfield framed for immorality (lines 32–4). Lanfranc is concerned
both to put the record straight and to be seen to act only with papal approval. His
position was much strengthened when Alexander II commended him to the
king as acting papal legate (no. 7, lines 41–4).

Vniuersae Christi aecclesiae summo rectori Alexandro indignus
Anglorum episcopus^a Lanfrancus finem bonum inferre bono
principio.

Necessitate urgente expectare non potui quoadusque redirent
5 quos ad uos transmisi priores legati nostri. Hermannus siquidem
nostrae regionis episcopus, qui tempore uenerandae memoriae
Leonis papae antecessoris uestri relicto episcopatu monachicam
uitam petiit, nunc iterum hoc idem facere omnibus modis petit.¹

ᵉ et sancte V

---

2 NV
ᵃ archiepiscopus V

at your expense for three months or longer.[4] But I could not have done this without great inconvenience, both physical and financial; God and his angels are my witness. There were many different factors preventing me, more than can be included in the brief compass of a letter. But if the King above grant me life and health with sufficient means, I do long to visit the holy apostles and both you and the holy Roman Church. If this is to come about, I urge you to entreat God mercifully to grant long life to my lord the king of the English, to establish him in security from all his enemies and to stir up his heart to love him and his holy Church with all godly devotion. While the king lives we have peace of a kind, but after his death we expect to have neither peace nor any other benefit.

2

Lanfranc to Pope Alexander II   *24 Apr.–Oct. 1071*

To Alexander, supreme ruler of the universal Church of Christ, Lanfranc, an unworthy bishop of the English, wishes that from a good beginning he may derive a good conclusion.

On this urgent matter I could not wait until the messengers whom I had already sent to you returned. There is a bishop in our province called Hermann, who gave up his office in the time of your predecessor Pope Leo of revered memory and tried to become a monk; he is now trying to do so once more by every means he can.[1]

---

[4] Lanfranc was in Rome in Oct. 1071 (no. 3, n. 7); thus 'sequenti anno' (as distinct from 'hoc anno') refers to Christmas 1072.

---

2 [1] Hermann of Ramsbury (1045–78) retired *c.* 1054 to S. Bertin (dioc. S. Omer), returned to England by 1058 and moved his see to Sherborne; despite his renewed desire for the monastic life he lived to transfer it again to Old Sarum (1075: no. 11, lines 47–8), where he died—still a bishop—in 1078.

Et nisi ego censura canonica obstitissem, iampridem aut regi
10 episcopium reddidisset, aut clam ad monasterium confugisset.
Et quidem dum uirili robore atque iuuenta uiguit, scientia diuinarum atque mundanarum rerum preditus ad pastorale officium
satis utilis persona extitit. Sed iam senili aetate prolixaque egritudine confectus debito officio curam impendere ulterius non ualet.
15 Nec existimet sancta colendaque beatitudo uestra quod aut
quibuslibet iniuriis lacessitus aut regalibus angariis ultra uires
pregrauatus hoc facere uelit. Deum omnipotentem dulcissimam-
que uestram gratiam testor quod nec in uerbis eius, dum familiari
colloquio consilium animae suae a me quereret suasque michi
20 neglegentias confitendo aperiret, deprehendere id ualui nec a
quoquam hominum tale aliquid de eo unquam audiui. Sed sicut
f. 3 puto et reuera / est, exactis in hac uita compluribus annis iam
tandem proximus morti, priusquam moriatur a uinculis ac mole
tanti oneris[b] desiderat absolui ac liberari, et in extremo saltem
25 uitae suae psalmis, ymnis, orationibus, lectionibus occupari.
Propterea apostolicae sedis celsitudinem consulendum putaui,
quatinus ab ea instructi certissime teneamus quid in tam excellenti
tamque necessaria re concedere uel facere debeamus. Nec id
differri oportet; quia ualde timendum est, nisi sollercia uestra
30 prouideat, ne eius corporalis incommoditas multis animabus causa
perditionis existat. De hac re ista sufficiant.

Licifeldensis uero episcopus[2] qui apud legatos uestros de
incontinentia carnis, cui uxor publice habita filiique procreati
testimonium perhibebant, aliisque criminibus accusatus ad
35 sinodum tamen eorum uenire noluit; unde et predicti legati
uestri eum excommunicauerunt, regique substituendi successorem
ut dicitur licentiam concesserunt.[3] In Paschali solennitate ad
curiam uenit,[4] de illatis culpis causam inire noluit, regi in conuentu
episcoporum atque laicorum episcopatum reddidit, se amplius
40 non habiturum nec successori calumniam aut damnum illaturum
iureiurando spontanea uoluntate firmauit; dehinc ad monasterium
in quo ab infantia nutritus monachus fuerat repedauit.[5] Ego

---

[b] hoñis V

[2] Leofwine, abbot of Coventry (c. 1043–53) and bishop of Lichfield (1053–70)
returned to be a monk at Coventry; cf. no. 27.
[3] The bishop was deposed at the council of Winchester, Easter 1070: H. E. J.
Cowdrey, 'Bishop Ermenfrid of Sion and the penitential ordinance following the

Indeed if I had not countered with a legal prohibition, he would long ago have either resigned his bishopric to the king or secretly fled to a monastery. And to tell the truth when he was a young man and had his strength he was a suitable enough person for the office of bishop, for he was conversant with both sacred and secular affairs. But now that he is old and chronically ill he is no longer able to attend to his official duties. Your holy and revered beatitude must not suppose that it is because of any injustices that he has suffered or because he is unduly burdened with services to the king that he wishes to take this step. I call to witness almighty God and your most sweet grace that I have been able to detect nothing of that in what he said in private conversation when he sought spiritual counsel and acknowledged to me his shortcomings, nor have I ever heard such a report of him from anyone else. I think the truth really is that after many years in this world he is now at last close to death; and before he dies he wishes to be released and set free from the heavy chains of such great responsibility and to spend at least the close of his life in psalms, hymns, prayers and the reading of Scripture. It was for this reason that I decided to consult your highness in the apostolic see, so that with your guidance we can be quite sure what to allow or what action to take in a matter of such urgency and importance. There should be no delay; for the danger is very real that unless you make some wise provision for him his physical incapacity will bring spiritual ruin to many. So much for this problem.

The bishop of Lichfield,[2] who was accused before your legates of carnal incontinence (the proof being his wife, whom he openly recognized, and the children he had fathered) and of other misdemeanours, refused to come to their synod; so these same legates excommunicated him and, it is said, gave the king licence to appoint a successor in his place.[3] The bishop came to court at the festival of Easter[4] and did not attempt to dispute the charges in detail; but in the assembly of bishops and laity he returned his bishopric to the king, affirming voluntarily and on oath that he would have it no longer and that he would not implead or injure his successor. Then he made his way back to the monastery where he had been brought up as a monk from his childhood.[5] Now I am

battle of Hastings', *Journal of Ecclesiastical History* xx (1969), 230. See further *Councils and Synods* ad loc.
    [4] Easter 1071: the bishop's capitulation to the king cannot be dated to the same week as his defiance of the legates.   [5] See p. 36 n. 2.

tamen nouus Anglus rerumque Anglicarum, nisi quantum ab
aliis accipio, adhuc pene inscius[6] in locum eius non presumpsi uel
45 episcopum consecrare uel consecrandi licentiam aliis episcopis
f. 3ᵛ dare, quoadusque preceptio uestra ueniat, quae in tanto / negotio
quid oporteat fieri informare nos debeat.[7] Nec id quoque differat
amanda paternitas uestra, quia diu est ex quo illa miserrima
aecclesia pastore est destituta.
50 Omnipotens Dominus det nobis semper audire de uobis quod
audire coepimus et audire desideramus, diligende, colende,
reuerende pater.

3

Memorandum on the primacy of Canterbury
21 Apr. 1073–28 Aug. 1075

A memorandum bearing on (*a*) the primatial jurisdiction of Canterbury over
York and (*b*) the metropolitan jurisdiction of Canterbury over the three bishoprics
on the northern border of the province: Worcester, Lichfield and Dorchester.
It is in five parts: (i) lines 1–50, autumn 1070: Lanfranc's arrival, his claim to
primacy over Archbishop Thomas and its provisional settlement; (ii) lines 51–82,
Oct. 1071–Apr. 1072: Lanfranc's visit to Rome and the resulting council of
Winchester; (iii) lines 83–96, *c.* 8 Apr. 1072: Archbishop Thomas's profession;
(iv) lines 97–138, *c.* 8 Apr. 1072: text of the council of Winchester; (v) no. 4,
Apr.–May 1072: Lanfranc's report to Pope Alexander II. Two of these sections
derive from existing material: section ii is based on section v (lines 52–7 = no.
4, lines 111–14, 5–9; lines 70–7 = no. 4, lines 14–18, 96–9); section iv is
based on a document similar to Cantaβ. The memorandum as a whole was
probably assembled soon after the death of Alexander II (line 4) and almost
certainly before the council of 1075 (no. 11). It is quoted extensively in A.L.,
pp. 287–8 (App. C below) and in *Gesta Pontificum*, pp. 39–43 (= lines 1–134).

i. ᵃAnno dominicae incarnationis millesimo septuagesimo in-
trauit Anglicam terram Lanfrancus Cadomensis coenobii abbas,
monentibus atque precipientibus Willelmo glorioso Anglorum
rege et felicis memoriae Alexandro totius sanctae aecclesiae summo
5 pontifice. Is post paucos sui introitus dies Dorobernensem
aecclesiam regendam suscepit.[1] Consecratus est autem quarto
kalendas Septembris in sede metropoli a suffraganeis ipsius sedis
Willelmo Londoniensi episcopo, Walchelino Uuentano, Remigio

3 NVLd (*from line* 83) Le Cantaβ (*from line* 97)
ᵃ No. 3 is quoted in extenso in V.L. caps. 10–11, with one notable interpolation (line 52 below). See further *Councils and Synods* ad loc.

a novice Englishman, virtually ignorant as yet of English affairs, except for what I learn at second hand;[6] and I have not presumed either to consecrate a bishop in his place, or to give other bishops licence to consecrate, until instructions come from you, directing us how to proceed in a matter of such consequence.[7] Here too, beloved father, you should not delay, for that most unhappy church has now been without its minister for a long time.

May almighty God grant us ever to hear that news of you which we have begun to hear and desire to hear, o dear, revered and reverend father!

3

Memorandum on the primacy of Canterbury
21 Apr. 1073–28 Aug. 1075

i. In the year of our Lord 1070 Lanfranc, abbot of the monastery of Caen, entered the land of England at the desire and command of William, the glorious king of the English, and Alexander of happy memory, supreme pontiff of the holy and universal Church. A few days after he arrived, he assumed control of the church of Canterbury.[1] On 29 August he was consecrated in his metropolitan cathedral by the suffragans of that see: William, bishop of London,

---

[6] Cf. the description of Archbishop Thomas as 'nouus . . . homo et anglicae consuetudinis penitus expers' (no. 3, lines 22–3). Having been archbishop only since Aug. 1070, Lanfranc had real difficulty in reconstructing a case that had been left unresolved the previous spring.

[7] Whatever the pope's advice (which does not survive), the consecration of the new bishop of Lichfield was deferred until at least the autumn of 1072 (A.L., p. 289): i.e. until Lanfranc had confirmed his own jurisdiction over the see (Mar. 1072: no. 3, lines 56–8, 104–17).

---

3 [1] Lanfranc was invested by King William I on 15 Aug. 1070: *Flor. Wig.* ii. 7.

Dorcensi siue Lincholiensi,[2] Siuuardo Rofensi, Herfasto Hel-
10 meanensi siue Tehfordensi,[2] Stigando Selengensi, Hermanno
Siraburnensi, Gisone Uuellensi. Ceteri qui absentes fuerunt
causas suae absentiae tam legatis quam litteris ostenderunt.[3]

Ipso anno Thomas Eboracensis aecclesiae electus antistes
Cantuarberiam ex prisca consuetudine ab eo sacrandus aduenit.
15 A quo cum Lanfrancus scriptam de oboedientia sua cum adiectione
iurisiurandi professionem custodito antecessorum more exposceret,
respondit Thomas se id nunquam facturum, nisi prius scriptas
de hac re auctoritates legeret, nisi testes huius antiquitatis asser-
f. 4 tores cerneret, postremo nisi congruas super hac / re rationes
20 audiret quibus id iuste et rationabiliter sine suae aecclesiae
preiudicio facere deberet. Hoc autem ignorantia magis quam
spiritus elati pertinatia agebat.[b] Nouus enim homo et Anglicae
consuetudinis penitus expers uerbis adulatorum plus aequo et
bono fidem exhibebat. Lanfrancus tamen, in presentia paucorum
25 episcoporum qui ad eum pro hac consecratione conuenerant,[c]
quod postulauit ostendit. At ille aspernatus omnia non sacratus
abscessit. Quod rex audiens grauiter accepit, existimans Lan-
francum iniusta petere et scientia litterarum magis quam ratione
et ueritate confidere, quamuis nec ipsi Thomae deesset scriptura-
30 rum peritia multo ingenio multoque studio comparata.[4] Paucorum
dierum spacio euoluto Lanfrancus ad curiam uenit, a rege audientiam postulauit, redditis rationibus eius animum mitigauit,
transmarinis qui aderant suae parti iusticiam adesse suasit et
persuasit. Angli enim,[d] qui rem nouerant, assertionibus eius per
35 omnia constantissime testimonium[e] perhibebant. Itaque regio
edicto communique omnium decreto statutum est ad praesens
debere Thomam ad matrem totius regni aecclesiam redire, professionem scribere, scriptam legere, lectam inter examinandum
in presentia episcoporum aecclesiastico more Lanfranco por-
40 rigere.[5] In qua preceptis quidem eius in omnibus quae ad Christianae religionis cultum pertinent se obtemperaturum absolute

---

[b] aiebat Le   [c] aduenerant V   [d] autem V   [e] testimonum N

---

[2] Remigius and Herfast are given the titles claimed in their professions of
obedience: Richter, nos. 32–3.

[3] The absent bishops are Leofric of Exeter, Walter of Hereford and Wulfstan
of Worcester; no letters of apology survive.

[4] He is said to have been taught by Lanfranc himself: Hugh the Chanter,

Walchelin of Winchester, Remigius of Dorchester or Lincoln,[2] Siward of Rochester, Herfast of Elmham or Thetford,[2] Stigand of Selsey, Hermann of Sherborne and Giso of Wells. Other bishops, who were absent, gave the reasons for their absence both by legates and in writing.[3]

In the same year Thomas, archbishop-elect of the church of York, by ancient custom came to Canterbury to be consecrated by Lanfranc. But when Lanfranc, following the practice of his predecessors, asked him for a written profession of obedience, fortified by an oath of loyalty, Thomas replied that he would never do that until he could read evidence of the claim and could see witnesses testifying to its antiquity; in short, until he should hear good reason why he should do it justly and reasonably, without prejudice to his own church. He acted in this way from ignorance rather than from a proud and obstinate spirit. For he was a newcomer, with no experience whatever of English usage, and he placed more confidence in the advice of flatterers than was right and proper. In the presence of a few bishops who had joined him for this consecration Lanfranc displayed the evidence that Thomas required. But he rejected everything and departed unconsecrated. When the king heard this, he was very displeased, for he thought that Lanfranc was trying to get more than his due and was relying more on worldly learning than on reason and truth, although Thomas himself was not without scholarly accomplishment, acquired by great natural ability and hard work.[4] A few days later Lanfranc came to court and requested an audience with the king; he calmed his anger with an explanation of the case and completely persuaded the Normans who were there that right was on his side. As for the English, who already understood the matter, they testified very firmly in support of his claims in all respects. So it was decided by the king's edict and the general decision of all those present that for the moment Thomas should return to the mother church of the whole kingdom, write a profession, read out what he had written and present to Lanfranc what he had read, while he was being examined in the presence of the bishops as is the custom of the Church.[5] In this document he should promise to obey Lanfranc's instructions absolutely and unconditionally in all matters relating to the practice of the Christian religion; but he should not render the same

---

History of the Church of York 1066–1127, s.a. 1070, ed. C. Johnson (N.M.T., 1961), p. 2.

[5] A bishop at his consecration normally made a confession of faith and a profession of obedience to his metropolitan: *PRG* i. 200–11. Canterbury was unusual, but not unique, in exacting a written profession and preserving it carefully. See Richter, pp. xi–xxiv *et passim*.

nulla interposita conditione promitteret; successoribus uero eius
non ita nisi prius uel coram rege[f] uel in episcopali concilio com-
petens ei ratio redderetur, qua antecessores suos Dorobernensis
45 aecclesiae primatibus id fecisse et facere debuisse euidentissime
f. 4[v] ostenderetur. / Igitur rediit, quae iussa sunt impleuit, sacratus
abscessit. Non post multos dies Lanfrancus ab uniuersis Anglici
regni episcopis qui diuersis temporibus diuersis in locis ab aliis
archiepiscopis uel a papa tempore Stigandi sacrati sunt profes-
50 siones petiit et accepit.[6]

ii. Sequenti anno cum prefato[g] archiepiscopo Romam iuit,[7]
et honorifice a sede apostolica susceptus[h] unum quidem pallium
de altari Romano more accepit, alterum uero in[i] indicium uidelicet
sui amoris cum quo missam celebrare solebat Alexander ei papa
55 sua manu porrexit. In cuius presentia Thomas calumniam mouit
de primatu Dorobernensis aecclesiae, et de subiectione trium
episcoporum Dorcensis siue Lincoliensis, Wigorniensis, Licifeldensis qui nunc est Cestrensis,[8] dicens Cantuariensem aecclesiam
atque Eboracensem parem ad se inuicem honorem habere, nec
60 alteram alteri secundum beati Gregorii constitutionem debere
ullatenus subiacere, excepto quod alterutrius archiepiscopum
priorem et digniorem oporteat esse eo quem constiterit fuisse
posterius ordinatum;[9] praedictos uero tres episcopos suae sedi
suisque antecessoribus ab antiquis temporibus extitisse subiectos.
65 Lanfrancus hoc audiens etsi moleste tulit modesta tamen discretione uerba illius ueritate penitus carere respondit, asseuerans
Gregorianam illam constitutionem non de Cantuariensi et
Eboracensi aecclesia, sed de Londoniensi et Eboracensi esse
promulgatam. De qua re et de tribus episcopis multis hinc inde
70 uerbis prolatis, decreuit Alexander papa oportere hanc causam in /
f. 5 Anglica terra audiri, et illic tocius regni episcoporum et abbatum

---

[f] *om.* V   [g] Le *adds* Eboracensi   [h] V.L. *adds*: est. Siquidem uenienti papa
assurrexisse dicitur, tum pro sua magna religione et eminenti scientia tum quia
dum esset in Normannia uenientes Romane ecclesie ministros honorifice susci-
piebat, et quosdam pape consanguineos studiose docuerat. Fertur etiam papam
dixisse, Non ideo assurrexi ei, quia archiepiscopus Cantuarie est, sed quia
Becci ad scholam eius fui et ad pedes eius cum aliis auditor consedi. Itaque
duo pallia illi dedit   [i] in *om.* Le

---

[6] Professions are extant from two of the border sees (Worcester and Dorchester: Richter, nos. 31–2; cf. Barlow, *English Church*, pp. 302–10); the bishop
of Lichfield had been deposed. The profession of Herfast of Elmham, who had
been consecrated after Stigand's deposition, is textually related to the others

obedience to his successors until satisfactory evidence was given him, either in the king's court or in an episcopal council, which would show beyond any doubt that his predecessors had made, and ought to have made, this profession to the primates of the church of Canterbury. So he came back, fulfilled what was required and went away consecrated. Not many days later Lanfranc required and received professions of obedience from all those bishops of the English realm who in the time of Stigand had been consecrated at various times and at various places by other archbishops or by the pope.[6]

ii. The following year Lanfranc went to Rome with the same archbishop[7] and was honourably received by the apostolic see: he took one pallium from the altar in the Roman manner, but Pope Alexander personally presented him with another in which he used to celebrate Mass, as a mark of his affection. In the pope's presence Thomas made his allegation about the primacy of the church of Canterbury and the obedience owed by the three bishops of Dorchester or Lincoln, Worcester, and Lichfield (now Chester);[8] he said that the churches of Canterbury and York were equal to each other in status, and that according to the constitution of St. Gregory neither should be subject to the other in any way, except that the earlier of the two to have been ordained shall take precedence over the archbishop who is known to have been ordained later.[9] As for the three bishops, they had been subject to his own see and to his predecessors since ancient times. Although Lanfranc was angry when he heard this, he replied temperately enough that the man's statement was completely false, maintaining that the Gregorian constitution had been promulgated in respect not of the churches of York and Canterbury but of the churches of York and London. After long argument over this and over the three bishops Pope Alexander ruled that this case should be heard in the land of

(Richter, no. 33). Even these three do not survive as originals; and lines 47–50 here are the only evidence that the other eight bishops who had been consecrated before Lanfranc's arrival renewed their professions also.

[7] Oct. 1071: the date is established by J.L. 4692 (see below). The party consisted of the two archbishops, Remigius, bishop of Dorchester (Richter, no. 32; Eadmer, *H.N.*, p. 11) and Baldwin, abbot of Bury St. Edmunds (J.L. 4692; Hermann the Archdeacon, *Miracula S. Eadmundi* 38, ed. F. Liebermann, *Ungedruckte anglo-normannische Geschichtsquellen* (Strassburg, 1879), pp. 249–50).

[8] The formal transfer of the see of Lichfield to Chester took place at the council of London in 1075 (no. 11, lines 43–9). Either 'qui nunc est Cestrensis' is a later gloss (incorporated by NVLe) or the memorandum itself is later than the council of London. In dating the memorandum 1073–5 I am committed to the former assumption.

[9] Gregory the Great, *Registrum* xi. 39, ed. L. M. Hartmann (Berlin, 1895: *MGH Epistolae* II. ii), pp. 312–13; cf. Bede, *H.E.*, i. 29, pp. 104–7.

testimonio et iudicio definiri. Lanfrancus quamuis alligatum illum[j] suo tempore facta ab eo professione teneret, maluit tamen pro successoribus laborare quam eis in posterum indiscussam
75 hanc tantam calumniam discutiendam reseruare. Vterque igitur in Paschali solennitate ad regem uenit, ibique prolatis in medium partium rationibus sententiam de negotio regalis curia[k] dedit. Iussum tunc est fieri scriptum totius causae continens finem.[10] Lanfrancus Alexandro papae epistolam[l] direxit in qua ei totius
80 negotii gestionem breuiter et ueraciter enarrauit.[11] Vtraque scripta subter annexa sunt, praemissa professione quam Thomas Lanfranco coram rege et eius curia manu in manum porrexit:[12]

iii. Decet[m] christianum quenque christianis legibus subiacere, nec his quae a sanctis patribus salubriter instituta sunt quibuslibet
85 rationibus contraire. Hinc nanque irae dissensiones inuidiae contentiones[13] ceteraque procedunt, quae amatores suos in poenas aeternas demergunt. Et quanto quisque altioris est ordinis, tanto impensius diuinis debet obtemperare preceptis. Propterea ego Thomas ordinatus iam Eboracensis aecclesiae metropolitanus
90 antistes auditis cognitisque rationibus absolutam tibi Lanfrance Dorobernensis archiepiscope tuisque successoribus de canonica oboedientia professionem facio, et quicquid a te uel ab eis iuste et canonice iniunctum michi fuerit seruaturum me esse promitto. De hac autem re dum a te adhuc ordinandus essem dubius fui,
95 ideoque tibi quidem sine conditione, successoribus uero tuis conditionaliter, obtemperaturum me esse promisi. /

f. 5[v] iv.[14] [n]Anno[o] ab incarnatione Domini nostri Iesu Christi millesimo septuagesimo secundo, pontificatus autem domni Alexandri papae undecimo, regni uero Willelmi gloriosi regis Anglorum et
100 ducis Northmannorum[p] sexto, ex praecepto eiusdem Alexandri papae annuente eodem rege, in presentia ipsius et episcoporum atque abbatum, uentilata est causa de primatu quem Lanfrancus Dorobernensis archiepiscopus super Eboracensem aecclesiam iure suae aecclesiae proclamabat, et de ordinationibus quorundam

---

[j] eum Le   [k] Le *adds*: ut per concilium finiretur   [l] ecclesiam *corrected* V   [m] Ld *begins*   [n] Le *adds*: Generale concilium regni Anglorum de iure et primatu dorobernensis aecclesiae   [o] Cantaβ *begin* [p] Normannorum V

[10] lines 97–138 = section iv.
[11] i.e. no. 4; cf. no. 5, lines 17–18.
[12] Richter, no. 34: cf. *Councils and Synods* ad loc. Thomas's earlier, limited profession (lines 35–47, 94–6) does not survive.

England and settled there by the testimony and judgement of the
bishops and abbots of the whole kingdom. Although for his own
lifetime Lanfranc could bind Thomas by the profession he had
made, he was still ready to exert himself on behalf of his successors
rather than leave such a serious claim undiscussed for them to have
to treat later on. So both archbishops came to the king at the festival
of Easter and there when the arguments on both sides had been put
forward, the king's court gave judgement on the matter. Then they
ordered a document to be drawn up recording the settlement of the
whole case.[10] Lanfranc sent a letter to Pope Alexander in which he
gave him a succinct and accurate account of how the whole affair
had gone.[11] Both texts are appended below, preceded by the profession which Thomas gave to Lanfranc personally in front of the
king and his court:[12]

iii. [Archbishop Thomas's profession:] It is right that every
Christian should be subject to Christian laws, not opposing by
arguments of any kind what has been soundly established by the
holy Fathers. Such disputatiousness is the source of wrath, dissen-
sions, envy, disputes and other evils,[13] which plunge their addicts
into eternal torments. The loftier a man's estate, the greater too his
obligation to observe the commandments of God. Wherefore I
Thomas, now ordained metropolitan bishop of the church of York,
having heard and understood the case for doing so, make to you
Lanfranc, archbishop of Canterbury, and to your successors an
absolute profession of canonical obedience; and whatever shall be
justly and canonically enjoined on me by you or by them I promise
to observe. When I first sought ordination from you I was uncertain on this point, and so I promised obedience to you unconditionally but to your successors conditionally.

iv. [Council of Winchester; Easter 1072:][14] In the year of our
lord Jesus Christ 1072, the eleventh year of the pontificate of the
lord Pope Alexander and the sixth of the reign of William, glorious
king of the English and duke of the Normans, at the command of
the same Pope Alexander and with the consent of the aforesaid
king, in the presence of the king himself and the bishops and
abbots, there was a formal examination of the case for primacy,
which Archbishop Lanfranc of Canterbury was advancing as a
right of his own church over the church of York, and of the case
for ordaining certain bishops, where it was not at all clear to whose

[13] Cf. 2 Cor. 12: 20.
[14] Following Lanfranc's own report to Alexander II (no. 4, line 17), the
author of the memorandum places the royal judgement at Easter (no. 3,
line 76), hence at Winchester; he makes no reference to a further meeting at
Whitsun.

105 episcoporum de quibus ad quem specialiter pertinerent certum
    minime constabat. Et tandem aliquando diuersis diuersarum
    scripturarum auctoritatibus probatum atque ostensum est quod
    Eboracensis aecclesia Cantuariensi debeat subiacere, eiusque
    archiepiscopi ut primatis totius Britanniae dispositionibus in iis
110 que ad christianam religionem pertinent in omnibus oboedire.[15]
    Subiectionem uero Dunelmensis hoc est Lindisfarnensis episcopi,
    atque omnium regionum a terminis Licifeldensis episcopii et
    Humbrae magni fluuii usque ad[q] extremos Scotiae fines, et quic-
    quid ex hac parte praedicti fluminis ad parrochiam Eboracensis
115 aecclesiae iure competit, Cantuariensis metropolitanus Eboracensi
    archiepiscopo eiusque successoribus in perpetuum obtinere
    concessit: ita ut si Cantuariensis archiepiscopus concilium cogere
    uoluerit, ubicunque ei uisum[r] fuerit, Eboracensis archiepiscopus
    sui praesentiam cum omnibus sibi subiectis episcopis[s] ad nutum
120 eius exhibeat, et eius canonicis dispositionibus oboediens existat.[16]
    Quod autem Eboracensis archiepiscopus professionem Can-
f. 6 tuariensi archiepiscopo facere / etiam cum sacramento debeat
    Lanfrancus Dorobernensis archiepiscopus ex antiqua anteces-
    sorum consuetudine ostendit, sed ob amorem regis Thomae
125 Eboracensi archiepiscopo sacramentum relaxauit, scriptamque
    tantum professionem recepit, non preiudicans successoribus suis
    qui sacramentum cum professione a successoribus Thomae
    exigere uoluerint. Si archiepiscopus Cantuariensis uitam finierit,
    Eboracensis archiepiscopus Doberniam ueniet, et eum qui
130 electus fuerit cum ceteris prefatae aecclesiae episcopis ut primatem
    proprium iure consecrabit.[17] Quod si archiepiscopus Eboracensis[t]
    obierit, is qui ei successurus eligitur, accepto a rege archiepiscopa-
    tus dono, Cantuariam uel ubi Cantuariensi archiepiscopo uisum
    fuerit[u] accedet, et ab ipso ordinationem canonico more suscipiet.
135 Huic constitutioni consenserunt prefatus rex et archiepiscopi,
    Lanfrancus Cantuariensis et Thomas Eboracensis, et Hubertus
    sanctae Romanae aecclesiae subdiaconus et prefati Alexandri
    papae legatus,[v] et caeteri qui interfuerunt episcopi et abbates.[w][18]

---

[q] *om.* V   [r] uisum ei LeCantaβ   [s] *om.* LdCantβ; Le[1] *adds interlin.*
[t] Eboracensis archiepiscopus LdCantaβ   [u] uisum fuerit NV; placuerit
LdLeCantaβ   [v] et Hubertus... legatus *om.* LdCantaβ   [w] et abbates
om. LdCantaβ

[15] The proofs are enumerated in no. 4, lines 26–71. Archbishop Thomas's
second profession is to the archbishop of Canterbury as such (lines 107–10) rather
than to Lanfranc personally (lines 40–2 above).

jurisdiction they belonged. Finally it was established and demonstrated by written proofs of various kinds that the church of York
should be subject to Canterbury and should obey the directions of
its archbishop, as primate of the whole of Britain, in all matters
relating to the Christian religion.[15] Jurisdiction over the bishop of
Durham, that is Lindisfarne, and over all the territory from the
borders of the see of Lichfield and the great river Humber to the
furthest limits of Scotland, and whatever on the southern side of
the same river lawfully falls within the diocese of York the metropolitan of Canterbury has confirmed in perpetuity to the archbishop of York and his successors. If for instance the archbishop
of Canterbury should wish to summon a council, wherever he may
see fit, the archbishop of York shall present himself at his command, with all his suffragan bishops, and be obedient to his lawful
instructions.[16] Archbishop Lanfranc of Canterbury demonstrated
that according to the ancient right of his predecessors an archbishop of York should profess obedience to the archbishop of
Canterbury with a public oath as well; but out of love for the king
he waived the oath for Archbishop Thomas of York and accepted
a written profession only, without prejudice to his own successors,
who might wish to exact from Thomas's successors an oath as well
as a profession. If the archbishop of Canterbury reaches the close
of his life, the archbishop of York shall come to Canterbury and
duly consecrate the archbishop-elect as his own primate, with the
help of other bishops of that church.[17] But if the archbishop of York
dies, when his chosen successor has received the archbishopric
from the king, he shall come to Canterbury or wherever the archbishop of Canterbury thinks fit, and receive ordination from him
according to the custom of the Church. This constitution has received the assent of the aforesaid king and archbishops, Lanfranc
of Canterbury and Thomas of York, and of Hubert, subdeacon of
the holy Roman Church and legate of the aforesaid pope Alexander, and of the other bishops and abbots[18] who were present.

---

[16] Archbishop Thomas attended the councils of London, 1075 (no. 11, lines
8, 77) and Gloucester, 1081 (consecration of William of St. Carilef: A.L.,
p. 289); the membership of Lanfranc's other councils is not known.
[17] The issue arose in 1093: see the conflicting accounts of Eadmer, *H.N.*,
pp. 42–3, and Hugh the Chanter, *History of the Church of York 1066–1127*,
s.a. 1093, ed. C. Johnson (N.M.T., 1961), pp. 7–8.
[18] Cf. lines 101–2 above.

[Ventilata est autem haec causa prius apud Uuentanam ciuitatem
140 in Pascali solemnitate in capella regia quae sita est in castello,[19]
postea in uilla regia quae uocatur Uuindisor ubi et finem accepit
in praesentia regis episcoporum abbatum diuersorum ordinum
qui congregati erant apud curiam in festiuitate Pentecostes.][x]

4

Lanfranc to Pope Alexander II   8 Apr.–27 May 1072

This letter is section v of the memorandum on the primacy of Canterbury
(no. 3 = sections i–iv). It is Lanfranc's report to Alexander II on the council
to which he had referred the dispute between Lanfranc and Thomas of York
(lines 4–16; cf. no. 3, lines 69–72). Lanfranc describes the summoning and the
authority of the council of Winchester (lines 16–26), the arguments and proofs
advanced by the disputants (lines 26–85) and the judgement in favour of
Canterbury (lines 85–99). He encloses a copy of the document recording that
judgement (lines 99–101); it is his hope that the pope will confirm it forthwith
in a privilege (lines 104–5). See further Introduction, pp. 3–4.

Domino totius christianae religionis summo speculatori A.
papae L.[a] sanctae Dorobernensis aecclesiae antistes debitam cum
omni seruitute oboedientiam.

---

    [x] Ventilata . . . Pentecostes LdLeCant*β* *only*

---

4 NVLe
[a] Le *adds* indignus

[This case was examined first in the city of Winchester at the festival of Easter, in the royal chapel which is in the castle,[19] and then on the royal estate called Windsor, where it was settled in the presence of the king, the bishops, abbots, and the men of various ranks who had assembled there at court at the feast of Whitsun.]

AUTOGRAPH SIGNA IN CANTα:[20]

William I; Queen Matilda; Hubert, the papal legate; Lanfranc, archbishop of Canterbury; Thomas, archbishop of York; Walchelin, bishop of Winchester; Remigius, bishop of Dorchester; Herfast, bishop of Thetford; Wulfstan, bishop of Worcester.

AUTOGRAPH SIGNA IN CANTβ:

William I; Queen Matilda.

SUBSCRIPTIONS TO CANTβ:

Hubert the papal legate;

Archbishops: Lanfranc of Canterbury; Thomas of York;

Bishops: William of London; Hermann of Sherborne; Wulfstan of Worcester; Walter of Hereford; Giso of Wells; Remigius of Dorchester; Walchelin of Winchester; Herfast of Elmham; Stigand of Chichester; Siward of Rochester; Osbern of Exeter; Odo of Bayeux; Geoffrey of Coutances;

Abbots: Scotland of St Augustine's; Ælfwine of Ramsey; Ælnoth of Glastonbury; Thurstan of Ely; Wulfwold of Chertsey; Æthelwig of Evesham; Frederick of St Albans; Geoffrey of Westminster; Baldwin of Bury St Edmunds; Turold of Peterborough; Adelelm of Abingdon; Riwallon of New Minster.

4

Lanfranc to Pope Alexander II   8 Apr.–27 May 1072

To the lord Pope Alexander, most lofty guardian of the whole Christian religion: Lanfranc, archbishop of the holy church of Canterbury, offers unstinted service and due obedience.

[19] Cf. M. Biddle and D. J. Keene, 'Winchester in the eleventh and twelfth centuries', in *Winchester in the Early Middle Ages*, ed. F. Barlow and others (Oxford, 1976: *Winchester Studies* i), pp. 302–4.

[20] The precedence of the bishops was not firmly agreed until 1075 (no. 11, lines 6–32). Here Walchelin has precedence in his own city (Cantα), but stands in order of consecration at Windsor (Cantβ).

Meminisse debet humiliter excellens excellenterque humilis
5 beatitudo uestra quia quo tempore apud uos fuimus[1] Eboracensis
aecclesiae antistes aduersum me palam murmurauit, clam de-
traxit, in praesentia celsitudinis uestrae calumniam suscitauit,
dicens me iniuste uelle agere eo quod super se suamque aecclesiam /
f. 6ᵛ iure nostrae aecclesiae primatum niterer obtinere. De quorundam
10 quoque subiectione episcoporum quos aecclesiae suae conatus est
aggregare, antiquam sua querela non est ueritus consuetudinem
temerare.[2] Quibus de rebus uos sicut sanctum prudentemque
pastorem decuit et oportuit per scriptum sententiam promulgastis
quatinus conuentus Anglicae terrae episcoporum abbatum cetera-
15 rumque religiosi ordinis personarum utriusque partis rationes
audiret, discuteret, definiret. Factumque est ita; conuenerunt
enim ad regalem curiam apud Uuentanam ciuitatem in Paschali
solennitate[3] episcopi abbates ceterique ex sacro ac laicali ordine
quos fide et actione morumque probitate par fuerat conuenisse.
20 In primis adiurati sunt a nobis ex uestra auctoritate per sanctam
oboedientiam, deinde regia potestas per semetipsam contestata
est eos per fidem et sacramentum quibus sibi colligati erant,
quatinus hanc causam intentissime audirent, auditam ad certum
rectumque finem sine partium fauore perducerent. Vtrumque
25 omnes concorditer susceperunt, seseque ita facturos sub prefata
obligatione spoponderunt. Allata est igitur *Aecclesiastica gentis
Anglorum ystoria* quam Eboracensis aecclesiae praesbiter et
Anglorum doctor Beda composuit;[4] lectae sententiae quibus pace
omnium demonstratum est a tempore beati Augustini primi
30 Dorobernensis archiepiscopi usque ad ipsius Bedae ultimam
senectutem, quod fere centum et quadraginta annorum spatio /
f. 7 terminatur, antecessores meos super Eboracensem aecclesiam
totamque insulam quam Britanniam uocant necnon et Hiberniam
primatum gessisse, curam pastoralem omnibus impendisse, in ipsa
35 Eboracensi urbe persepe locisque finitimis ubi eis uisum fuit
episcopales ordinationes atque concilia celebrasse, ᵇEboracenses
antistites ad ipsa concilia uocasseᵇ et cum res poposcisset de suis
eos actibus rationem reddere compulisse. Episcopos quoque
quorum subiectionem in questionem adduxerat infra illud centum
40 et .xl. annorum spacium per Dorobernenses archiepiscopos fuisse
sacratos, ad concilia uocatos, quosdam quoque exigentibus culpis

ᵇ⁻ᵇ N *adds in margin: see Introduction, p. 16*

Exalted in lowliness and lowly when exalted your beatitude must recall that, while we were with you,[1] the archbishop of the church of York publicly criticized and privately disparaged me, and in your highness's presence made this accusation: I was meditating an injustice, in that I was endeavouring to acquire primacy over him and his church as a right of our own church. In his accusation he did not scruple to challenge the long-established right of jurisdiction over certain bishops, whom he attempted to attach to his own church.[2] In this affair, as was right and proper in a holy and skilful ruler, you issued a written directive that an assembly of the bishops, abbots and other persons of religious profession in the land of England should hear the case for both sides, consider it and reach a decision. This has been done: the bishops, abbots and others of the clergy and laity whom it was right to summon for their orthodoxy, their edifying life and their blameless character assembled at the royal court in the city of Winchester at the festival of Easter.[3] First on your authority we exhorted them by holy obedience, and then on his own authority the king enjoined them by the sworn fealty with which they were bound to him, to hear this case with the greatest care and then bring it impartially to a definitive and just conclusion. They all agreed to both proposals without dissent, promising to do so by the duty that bound them. So we brought in *The Ecclesiastical History of the English People*, the work of Bede, a priest of the church of York and Doctor of the English;[4] passages were read out which proved to everyone's satisfaction that from the time of St. Augustine, the first archbishop of Canterbury, until the last years of Bede himself, which is a period of almost 140 years, my predecessors exercised primacy over the church of York and the whole island which men call Britain and over Ireland as well; they extended pastoral care to all: they ordained bishops and held councils where they thought fit, often in the city of York itself and in places nearby; they summoned the archbishops of York to these councils and when necessary compelled them to give an account of their actions. The bishops too whose proper obedience Thomas had called in question had during that period of 140 years been consecrated by the archbishops of Canterbury and called to their councils, while some for the gravity of their misdemeanours had

---

4 [1] Oct. 1071: see no. 3, n. 7.

[2] Worcester, Lichfield, Dorchester: no. 3, lines 56–8.   [3] 8 Apr. 1072.

[4] Archbishop Thomas's case is thus undermined by the greatest scholar of his own province. Lanfranc was no doubt impressed by the jurisdiction of Archbishop Theodore (668–90: Bede, *H.E.* iv. 2–6, pp. 332–55); nevertheless all this evidence (lines 26–44) refers to the period before the see of York was fully established: after Bede's death (735) the picture was very different.

ab eis cum Romanae sedis auctoritate depositos; multaque in hunc modum quae epistolaris modestia per singula explicare non potest. Diuersa ad legendum porrecta concilia quae diuersis
45 temporibus diuersis de causis a meis sunt antecessoribus celebrata. Quae tametsi non eandem suae institutionis habuere materiam, eandem tamen de primatu et subiectionibus episcoporum tenuere sententiam. Recitatae eorundem de quibus questio uersabatur episcoporum ante predecessores meos factae electiones et per eos
50 ordinationes, qui Dorobernensi aecclesiae de sua oboedientia scriptas reliquerunt professiones;[5] urbs nanque que nunc Cantu- arberia nominatur antiquis temporibus ab ipsius terrae incolis Dorobernia uocabatur. Accesserunt omnium testimonia qui
54 omnia quae scripta sonuerunt se suis quisque temporibus uidisse
f. 7ᵛ et audisse constantissime firmauerunt. / Nec defuere[c] gesta quibus reseratum est, cum Anglia per plures esset regulos diuisa, Nor- danymbrorum regem ubi sita est ciuitas Eboraca accepto precio cuidam simoniaco episcopium uendidisse, pro qua culpa a Doro- bernensi archiepiscopo ad concilium uocatum fuisse, nolentemque
60 uenire pro sua inoboedientia excommunicationis sententiam pertulisse. Cuius communionis atque consortii omnis illarum parcium aecclesia tamdiu abstinuit quoadusque concilio seipsum exhibuit, culpam dixit, quod male gestum est correxit, de reliquo emendaturum se fore spopondit.[6] Quae res non mediocre tulit
65 indicium, antecessores meos super illam[d] terram illamque aeccle- siam habuisse primatum. Vltimum quasi robur totiusque causae firmamentum prolata sunt antecessorum uestrorum Gregorii, Bonefacii, Honorii, Vitaliani, Sergii, item Gregorii, Leonis,[e] item ultimi Leonis[e] priuilegia atque scripta, quae Dorobernensis
70 aecclesiae presulibus Anglorumque regibus aliis atque aliis tem- poribus uariis de causis sunt data aut transmissa.[7] (Reliqua enim reliquorum tam autentica quam eorum exemplaria in ea combu- stione atque abolitione quam aecclesia nostra ante quadriennium perpessa est penitus sunt absumpta.[8]) His atque aliis quae particu-

---

[c] defuerunt Le   [d] ipsam V   [e] Johannis: *William of Malmesbury, Gesta Pontificum p. 46*; see *Introduction, p. 22*.

---

[5] Pre-Conquest professions survive for Worcester (Richter, nos. 3, 11) and Lichfield (Richter, nos. 9, 15, 17, 21). No Dorchester professions survive; but as Remigius also took the title 'Legoracensis' the two Leicester professions (Richter, nos. 10, 20) may have been invoked here.

even been deposed by these archbishops on the authority of the Roman see. There was much further evidence of this kind which cannot be set out in detail within the modest scope of a letter. The texts of various councils were rehearsed, which for different reasons my predecessors held at various times. These, although not relating to the same subject, still adopted the same position on the primacy and the jurisdiction over the bishops. We enumerated the elections of those disputed bishops, made in the presence of my predecessors, and their ordination by my predecessors; they have left written professions of obedience to the church of *Dorovernia*.[5] (The city which now has the name of Canterbury was in ancient times called *Dorovernia* by the inhabitants of this country.) Similar testimony was given by all, who affirmed with the utmost consistency that each man had seen and heard in his own lifetime everything that these writings declared. Annals there were too, which disclosed that, when England was divided among many local kings, the king of the Northumbrians where York is situated sold the episcopal office for a sum of money to a simoniac; for that crime the king had been called to a council by the archbishop of Canterbury and when he refused to come had suffered excommunication for his recalcitrance. The whole Church in that part of the world abstained from communion with him or contact of any kind until he presented himself at a council, admitted his fault, corrected the error and promised that he would amend his life in future.[6] This affair supplied notable proof that my predecessors had primacy over that land and its church. Finally we produced as the cornerstone of our entire case the privileges and letters of your own predecessors—Gregory, Boniface, Honorius, Vitalian, Sergius, again Gregory, Leo and the most recent Leo—which were given or sent to the rulers of the church of Canterbury and the kings of the English at one time or another for various reasons.[7] (Other documents from other hands were utterly consumed—both the originals and the copies—in that destructive fire which our church suffered four years ago.[8]) When this and other evidence, which brevity

---

[6] This incident is otherwise unrecorded.

[7] Most of the popes here named appear as the authors of the forged privileges which in 1123 were presented at Rome in support of the primacy of Canterbury. Either Lanfranc is referring to these forgeries (but prudently not quoting them), or the forgeries were constructed on the basis of Lanfranc's list of popes. See further Southern, 'Canterbury Forgeries', pp. 193–226 and Gibson, App. C.

[8] 6 Dec. 1067: *A.S. Chron.* D s.a. 1067.

75 latim breuiterque explicari non possunt ex parte nostrae aecclesiae
in causa peroratis, contra tantam tantarum auctoritatum euiden-
tiam paucissimas contradictiones opposuit, epistolam illam precipue ferens in medium qua beatus Gregorius Londoniensem atque
79 Eboracensem aecclesiam pares esse nec alteram alteri subiacere
f. 8 instituit.⁹ / Quam scripturam cum in rem nichil facere concordi
sententia cuncti protinus definissent, pro eo quod nec ego Londoniensis episcopus essem nec de Londoniensi aecclesia esset quaestio
instituta, uertit se ad alia egena atque infirma argumenta quae
post paucam moram Christo reuelante paucis sunt obiectionibus
85 abolita. Quem cum rex dulci paternaque reprehensione argueret
quod contra tantam argumentorum copiam tam inops rationum
uenire presumpsisset, respondit se antea ignorasse Dorobernensem aecclesiam tot tantisque auctoritatibus tamque perspicuis
rationibus esse munitam. Versus itaque ad preces est; rogauit
90 enim regem ut me rogaret quatinus omnem mentis rancorem
aduersus eum pro hac causa conceptum omitterem, pacem diligerem, concordiam facerem, aliqua quae mei essent iuris studio
ei caritatis concederem.¹⁰ Cui peticioni ego libenter et cum gratiarum actione assensum prebui, quia miserante Deo non ego sed
95 ille prisce consuetudinis uiolator causa erat istius scandali. Facta
est igitur communi omnium astipulatione de hac re quaedam
scriptura, cuius exemplaria per principales Anglorum aecclesias
distributa futuris semper temporibus testimonium ferant ad
quem finem causa ista fuerit perducta.¹¹ Cuius exemplar uobis
100 quoque quibus sanctam totius mundi aecclesiam constat esse
commissam transmittendum curaui, ut ex hoc atque aliis quae
transmissa sunt perspicue cognoscatis ex more antecessorum
quid michi Christique aecclesiae quam regendam suscepi con-
f. 8ᵛ cedere debeatis. ᶠQuod / peto honeste et sine dilatione per indultum
105 sedis apostolicae priuilegium fieri, quatinus ex hoc quoque
quantum me diligatis euidenter possit ostendi;¹² de me autem
reuera estimate quod de fideli ac seruo beati Petri ac uestro
sanctaeque aecclesiae Romanae.¹³ Nunquam enim res quaelibet de
archa mei pectoris eicere quauis occasione poterit inauditam illam
110 humilitatem quam michi extremo hominum tantis indigno

ᶠ⁻ᶠ Quod peto . . . curaui (*line* 121) *om.* Le

---

⁹ Gregory the Great, *Registrum* xi. 39, ed. L. M. Hartmann (Berlin, 1895:
MGH Epistolae II. ii), pp. 312–13; cf. Bede, *H.E.* i. 29, pp. 104–7.

forbids us to set out in detail, had been marshalled on behalf of our church, Archbishop Thomas countered these overwhelming and authoritative proofs with the most trivial objections, making special play of that letter in which St. Gregory laid down that the churches of London and York were equal, neither being subject to the other.[9] When the whole company had at once ruled unanimously that this document was irrelevant to the matter in hand, in that I was not bishop of London nor did the case refer to the church of London, he turned to other proofs, slight and weak, which by Christ's help were soon demolished at a few strokes. When the king rebuked him with paternal mildness for having presumed to come so poorly supplied with arguments against such a battery of proofs, he replied that he had not previously understood that the church of Canterbury was fortified with so many mighty proofs and such convincing arguments. So he became a suppliant; he pleaded with the king to persuade me to put aside all the hostility towards him that this lawsuit had engendered, to choose peace and make a settlement with him, and to concede him out of charity some points which were mine by right.[10] This request I granted freely and thankfully, for by God's mercy it was not I but he who in breaking with ancient usage had initiated the dispute. So by common consent a written record was made of this agreement and copies sent to the major churches of England, which in future ages will always testify to how that lawsuit has been concluded.[11] Nor have I neglected to send a copy to you, to whom the holy Church throughout all the world has indisputably been committed, so that from this and the other documents sent you may clearly understand what you should confirm in the tradition of your predecessors to me and to Christ Church, whose government is in my hands. I ask that it be expressed as a privilege by grace of the apostolic see in due form and without delay, so that here too there may be an open declaration of the strength of your love for me;[12] on my part reckon my love to be truly that of St. Peter's faithful servant and your own and that of the holy Roman Church.[13] Nothing could ever cast out of my heart's treasury that unprecedented condescension which in Rome you showed to me the least of men, unworthy of such honours, in

[10] i.e. to be excused the public oath: no. 3, lines 121–8.

[11] See Hugh the Chanter, *History of the Church of York 1066–1127*, s.a. 1072: 'Plurima autem carte illius exempla miserunt (monachi Cantuarienses) in ecclesias et monasteria ut in armariis conseruarentur', ed. C. Johnson (N.M.T., 1961), p. 5. The text circulated was Cantβ: see *Councils and Synods* ad loc.

[12] The argument turns on 'ex hoc quoque' (line 105): let one declaration of favour (the two pallia) be matched with another (the primatial privilege).

[13] A second line of argument: Lanfranc's faithful service to his lord.

honoribus Rome exhibuistis, quodque duo pallia, unum de altari
ex more et alterum quo sanctitas uestra missas celebrare con-
sueuerat, ad ostendendam circa me beniuolentiam uestram michi
impendistis;[14] illud quoque quod omnibus quorum mediator
115 extiti quicquid iuste ac salubriter petierunt me interueniente
protinus concessistis:[15] ut taceam alia plura quae in hac parte ab
his minime discrepant, quaeque michi memoriam uestri nominis
si quid boni facio[g] dulciter representant.

Epistolam quam Beringerio[h] scismatico dum adhuc Cadomensi
120 cenobio praeessem transmisi[16] paternitati uestrae sicut precepistis
transmittere curaui.[f]

Omnipotens Dominus uitam uestram ad honorem sanctae
aecclesiae uestris dispositionibus diuinitus commissae in tempore
prolixam faciat, quatinus post tempus quae sine tempore sunt
125 prolixa aeternitatis spacia uobis concedat.

5

Lanfranc to Archdeacon Hildebrand

8 Apr.–27 May 1072

Dispatched as a supporting letter to no. 4; Hildebrand's reply is no. 6. Lanfranc
and Hildebrand no doubt met at the papal court in 1067 (Orderic, *Hist.
Eccles.* ii. 200) and 1071 (no. 3, n. 7); their acquaintance may even have
begun under Leo IX, at whose court Lanfranc spent some months in 1050.
Nevertheless Lanfranc's unusually ornate style suggests that he is not addressing
a trusted friend and colleague.

Domino sanctae Romanae aecclesiae archidiacono Hildebrando
L. suus 'sanctis principiis sanctum coniungere finem'.[1]

Explicare litteris mens mea non potest quanta dilectione uestrae
f. 9 sinceritati / conectitur, quantaque dulcedine gratiarum uestrarum
5 quas michi tam praesenti quam absenti benignitas uestra semper
exhibuit indesinenter reminiscitur. Propterea si donante Deo in
quibuslibet rerum generibus aliquid boni facio, salutem uestram
tam temporalem quam tempore carituram tradere obliuioni non
ualeo.[2] Et hoc oro omnipotentem Deum, quatinus uitam uestram
10 ad honorem et firmamentum sanctae aecclesiae suae prolixam
in hoc seculo faciat, incontaminatam ab omni peccati contagione

---

[g] boni bonifacio N   [h] Berigerio N

5 NV

that as a mark of your favour towards me you assigned to me two pallia, one from the altar as was usual and another with which your holiness had been accustomed to celebrate Mass,[14] and also in that whenever I was anyone's advocate at my intercession you at once granted his request, if it was just and profitable.[15] I say nothing of many other instances which in this respect are no different from these and which pleasantly bring back the memory of your name to me when I do anything good.

Nor have I neglected to send to you, father, as you directed, the letter which I sent to the schismatic Berengar[16] when I was still abbot of the monastery in Caen.

May the Lord almighty make your life long within time to the honour of the holy Church that is providentially committed to your care, so that he may grant you a wide measure of timeless eternity when time is no more.

5

Lanfranc to Archdeacon Hildebrand

8 Apr.–27 May 1072

To the lord Hildebrand, archdeacon of the holy Roman Church, his devoted servant Lanfranc wishes that 'he may bring holy enterprises to a holy conclusion'.[1]

Language cannot express with what affection my mind is bound to your honour and how sweet is the continual remembrance of the favours that in your benevolence you have always extended to me, whether present or absent. If by the grace of God I achieve anything worthwhile in any spheres of action, I cannot be unmindful of your welfare both temporal and in the future state beyond time.[2] This I pray almighty God, to give you long life in this world to the honour and support of his holy Church, to preserve your life spotless from all contagion of sin, and in the world to come generously

---

[14] Oct. 1071 (no. 3, n. 7); for other versions of this anecdote see Gibson, App. A, no. 2.

[15] Lanfranc intervened on behalf of Remigius of Dorchester (Richter, no. 32) and allegedly too on behalf of Archbishop Thomas himself (Eadmer, *H.N.*, p. 11). The argument continues: When I was another man's advocate, you listened to me; now I am my own . . .

[16] L.D.C.S.D.: see further nos. 46, 49.

5 [1] *Locum non inueni.* Contrast the more moderate address to the pope himself: 'finem bonum inferre bono principio' (no. 2, lines 2–3).

[2] Cf. no. 4, lines 117–18.

custodiat, et in futuro centuplicatis operibus uestris uitam uobis
permanentem copiosus remunerator retribuat.[3]

Porro calumnia quam Eboracensis aecclesiae antistes aduersum
15 me mouit de primatu et de[a] subiectione quorundam episcoporum
secundum preceptum apostolicae sedis audita ac determinata est.
Cuius negotii gestionem breuiter ex ordine scriptam domino
nostro papae transmisi,[4] quam uolo et rogo a uobis competenti
diligentia legi, quatinus caritas uestra certissimum teneat quid
20 michi aecclesiaeque meae sedes apostolica confirmando concedere
et concedendo confirmare per priuilegium debeat.[5]

6

Archdeacon Hildebrand to Lanfranc   *summer 1072*

The reply to no. 5, possibly also to no. 4. If Hildebrand's letter seems curt in the
circumstances, this was one of the points at issue: whether to transact business
personally or by letter.

Lanfranco uenerabili Cantuariorum archiepiscopo Hildebrandus
sanctae Romanae aecclesiae archidiaconus salutem in Domino.

Verba legatorum uestrorum gratanter accepimus, sed quod uoluntati uestrae in mittendo absenti personae uestrae priuilegio ut
5 illi petebant rite non potuimus satisfacere ualde doluimus. Neque
f. 9ᵛ id egre ferat uestra prudentia; / quoniam si alicui archiepiscoporum
nostris temporibus absenti hoc concessum fuisse uidissemus,
profecto religioni uestrae promptissima caritate honorem hunc
absque uestra fatigatione impenderemus. Vnde necessarium nobis
10 uidetur uos apostolorum limina uisitare, quatinus de hoc et ceteris
una uobiscum efficatius quod opportuerit consulere ualeamus
atque statuere.[1] De cetero si legatos nostros ad uos uenire contigerit solita caritate recipite, et quae uobis in aure dixerint prout
carissimum sanctae Romanae aecclesiae filium et religiosum
15 decet sacerdotem procurare studete.

ᵃ *om.* V

---

6 NV

to recompense you a hundredfold for your works with the life that endures for ever.[3]

The accusation which the archbishop of York made against me concerning the primacy and the obedience owed by certain bishops has been examined and concluded according to the instructions of the apostolic see. I have sent our lord the pope a summary account of the affair;[4] I do earnestly request you to read it with due attention, so that you may as a friend fully understand what kind of privilege the apostolic see should ratify and confirm to me and my church.[5]

6

Archdeacon Hildebrand to Lanfranc   *summer 1072*

To the reverend Lanfranc, archbishop of Canterbury, Hildebrand, archdeacon of the holy Roman Church, sends greetings in the Lord.

We were glad to receive your legates' message; but much to our regret we could not legally accede to your wish that the privilege should as they requested be sent to you in your absence. As a man of experience you need not be distressed at our refusal: if in our time we had ever seen this granted to an archbishop in his absence, then as a mark of our love we should have hastened to bestow the honour on you, reverend sir, without any effort on your part. But it does seem to us essential that you should visit the courts of the Apostles, so that we can discuss this and other problems with you in person and decide more effectively how to resolve them.[1] Finally if our legates should visit you, receive them with your accustomed charity and act promptly on any advice that they may give you, as befits a very dear son of the holy Roman Church and a godly bishop.

[3] Cf. Matt. 19: 29.
[4] Sc. no. 4; cf. Cicero, *De inventione* i. 38: 'In gestione autem negotii . . . etc.'. The same phrase is used in no. 3, lines 79–80.
[5] Cf. no. 4, lines 103–4.

6 [1] Lanfranc never returned to Rome: in 1080 he gave a spirited justification for not doing so (no. 38, lines 12–20); in 1082 Gregory VII was demanding his attendance under threat of excommunication (G. VII, *Reg.* ix. 20), but without result.

7

Pope Alexander II to King William I   Oct. *1071*

Written when Lanfranc and his colleagues visited Rome in the autumn of
1071 (no. 3, n. 7); cf. lines 44–8 below. The letter indicates the degree of
jurisdiction that Alexander, in contrast with his successor, was ready to delegate
to Lanfranc: he can reverse a legatine judgement (lines 30–6) and he can in
principle act on the pope's behalf (lines 41–4). This letter passed into collections of canon law, e.g. LcLeCd; for further manuscripts see *Councils and
Synods*, 24 May, 1070.

ᵃAlexander episcopus seruus seruorum Dei carissimo filio W.
glorioso regi Anglorum salutem et apostolicam benedictionem.

Omnipotenti Deo laudes gratiasque referimus quod hoc in
tempore, licet mundus in maligno positus¹ plus solito prauis
5 incumbat studiis, tamen inter mundi rectores et principes egregiam
uestrae religionis famam intelligimus, et quantum honoris sanctae
aecclesiae tum simoniacae haeresis uires opprimendo tum catholi-
cae libertatis usus et officia confirmando uestra uirtus impendat
non dubia relatione cognoscimus.² Sed quoniamᵇ non iis qui bona
10 demonstrant initia sed in fine probatis³ premium et corona
promittitur, excellentiam uestram plena dilectione monemus ut in
studio christianissimae deuotionis uestrae persistatis, et primo
quidem aecclesias Christi quae in regno uestro sunt religioso
14 cultu et iustis dispositionibus exornetis, commissa uobis regni
f. 10 gubernacula ita iusticiam tenendo tractetis / ut ex operum
rectitudine quod scriptum est, 'Cor regis in manu Dei',⁴ uobis
manifeste congruat.ᶜ Rogamus etiam dilectionem uestram ut aec-
clesiasticas personas ab iniuria defendatis, uiduas et orphanos et
oppressos misericorditer releuando protegatis; quoniam licet ille
20 rex regum et supernus arbiter totius regni quod uobis tradidit
rationem a uobis exigat, pro his tamen districtius appellabit
quibus hic non sunt uires et arma nisi uestra potentia. Ad haec
igitur perficienda et aliarum uirtutum incrementa percipienda
fratris nostri Lanfranci Cantuariensis archiepiscopi monitis et
25 consiliis gloriam uestram ortamur adquiescere; quem carissimum
membrum et unum ex primis Romanae aecclesiae filiis lateri
nostro assidue non adiunctum esse dolemus,⁵ sed ex fructu quem

---

7 NVLcLeCd *with some use of* [Ct]

ᵃ De causa Ailrici episcopi cicestrensis LcCd   ᵇ quia V   ᶜ congruet
Le

---

¹ 1 John 5: 19.

7

Pope Alexander II to King William I   *Oct. 1071*

Bishop Alexander, servant of the servants of God, greets his dearest
son William, the glorious king of the English, and sends him his
apostolic blessing.

We praise and thank almighty God that although the world that
'lieth in wickedness'[1] is tending more than usual towards evil pur-
suits, we learn at this time of your outstanding reputation for piety
among the rulers and princes of the world and we receive unmistakable evidence of your support for the Church: you do battle
against the forces of simoniacal heresy and you defend the freedom
of catholic rites and customs.[2] But since the crown of reward is
promised not to those who begin well but to those who are proven
at the end,[3] from our heart we urge your excellency zealously to
persevere in your most Christian devotion. In the first place you
must adorn the churches of Christ in your realm with true religion
and just government, and rule the kingdom that is in your care so
justly that in your upright dealings the text 'The heart of the king
is in the hand of God'[4] may manifestly apply to you. We further
admonish you, dear son, to defend members of the clergy from
injustice and to protect widows, orphans, and the oppressed, mercifully coming to their succour; for although that King of kings, the
supreme Judge on high, calls you to account for the whole kingdom
which he has entrusted to you, yet he will summon you more
strictly to answer for those who have here no resource or defence
except your power as king. To achieve these ends and to gain increase of other virtues we exhort your highness to follow the advice
and counsel of our brother Lanfranc, archbishop of Canterbury;
as our most cherished member, one of the leading sons of the
Roman Church, we are grieved that he is so rarely at our side,[5] but

---

[2] Alexander no doubt refers principally to the legatine councils of Easter and
Whitsun 1070: *Councils and Synods*, ad loc.

[3] Cf. Rev. 2: 10.

[4] Cf. Prov. 21: 1.

[5] For the metaphor of head and limbs implicit here see 1 Cor. 12: 12–27.

aecclesiae in regnoo uestr tribuit consolationem eius absentiae
sumimus.

30 Praeterea eminentiae uestrae notum esse uolumus quod causa
Alricii, qui olim Cicestrensis aecclesiae presul dictus a suppositis
legatorum nostrorum depositus est, non ad plenum nobis tractata
uidetur. Ideoque sicut in canonibus cautum est in pristinum locum
debere restitui iudicauimus,[6] deinde causam eius iuxta censuram
35 canonicae traditionis diligenter retractandam et diffiniendam
predicto fratri nostro archiepiscopo Lanfranco commisimus.[7]
Item sibi negotium de discernenda lite quae inter archiepiscopum
Eboracensem et episcopum Dorcacestrensem de pertinentia[d]
diocesis eorum est firmiter iniungendo commendauimus, ut hanc
40 causam diligentissima perquisitione pertractet et iusto fine
f. 10ᵛ determinet.[8] In causis autem / pertractandis et diffiniendis ita
sibi nostrae et apostolicae auctoritatis uicem dedimus, ut quicquid
in eis iusticia dictante determinauerit, quasi in nostra presentia
definitum deinceps firmum et indissolubile teneatur. Multa uobis
45 preter haec significata dedissemus, nisi quod ea in huius dilectissimi
fratris nostri Lanfranci et eiusdem fidelissimi uobis ore posuimus,
ut eius uiua uoce et nostrae dilectionis affectum plenius cognoscatis,
et reliqua nostrae[e] legationis uerba[9] attentius audiatis.[f]

Deus autem omnipotens det uobis quaecunque sibi sunt placita[g]
50 uelle et posse,[10] ut et hic auctor sit uestri gubernaculi et retributor
in gloria sempiterni gaudii.

---

[d] pertinentia N¹V; pertinatia N   [e] uestrae LcCd   [f] [Ct adds:
praeterea rogamus prudentiam uestram ut Tedaldum communem fidelem
nostrum Cestrensi Ecclesiae episcopum praeponatis]   [g] LcLeCd add et

---

[6] e.g. Zephyrinus, *Epistola Aegiptiis directa* (Hinschius, p. 133); cf. M. Brett,
The English Church under Henry I (Oxford, 1975), p. 92, with references.

[7] Aethelric of Chichester was deposed at the council of Windsor, Whitsun
1070 (*Councils and Synods*, ad loc.) and his successor, Stigand (nominated 23
May 1070), probably consecrated before Lanfranc's arrival. Aethelric seems
to have spent the next six years in limbo. Although he was sent 'ex precepto
regis' to be a witness at Penenden Heath in 1072 (J. Le Patourel, 'The Reports
of the Trial on Penenden Heath', *Studies in Medieval History presented to F. M.
Powicke*, ed. R. W. Hunt and others, Oxford, 1948, p. 23), there is no evidence,
apart from the present letter, that he was ever reinstated as bishop. He was
definitively deposed at the council of Winchester, Easter 1076: *Councils and
Synods*, ad loc.

[8] There were two points at issue between Dorchester and York. Should the
bishop of Dorchester acknowledge York as his metropolitan? This question
was discussed at the council of Winchester, Easter 1072 (no. 4, lines 38–9;

we are consoled for his absence by the increment which he renders to the Church in your realm.

We wish to draw your eminence's attention to the case of Alricius, formerly entitled bishop of Chichester, who was deposed by representatives of our legates: it does not seem to us to have been fully examined. So we have ruled that he should be restored to his original position, as canon law decrees;[6] and have referred the case to our brother whom we have just mentioned, Archbishop Lanfranc, to be thoroughly re-examined and concluded in accordance with canon law.[7] We have also committed to him the task of deciding the dispute between the archbishop of York and the bishop of Dorchester over the boundary between their dioceses, urging him to examine this case very carefully and bring it to a just conclusion.[8] The personal and apostolic authority that we have delegated to him for the conduct and conclusion of disputes is such that whatever he may decide in these affairs, so long as it is just, can thereafter be considered no less firm and binding than if the matter had been concluded in our own presence. We should have written to you at much greater length, had we not put our words in the mouth of our beloved brother Lanfranc, who is also your most faithful servant, so that from him in person you may both learn more fully the warmth of our affection and listen the more attentively to the rest of our business.[9]

May almighty God give you the will and the power to do whatever is pleasing to him,[10] that he may both direct your rule in this world and reward you with eternal joy in glory.

---

cf. no. 3, lines 102–6) and judgement given against York. The second question concerned certain lands south of the Humber (cf. no. 3, lines 113–15). Did these lie within the *diocesan* jurisdiction of York or Dorchester? Lanfranc appears to have been instructed to examine this separate dispute, which had no bearing on the rights of Canterbury, as a preliminary to the council of Winchester.

[9] This phrase must cover the instructions to initiate the council of Winchester (no. 3, lines 97–138).

[10] Cf. Phil. 2: 13.

8

Pope Gregory VII to Lanfranc c. July 1073

J.L. 4801; Cowdrey, *Epistolae Vagantes*, no. 1. Gregory writes not long after his consecration (30 June 1073: cf. note 1) and in any event almost certainly before Lanfranc wrote to the Irish kings (nos. 9–10).

[a]Gregorius episcopus seruus seruorum Dei carissimo fratri in Christo L. uenerabili Cantuariorum archiepiscopo salutem et apostolicam benedictionem.

Qualiter nobis apostolici regiminis honor et onus inpositum sit et
5 quantis undique stringamur angustiis presentium tibi portitor indicabit, cui respectu tuae dilectionis etiam nonnulla nostris adhuc familiaribus occulta aperuimus. De cetero inprimis fraternitatem tuam rogamus ut Deum pro nobis iugiter exorare non pigeat et subditos sibi uel coniunctos fratres suis nos orationibus
10 apud Deum iuuare commoneat.[1] Quanto enim in maiore periculo positi sumus, tanto amplius tuis et bonorum omnium suffragiis indigemus. Nos etenim si diuinae uindictae iudicium effugere uolumus, contra multos insurgere et eos in animam nostram
f. 11 pro/uocare compellimur. Nam dum omnes fere sicut ait apostolus
15 'quae sua sunt non quae Iesu Christi quaerunt',[2] regnorum principes et huius mundi potentes ut cupiditates suas expleant legem Dei et iusticiam non iam neglegenter deserunt, sed summis conatibus impugnant; ut illud prophetae nunc sub oculis uideamus impletum: 'Astiterunt reges terrae et principes conuenerunt in
20 unum aduersus Dominum et aduersus Christum eius.'[3] Episcopi uero et qui pastores animarum esse deberent mundi gloriam et delicias carnis insatiabili desiderio prosequentes non solum in semetipsis quae sancta quaeque sunt religiosa confundunt, sed subditos suos ad omne nefas operum suorum exemplo per-
25 trahunt. Quibus non contraire quam nobis periculosum, resistere autem et eorum nequiciam refrenare quam difficile sit tua prudentia[b] nouit. Sed quoniam quos dolores inter has patiamur angustias ut supra diximus huic communi filio nostro tibi referendum exeruimus, plura de his dicere supersedemus.

30 Tuam uero fraternitatem, etsi monitore non egeat, impellente

8 NVLcCd
[a] LcCd *add*: Decretum Gregorii pape. ut Lanfrancus archiepiscopus Cantuariensis curam Christianitatis exerceret super Scotiam [b] prouidentia LcCd

8

Pope Gregory VII to Lanfranc   c. *July 1073*

Bishop Gregory, servant of the servants of God, sends to the venerable Lanfranc, archbishop of Canterbury, his dearest brother in Christ, greetings and apostolic blessing.

The bearer of this letter will tell you how the honour and the burden of apostolic rule were laid upon us, and also what great difficulties beset us on all sides; out of regard for you, dear friend, we have apprised him even of certain matters which are still unknown to our colleagues here. But first of all we entreat you as our brother not to neglect continual intercession on our behalf; enjoin your monks too and those of associated communities to commend us to God in their own prayers.[1] For the greater the peril in which we lie, the more we need support from you and all good men. We ourselves, if we would escape the sentence of divine punishment, are constrained to rise up against many and provoke them against our life. For while, as the Apostle says, nearly 'all seek their own, not the things which are Jesus Christ's',[2] in these days the rulers of the kingdoms and the mighty of this world are not merely neglecting but wholeheartedly opposing justice and the law of God in order to indulge their own lusts. Now we see before our eyes the words of the prophet fulfilled: 'The kings of the earth have stood up and the rulers taken counsel together against the Lord and against his anointed.'[3] Bishops, the very men who should be shepherds of souls, in their endless craving for worldly glory and the delights of the flesh are not only choking all holiness and piety within themselves but the example of their conduct is luring their charges into every kind of sin. A man of your experience knows the danger to us if we do not oppose them, yet how difficult it is to resist them and restrain their wickedness. But since (as we said above) we have disclosed to this our son and yours the anxieties we suffer in these hard times, so that he may give you a full account, we say no more of these matters here.

Though you, brother, need no guide, still we are moved by our

---

8 [1] Cf. Gregory's early letters to Hugh of Cluny and others, asking for their prayers: G.VII, *Reg.* i. 1–4.

[2] Phil. 2: 21.

[3] Ps. 2: 2.

tamen nos sollicitudine admonemus quatinus grauiora usquequaque resecare uitia studeat, et inter omnia et prae omnibus
nefas quod de Scottis audiuimus, uidelicet quod plerique proprias
uxores non solum deserunt sed etiam uendunt, modis omnibus
35 prohibere contendat. Ad haec enim apostolica te auctoritate
fultum esse uolumus, ut non solum in Scottis hoc scelus sed
etiam in aliis si quos in Anglorum insula tales esse cognoueris /
f. 11ᵛ dura animaduersione punias, et radicem tanti mali prudenti
sarculo correctionis penitus extirpare non differas.[4]

9

Lanfranc to Guthric, king of Dublin
29 Aug. 1073–autumn 1074

Dated by Bishop Patrick's consecration (lines 3–8; cf. A.L., p. 289). Although
Lanfranc is no doubt writing with Gregory VII's letter (no. 8) in mind, his own
criticisms are more radical: he condemns marriage within the kindred (lines
19–20) as well as easy divorce (lines 20–2; no. 8, lines 33–4). For the law of
marriage in Ireland, which differed radically from Roman civil law and still
more markedly from the teaching of such canonists as Peter Damian, see K.
Hughes, *Early Christian Ireland: Introduction to the sources* (New York, 1972),
pp. 46–7 and 79, with references. Similar issues arose in Scotland: see Turgot,
Vita S. Margaretae Scotorum Reginae viii, ed. J. Hodgson Hinde (Durham,
1867: Surtees Soc. li), pp. 243–5.

Lanfrancus non suis meritis sed gratia Dei archiepiscopus glorioso
Hiberniae regi[1] Gothrico salutem cum orationibus.

Venerabilem fratrem ac coepiscopum nostrum Patricium quem,
karissime fili, excellentia uestra ad nos consecrandum transmisit
5 honeste suscepimus, debitis officiis secundum canonicam institutionem Sancti Spiritus gratia cooperante sacrauimus, sacratum
ad sedem propriam cum testimonio litterarum nostrarum more
antecessorum nostrorum remisimus.[2] Qui quamuis de gloria
uestra multa nobis bona multisque laudibus digna retulerit, non
10 ab re tamen esse credimus si predicanda studia uestra nostra

---

[4] Given the letters that follow to Guthric and Toirrdelbach (nos. 9–10),
I have assumed that here also it is the Irish whose marriage customs are under
fire.

---

9 NV

own pastoral concern to remind you to endeavour to extirpate
serious moral offences wherever they occur, specifically and pre-
eminently that you strive by every means open to you to ban the
wicked practice which we have heard rumoured of the Irish:
namely that many of them not only desert their lawful wives but
even sell them. In these matters we wish you to be sustained with
apostolic authority, so that you may punish this crime with stern
chastisement not only among the Irish but among others too, if you
know of any such men in the island of the English, and be prompt
to cut out the root of such a great evil completely with the skilful
hoe of discipline.[4]

9

Lanfranc to Guthric, king of Dublin
                              29 Aug. 1073–autumn 1074

Lanfranc, archbishop not by his own merits but by the grace of
God, sends Guthric, the glorious king of Ireland,[1] his prayerful
greetings.

Dearest son, we received with honour our venerable brother and
fellow bishop Patrick, whom your excellency sent to us to be
consecrated; with the grace of the Holy Ghost to help us we
consecrated him in due form to his appointed duties; after his
consecration we sent him back to his own see with our letter of
commendation, as was the custom of our predecessors.[2] Now
although he brought us many good reports of you, glorious king,
matters worthy of much commendation, even so we think that it
may be useful to encourage you in your laudable endeavours with

---

9 [1] Guthric of Dublin (Gofraid mac Amlaíb meic Ragnaill: *c.* 1072–5) was
far from being 'king of Ireland'; he ruled the small Norse enclave of Dublin
and recognized Toirrdelbach Ua Briain, king of Munster (see no. 10), as his
overlord.

[2] Patrick bishop of Dublin (1074–84) was an Irishman educated and pro-
fessed in Worcester: A. Gwynn, *The Writings of Bishop Patrick 1074–84*
(Dublin, 1955: *Scriptores Latini Hibernenses* i), pp. 1–7, with references. See also
App. B. ii (letter petitioning that Patrick be consecrated) and Richter, no. 36.

adhortatione pulsamus. Sicut enim ignis flante uento clarius lucet et maior efficitur, sic uera uirtus ueris preconiis pulchrius enitescit et in melius augmentatur. Rogamus igitur sicut rogari oportet preciosum sanctae aecclesiae filium, quatinus fidem rectam ab ipso Deo et sanctis apostolis eius atque orthodoxis patribus traditam cum omni mentis sinceritate inuiolatam teneatis, fidei congrua opera in quantum uires suppetunt exhibeatis, superbis austeram humilibus placabilem uestram celsitudinem ostendatis.

In regno uestro perhibentur homines seu de propria seu de mortuarum uxorum parentela coniuges ducere, alii legitime sibi copulatas pro arbitrio et uoluntate relinquere, nonnulli suas aliis dare et aliorum infanda commutatione recipere.[3] Haec et siqua sunt alia crimina propter Deum et animam uestram in terra / potestatis uestrae corrigi iubete, talesque uos cum diuino adiutorio uestris subditis exhibete, ut et[a] amatores boni bona amplius diligant, et appetitores mali prauas actiones nequaquam exercere praesumant. Hoc enim facientes et diutius cum rerum temporalium felicitate in terra regnabitis, et post terrenum regnum sine fine regnaturi ad coelestia regna migrabitis.

Plura et prolixius uobis scripsissem, sed habetis uobiscum predictum antistitem uestrum monasticis institutionibus a pueritia enutritum, scientia diuinarum litterarum strenuissime eruditum,[4] bonorum operum ornamentis in quantum cognosci a nobis potuit decentissime adornatum. Quem de anima uestra uobis sepius loquentem si intento corde audieritis, audientes ut patri spirituali in his quae ad Deum pertinent oboedieritis, oboedientes ea quae uobis ab eo prolata fuerint in archa pectoris uestri reposueritis, speramus per misericordiam Dei quia neque uos perniciose errabitis neque subditos uobis in prauarum actionum pertinacia stare diu permiseritis.

Omnipotens Dominus contra inimicos mentis et corporis brachio uirtutis suae[5] excellentiam uestram defendat, et post longam huius seculi uitam ad eam quae finem non habet feliciter uos perducat.

---

[a] et ut V

[3] Marriage within the kindred is condemned in Lanfranc's letter to Toirrdel-bach (no. 10, lines 21–4) and by the council of London, 1075 (no. 11, *can.* vi). For casual divorce see no. 8, lines 32–4 and no. 10, lines 19–24.
[4] Gwynn, *Writings, passim.* Patrick's verses and homilies are the major witness to Latin scholarship at Worcester in the time of Wulfstan.

some words of advice. For just as a fire glows more brightly and flares up when the wind blows, so true worth shines forth more fair and grows better still when it is sincerely praised. We ask you then, as befits a cherished son of holy Church, to hold inviolate in all purity of heart the true faith handed down by God himself and his holy Apostles and the orthodox Fathers, to perform to the limit of your capacity the works that complement that faith and to show your sublime self harsh to the proud and amenable to the lowly.

There are said to be men in your kingdom who take wives from either their own kindred or that of their deceased wives; others who by their own will and authority abandon the wives who are legally married to them; some who give their own wives to others and by an abominable exchange receive the wives of other men instead.[3] For the sake of God and your own soul command that these offences and any others like them be corrected throughout the land which you rule, and with God's help so treat your subjects that those who love good may cherish it the more and those who lust after evil may never venture to do wrong. If you act in this way, not only will you reign longer on earth and have good fortune in the affairs of this world, but after this earthly kingdom you will go to the realms of heaven and reign there for ever.

I would have written you a longer and more detailed letter, but that you have with you the bishop whom we spoke of above. He has been nurtured in the monastic life since his youth; he is deeply versed in sacred learning;[4] and from what we could discover he has an exceptional distinction in good works. Listen often and carefully to him when he speaks to you about your soul; when you listen, obey him as a spiritual father in all that concerns God; and as you obey store up what he has told you in the treasury of your heart: then we trust that by the mercy of God you will neither stray into ruin yourself nor permit your subjects to continue for long in their stubborn evil practices.

May the Lord almighty defend your excellency by the strength of his arm[5] against the enemies of soul and body, and after long life in this world grant you an auspicious passage to the life which has no end.

[5] Ps. 88: 11.

10

Lanfranc to Toirrdelbach Ua Briain, king of Munster

c. *1074*

A companion letter to no. 9, probably of the same date. Toirrdelbach too is
exhorted to condemn marriage within the kindred and uncanonical divorce,
but unlike Guthric he is in a position to call a council: so he is given a specific
agenda (lines 18–42). These instructions may be contrasted with the very
general letter of encouragement sent to him by Gregory VII (Cowdrey, *Epistolae
Vagantes*, no. 57).

Lanfrancus peccator et indignus sanctae Dorobernensis aecclesiae
archiepiscopus magnifico Hibernie regi[1] Terdeluaco benedictionem cum seruicio et orationibus.

4   Nullam Deus maiorem terris misericordiam impendit quam cum
f. 12ᵛ pacis ac iusticiae amatores ad animarum / seu corporum gubernacula prouehit, et maxime cum bonis regibus regna huius mundi
regenda committit. Hinc namque pax oritur discordia sopitur et, ut
breuiter cuncta complectar, Christianae religionis obseruantia
stabilitur. Quod populis Hiberniae diuinitus tunc collatum fuisse
10 prudens inspector intelligit, quando omnipotens Deus excellentiae
uestrae ius regiae potestatis super illam terram concessit. Tot
enim tantaque bona de magnitudinis uestrae erga bonos pia
humilitate, contra prauos districta seueritate, circa omne hominumᵃ
genus discretissima aequitate frater et coepiscopus[2] noster
15 Patricius narrauit, ut quamuis uos nunquam uiderimus, tanquam
uisos tamen uos diligamus et tanquam uisis ac bene cognitis
uobis salubriter consulere et sincerissime seruire cupiamus.

Verum inter multa quae placent relata nobis sunt quaedam
quae displicent:[3] uidelicet quod in regno uestro quisque pro
20 arbitrio suo legitime sibi copulatam uxorem nulla canonica causa
interueniente relinquit et aliam quamlibet, seu sibi uel relicte
uxori consanguinitate propinquam siue quam alius simili im-
probitate deseruit, maritali seu fornicaria lege punienda sibiᵇ
temeritate coniungit; quod episcopi ab uno episcopo consecrantur;
25 quod in uillis uel ciuitatibus plures ordinantur; quod infantes
baptismo sine crismate consecrato baptizantur; quod sacri ordines
per pecuniam ab episcopis dantur. Haec omnia et siqua sunt
f. 13 similia contra euangelicam et apostolicam auctoritatem, / contra
sanctorum canonum prohibitionem, contra omnium orthodoxorum

10 NV
ᵃ humanum V   ᵇ sub V

10

Lanfranc to Toirrdelbach Ua Briain, king of Munster

c. *1074*

Lanfranc, a sinner and unworthy archbishop of the holy church of Canterbury, offers Toirrdelbach, the magnificent king of Ireland,[1] his blessing, his service and his prayers.

God grants the earth no greater mercy than when he promotes to the rule of souls or bodies men who love peace and justice, above all when he commits the kingdoms of this world to the rule of good kings. Then peace dawns, discord is hushed and—to sum everything up in a phrase—the practice of Christianity is firmly established. The wise observer knows that this was providentially granted to the peoples of Ireland when almighty God gave your excellency royal authority in that country. Patrick, our brother and fellow bishop,[2] has related so many remarkable instances of the godly humility with which your majesty treats good men, your stern severity to the wicked and your great wisdom and justice towards men of all conditions that though we have never seen you, we love you as though we had; and we desire to give you helpful advice and unfeigned service as though we not only had seen you but knew you well.

But among many things which are commendable certain reports have reached us which are quite the opposite:[3] namely that in your kingdom a man abandons at his own discretion and without any grounds in canon law the wife who is lawfully married to him, not hesitating to form a criminal alliance—by the law of marriage or rather by the law of fornication—with any other woman he pleases, either a relative of his own or of his deserted wife or a woman whom someone else has abandoned in an equally disgraceful way. Bishops are consecrated by a single bishop; many are ordained to villages or small towns; infants are baptized without the use of consecrated chrism; holy orders are conferred by bishops for money. No one who has the least familiarity with Christian learning is unaware that all these abuses and others like them are contrary to the Gospels and to apostolic teaching, that they are prohibited by canon law and are contrary to what has been established by all the orthodox Fathers who have gone before us. The more appalling

---

10 [1] Toirrdelbach (died 1086) was king of Munster and by *c.* 1073 high-king of Ireland: F. J. Byrne, *Irish Kings and High-Kings* (London, 1973), pp. 254–76.

[2] Patrick, bishop of Dublin (1074–84): see no. 9. Toirrdelbach is here apprised of Patrick's consecration.

[3] Cf. no. 9, n. 3.

30 patrum qui nos precesserunt fieri institutionem nullus qui sacras
litteras uel mediocriter legit ignorat. Quae quanto in conspectu
Dei sanctorumque eius amplius sunt horrenda, tanto studiosius
uestris sunt sine aliqua dilatione iussionibus prohibenda, et nisi
prohibita corrigantur districtissima terroris uestri seueritate puni-
35 enda. Nullum enim Deo uel maius uel gratius munus offerre
potestis quam si diuina et humana debitis legibus gubernare stu-
detis. Memores igitur diuini iudicii quo de commisso uobis regno
racionem reddituri estis Deo episcopos et religiosos quosque uiros
in unum conuenire iubete, sacro eorum conuentui praesentiam
40 uestram cum uestris optimatibus exhibete, has prauas con-
suetudines omnesque alias quae a sacris legibus improbantur a
regno uestro exterminare studete,[4] quatinus rex regum et dominus
dominantium cum uiderit regiam maiestatem uestram preceptis
suis in omnibus esse subiectam, seruis quoque ac fidelibus suis
45 pro timore et amore eius mansuetam, inimicis diuinae religionis
diuino zelo infestam, ipse quoque uos uestrosque fideles clamantes
ad se propiciatus exaudiat, hostes conterat, pacemque uobis in hoc
seculo stabilem et in futuro uitam aeternam concedat.

11

Council of London   *25 Dec. 1074–28 Aug. 1075*

Lanfranc summoned and presided over the council of London in William the
Conqueror's absence abroad (lines 51–2); hence it is not tied to a royal court
at Christmas, Easter or Whitsun. It was held after Christmas, within Lanfranc's
fifth year of office (A.L., p. 289); given the political disturbances of the spring
and summer (nos. 31–6), it should perhaps be dated to Easter rather than
Whitsun. Leaving aside the debate on the primacy (no. 3), *acta* survive for three
of Lanfranc's councils: Winchester 1072, London 1075 and Winchester 1076
(*Councils and Synods*, ad loc.). The *acta* of 1075 may be included here as evidence
of Lanfranc's status: he holds a council without the king; he exacts almost
complete attendance from both provinces (lines 8–18); he establishes precedence
among the leading bishops (lines 22–33).

Anno incarnationis dominicae millesimo septuagesimo quinto,
f. 13ᵛ regnante glorioso Anglorum rege Willelmo, anno / regni eius nono,
congregatum est Londoniae in aecclesia beati Pauli apostoli
concilium totius Anglicae regionis: episcoporum uidelicet abbatum
5 necnon et multarum religiosi ordinis personarum, iubente atque
eidem concilio presidente Lanfranco, sanctae Dorobernensis

11 NVJLe .

they are in the sight of God and his saints, the more uncompromis-
ingly should such practices be forbidden at once by your edicts and
punished, if they are not set right, great king, by the harshest
measures possible. You can offer God no greater or more pleasing
gift than your desire to govern divine and human affairs by the
appropriate laws. Remember the divine judgement at which you
will render account to God for the kingdom committed to you:
order the bishops and all men of religion to assemble together,
attend their holy assembly in person with your chief advisers, and
strive to banish from your kingdom these evil customs and all
others that are similarly condemned by canon law.[4] May the King
of kings and Lord of rulers, when he sees that your royal majesty
is in all things subject to his precepts, that as you fear and love him
you are merciful to his servants and followers, hostile to those who
oppose his worship and jealous for his rights, may he lend a propi-
tious ear to you and your followers who cry to him, may he beat
down your enemies and grant you lasting peace in this world and
eternal life in the next.

11

Council of London   *25 Dec. 1074–28 Aug. 1075*

In the year of our Lord 1075, in the ninth year of the reign of
William, glorious king of the English, a council of the whole land
of England was assembled in the church of St. Paul the Apostle in
London, namely of bishops, abbots and many ecclesiastics. The
council was summoned and presided over by Lanfranc, archbishop

---

[4] The first clearly-documented Irish council of this period was held by
Toirrdelbach's son, Muirchertach Ua Briain, in 1101; but there is reason
(apart from this letter) to think that Toirrdelbach himself did hold a council
on the lines that Lanfranc proposed: J. A. Watt, *The Church and the Two
Nations in Medieval Ireland* (Cambridge, 1970), pp. 5–9, with references.

aecclesiae archipresule totiusque Britannicae insulae primate,
considentibus secum uiris uenerabilibus Thoma Eboracensi archiepiscopo Willelmo Londoniensi episcopo Goisfrido Constantiensi,
10 qui cum transmarinus esset episcopus in Anglia multas possessiones habens cum ceteris in concilio residebat,[1] Walchelino
Wintoniensi Hermanno Siraburnensi Wulstano Wiricestrensi
Waltero Herefordensi Gisone Willensi Remigio Dorchacensi seu
Linconiensi Herfasto Helmeanensi seu Noruuicensi Stigando
15 Selengensi Osberno Exoniensi Petro Licifeldensi.[a][2] Rofensis aecclesia per idem tempus pastore carebat. Lindisfarnensis qui et
Dunelmensis episcopus canonicam excusationem habens concilio
interesse non poterat.[3]

Et quia multis retro annis in Anglico regno usus conciliorum
20 obsoleuerat,[4] renouata sunt nonnulla quae antiquis etiam noscuntur
canonibus definita.

i. Ex concilio igitur Toletano quarto Milleuitano atque
Bracharensi statutum est ut singuli secundum ordinationis suae
tempora sedeant, preter eos qui ex antiqua consuetudine siue
25 suarum aecclesiarum priuilegiis digniores sedes habent.[5] De qua
re interrogati sunt senes et aetate prouecti, quid uel ipsi uidissent
uel a maioribus atque antiquioribus ueraciter ac probabiliter /
f. 14 accepissent. Super quo responso petitae sunt induciae ac concesse
usque in crastinum. Crastina autem die concorditer perhibuere
30 quod Heboracensis archiepiscopus ad dexteram Dorobernensis
sedere debeat, Londoniensis episcopus ad sinistram, Wentanus
iuxta Eboracensem. Si uero Eboracensis desit, Londoniensis ad
dexteram Wentanus ad sinistram.[6]

ii. Ex regula beati Benedicti, dialogo Gregorii et antiqua regu-
35 larium locorum consuetudine ut monachi ordinem debitum teneant: infantes precipue et iuuenes in omnibus locis deputatis

[a] Licifeldensi] Lincoliensi Le

11 [1] Geoffrey witnesses as 'unus de Anglicae terrae primatibus', i.e. magnates:
n. 16 below; cf. no. 3 *ad fin*. See further J. Le Patourel, 'Geoffrey of Montbray,
bishop of Coutances, 1049–93', *E.H.R.* lix (1944), 129–61.

[2] After York, London and Winchester (for whom see lines 21–32) all these
bishops are in order of consecration, except for Worcester (1062), who has
'jumped' Hereford and Wells (both 1061). Another anomaly is Herfast's title
'Helmeanensi seu Noruuicensi', given that he is described in 1072 as bishop of
Elmham or Thetford (no. 3, lines 9–10) and that it was not until 1094-5 that
his successor but one formally moved to Norwich. But Norwich was already
the obvious choice on economic grounds: J. Campbell in *Historic Towns*, ed.
M. D. Lobel ii (London, 1975), Norwich, pp. 5–10.

of the holy church of Canterbury and primate of the whole island
of Britain; the venerable men sitting with him were Thomas, archbishop of York, William, bishop of London, Geoffrey of Coutances,
who though an overseas bishop was sitting with the others in the
council because he had a great deal of property in England,[1]
Walchelin of Winchester, Hermann of Sherborne, Wulfstan of
Worcester, Walter of Hereford, Giso of Wells, Remigius of Dorchester or Lincoln, Herfast of Elmham or Norwich, Stigand of
Selsey, Osbern of Exeter, Peter of Lichfield.[2] At that time the
church of Rochester lacked a pastor. The bishop of Lindisfarne,
that is Durham, for a canonically valid reason was unable to be
present at the council.[3]

Because the custom of holding councils had been in abeyance
in the realm of England for many years,[4] some legislation which is
already defined in ancient law was renewed.

    i. Thus in the fourth council of Toledo and the councils of
Mileum and Braccara it is decreed that each man shall sit according
to his date of ordination, except for those who have more honour-
able seats by ancient custom or by the privileges of their churches.[5]
Old men well stricken in years were questioned on this matter, as
to what they had either seen themselves or heard as true and convincing from their seniors and elders. They asked for time to
consider their answer and were given until the following day. Next
day they declared unanimously that the archbishop of York shall
sit on the right hand of the archbishop of Canterbury, the bishop
of London on his left and Winchester next to York. In the absence
of York, London shall sit on his right and Winchester on his left.[6]

    ii. Following the *Rule of St. Benedict*, Gregory's *Dialogue* and
the ancient custom of monasteries, monks shall observe a proper
mode of conduct. In particular the children and the young monks
shall everywhere be under supervision, suitable masters being

---

[3] Siward of Rochester was commemorated in Rochester on 14 Oct. (*Custu-
male Roffense*, ed. J. Thorpe, London, 1788, p. 37) and in Canterbury on
30 Oct. (Le Neve/Greenway, p. 75). If either of these is the day of his death,
the see had been vacant since Oct. 1074. For Walcher's preoccupations in the
north see no. 36.

[4] The phrase 'usus obsoleuerat' refers to the late Anglo-Saxon period.
Four councils had been held in the recent past: Easter and Whitsun 1070,
Easter and Whitsun 1072.

[5] IV Toledo, *can.* 3, Mileum (Numidia: now Mila, Algeria), *can.* 14, and I
Braga, *can.* 6: Hinschius, pp. 364, 318, 423; for Mileum see now C. Munier,
Concilia Africae a. 345–a. 525 (C.C.S.L. cxlix, 1974), p. 365.

[6] These arrangements are discussed by C. N. L. Brooke, 'Archbishop
Lanfranc, the English bishops, and the council of London of 1075', *Studia
Gratiana* xii (1967), 41–59.

sibi idoneis magistris custodiam habeant, nocte luminaria ferant;[7]
generaliter omnes nisi a prelatis concessa proprietate careant. Si
quis uero aliquid proprii sine prefata licentia habere in morte
40 fuerit deprehensus, nec ante mortem id reddiderit cum poenitentia
et dolore peccatum suum confessus, nec signa pro eo pulsentur
nec salutaris pro eius absolutione hostia immoletur nec in cime-
terio sepeliatur.[8]

iii. Ex decretis summorum pontificum Damasi uidelicet et
45 Leonis necnon ex conciliis Sardicensi atque Laodicensi, in quibus
prohibetur episcopales sedes in uillis existere, concessum est
regia munificentia et sinodali auctoritate prefatis tribus episcopis
de uillis ad ciuitates transire: Herimanno de Siraburna ad Seris-
49 beriam, Stigando de Selengeo ad Cicestrum, Petro de Licifelde
f. 14ᵛ ad Cestrum.[9] De quibusdam qui in uillis seu uicis adhuc / degebant
dilatum est usque ad regis audientiam, qui in transmarinis partibus
tunc temporis bella gerebat.[10]

iv. Ex multis Romanorum presulum decretis diuersisque
sacrorum canonum auctoritatibus, ne quis alienum clericum uel
55 monachum sine commendaticiis litteris retineat uel ordinet.[11]

v. Ad comprimendam quorundam indiscretorum insolentiam,
ex communi decreto sancitum[b] est ne quis in concilio loquatur
preter licentiam a metropolitano sumptam, exceptis episcopis et
abbatibus.

60 vi. Ex decretis Gregorii Maioris necnon et Minoris, ut nullus
de propria cognatione uel uxoris defunctae seu quam cognatus
habuit uxorem accipiat, quoadusque parentela ex alterutra parte
ad septimum gradum perueniat.[12]

vii. Vt nullus sacros ordines seu officium aecclesiasticum quod
65 ad curam animarum pertineat emat uel uendat. Hoc enim scelus a

---

[b] sanctitum N; sanccitum J

[7] *Benedicti Regula* lxx, ed. R. Hanslik (C.S.E.L. lxxv, 1960), p. 160; *Constitutions*, caps. 28 and 109, pp. 27 and 94.

[8] *Benedicti Regula* xxxiii, ed. cit., pp. 90–1; Gregory the Great, *Dialogi* iv, ed.
U. Moricca (Fonti per la Storia d'Italia 57, Rome, 1924), pp. 317–20.

[9] *Decreta Damasi* 19, *Decreta Leonis ad Africanos episcopos* 1, council of
Sardis, *can.* 6, council of Laodicaea, *can.* 57: Hinschius, pp. 512, 624, 267, 276.
In the short term Lanfranc and his colleagues may have been concerned with
the military security of these cathedrals as rebellion threatened in 1075. In the
longer term all the transfers, including Dorchester to Lincoln (1072) and Elmham to Thetford (1070–2) to Norwich (*c.* 1095) made economic sense; cf.
nos. 27 and 47.

[10] No further transfers were in fact agreed in William I's lifetime. Wells to

allotted to them, and they shall carry lights at night.[7] Monks of all ages shall eschew private property except with the permission of their superiors. If anyone is found on his deathbed to have private property without such permission, and he fails to return it before his death, confessing his sin with penitence and grief, no bells shall be rung for him nor shall the saving Host be offered for his absolution nor shall he be buried in the monastic graveyard.[8]

iii. Following the decrees of popes Damasus and Leo and also the councils of Sardis and Laodicaea, which prohibit the existence of episcopal sees in small townships, by the generosity of the king and the authority of the synod permission was granted to three of the bishops mentioned above to move from townships to cities: Hermann from Sherborne to Salisbury, Stigand from Selsey to Chichester, and Peter from Lichfield to Chester.[9] The case of certain others who remained in townships or villages was deferred until the king, who was at that time fighting overseas, could hear it in person.[10]

iv. Following many decrees of Roman popes and various texts of canon law, no one shall keep a strange clerk or monk in his household or ordain him without letters of commendation.[11]

v. To restrain the excesses of certain injudicious men it was unanimously decreed that with the exception of bishops and abbots no one shall speak in a council without permission from his metropolitan.

vi. Following the decrees of Gregory the Great and Gregory the Lesser, no one shall take a wife from his own or his deceased wife's kindred nor a kinsman's widow, as far as the seventh degree of kinship on either side.[12]

vii. No one shall buy or sell holy orders nor any position in the Church which carries pastoral responsibility. This crime was

Bath was formalized in 1088 (*Regesta* no. 314) and Thetford to Norwich was accomplished by Bishop Herbert Losinga in 1094–6.

[11] Similar legislation had been enacted at Winchester 1070, *can.* 3 and Winchester 1072, *can.* 6: *Councils and Synods*, ad locc.; cf. *Canones Apostolorum* 13 (Hinschius, p. 28). On the subject as a whole see C. Fabricius, 'Die *Litterae Formatae* im Frühmittelalter', *Archiv f. Urkundenforschung* ix (1926), 39–86, 168–94, and R. A. Fletcher, 'An *epistola formata* from León', *Bulletin of the Institute of Historical Research* xlv (1972), 122–8, with references.

[12] Gregory the Great, *Ep. ad Felicem episcopum* (Hinschius, p. 751); Gregory II, *Decreta* 9 (ibid., p. 754): see also Lanfranc's own commentary on the Pauline Epistles (*PL* cl. 355B: 1 Tim. 5: 4).

Petro apostolo in Simone Mago primitus dampnatum est, postea a
sanctis patribus uetitum et excommunicatum.[13]

    viii. Ne ossa mortuorum animalium quasi pro uitanda anima-
lium peste alicubi suspendantur, nec sortes uel auruspicia seu
70 diuinationes uel aliqua huiusmodi opera diaboli ab aliquo exer-
ceantur. Haec enim omnia sacri canones prohibuerunt, et eos
qui talia exercent data sententia excommunicauerunt.[14]

    ix. Ex conciliis Eliberitano et Toletano undecimo, ut nullus
episcopus uel abbas seu quilibet ex clero hominem occidendum
f.15 uel membris truncandum iudicet, / uel iudicantibus suae auctori-
76 tatis fauorem commodet.[15]

    Ego Lanfrancus Dorobernensis archiepiscopus subscripsi.
Ego Thomas Eboracensis aecclesiae archiepiscopus subscripsi.
Subscripserunt[16] et alii episcopi uel abbates qui interfuerunt.[c]

12

Thomas, archbishop of York, to Lanfranc
June 1072–Feb. 1073

Written after the resolution of the primacy dispute (May 1072: no. 3 above)
and before the consecration of Ralph, bishop of the Orkneys (3 Mar. 1073).
The year 1073, which is confirmed by Lv (no. 13: rubric), is preferable to
1077 (A.L., p. 289) in that 3 Mar. 1073 was a Sunday but 3 Mar. 1077 was not;
cf. Introduction, p. 5. Archbishop Thomas is exercising the jurisdiction
recently assigned to him in the north (no. 3, lines 111–17) and made more
practicable by the death of Adalbert, archbishop of Bremen (16 Mar. 1072).
The three preceding bishops in the Orkneys had been subject to Hamburg/
Bremen; Ralph was the first of three who recognized York: D. E. R. Watt,
Fasti Ecclesiae Scoticanae Medii Ævi ad annum 1638, 2nd edn. (Scottish Record
Society n.s. 1, Edinburgh, 1969), pp. 247–9.

Piissimo et sanctissimo Cantuariorum archiepiscopo totius quoque
Britanniae summo pastori L. Thomas fidelis suus et, nisi prae-
sumptuosum sanctitati suae uideatur, Eboracensis aecclesiae
archiepiscopus[1] coeli portas Petri uice iustis et iniustis iuste
5 aperire et claudere.

    [c] Subscripserunt . . . interfuerunt *om.* J (see note 16).

---

12 NVLv

---

    [13] Acts 8:18–24; cf. for instance Chalcedon, *can.* 2 (Hinschius, p. 285) and in
recent legislation Winchester 1070, *can.* 2 etc. (*Councils and Synods*, ad loc.).

originally condemned in Simon Magus by the Apostle Peter; later
on it was forbidden and outlawed by the holy Fathers.[13]

viii. The bones of dead animals shall not be hung up anywhere
as though to ward off cattle-disease; nor shall anyone cast lots, tell
fortunes and prophesy the future nor practise any similar works of
the devil. Holy canon law has forbidden all such things and after
due sentence excommunicated those who practise them.[14]

ix. Following the council of Elvira and the eleventh council of
Toledo, no bishop or abbot nor any of the clergy shall sentence a
man to be killed or mutilated; nor shall he lend the support of his
authority to those who are passing sentence.[15]

I Lanfranc, archbishop of Canterbury, have subscribed this
document.

I Thomas, archbishop of the church of York, have subscribed
this document.

The other bishops or abbots who were present have subscribed
also.[16]

12

Thomas, archbishop of York, to Lanfranc

June 1072–Feb. 1073

To the most reverend and holy Lanfranc, archbishop of Canterbury and supreme pastor of all Britain, Thomas his vassal and (if
it does not seem presumptuous to his holiness) archbishop of the
church of York:[1] may he open the gates of heaven to the just and
close them to the unjust as justly as St. Peter.

---

[14] Divination and soothsaying were condemned by the councils of Ancyra, *can.*
24, IV Carthage, *can.* 89 and IV Toledo, *can.* 28 (Hinschius, pp. 263, 306, 369).

[15] XI Toledo, *can.* 6 (Hinschius, p. 409); the reference to the council of
Elvira is an error (Brooke, *English Church*, p. 67).

[16] J adds subscriptions by the following: Bishops—William of London,
Walchelin of Winchester, Geoffrey of Coutances, Hermann of Sherborne,
Wulfstan of Worcester, Walter of Hereford, Giso of Wells, Remigius of Lincoln,
Herfast of Norwich, Stigand of Chichester, Osbern of Exeter, Peter of Chester.
Archdeacon—Ansketil of Christ Church, Canterbury. Abbots—Scotland of
St. Augustine's, Canterbury, Riwallon of New Minster (Winchester), Adelelm of
Abingdon, Wulfwold of Chertsey, Baldwin of Bury St. Edmunds, Theodwine
of Ely, Æthelwig of Evesham, Æthelnoth of Glastonbury, Ælfwine of Ramsey,
Galannus of Winchcombe, Serlo of Gloucester, Warin of Malmesbury,
Frederick of St. Albans, Edmund of Pershore, Liuuard of Muchelney, Ælfsige
of Bath, Leofwine of Coventry, Aldwin of Milton, Æsuuerdus of Abbotsbury,
Edward of Cerne, Osirich of Horton.

---

12 [1] Note the threefold recognition of Lanfranc's primacy: the formal title
('totius . . . pastori'), the vassal addressing his lord ('fidelis suus') and the possibly
ironic disclaimer ('et nisi . . . archiepiscopus').

Ecce pater sanctissime filius tuus ad te clamat, sed magis filia
Eboracensis uidelicet aecclesia ad eam cui dispositione diuina
presides aecclesiam tanquam ad maternum recurrens sinum[2] pie
postulat, ut ex abundantia maternarum deliciarum reparetur
10 inopia suarum se deserentium immo longe et inter barbaras
nationes positarum uirium.

Siquidem uenit ad nos quidam clericus[3] quem misit Paulus
comes[4] cum litteris sigillatis de Orchadum partibus, significans
in eis episcopatum suae terrae eidem clerico se concessisse. At ille
15 antecessorum suorum ordine custodito[5] postulat a nobis episcopum
se consecrari. Cui quod iuste petit iniuste denegare non possumus.
Precamur ergo ut nobis duos episcopos dirigat paternitas uestra,
quorum fulti orationibus et auxilio tante rei sacramentum canonice
19 compleamus. Illa autem procul arceatur suspicio quam nuperrime
f. 15ᵛ nobis noster frater et coepiscopus subintulit / Remigius, me
scilicet in posterum quaesiturum Dorcacestrensis uel Wigornensis
episcopi hac de causa subiectionem.[6] Dico enim coram Deo me
nunquam hoc facturum. Si placet igitur sanctitati uestrae ut
iuxta peticionem nostram nobis facere dignemini, locum Eboracum
25 tempus quinto nonas Martias nobis immutabiliter constituimus,
et uobis significamus.

Ergo uiuas et ualeas, et spiritualibus incrementis usquequaque
proficias.

13

Lanfranc to Wulfstan, bishop of Worcester, and
Peter, bishop of Chester[1]　　29 Aug. 1072–Feb. 1073

Sent in response to no. 12. The dating turns on the consecration of Peter,
bishop of Lichfield, which belongs to Lanfranc's third year of office (29 Aug.
1072–28 Aug. 1073); it took place in Gloucester and so perhaps at the Christmas
court of 1072: A.L., p. 289; cf. J. Tait, 'An alleged Charter of William the
Conqueror' in *Essays in History presented to R. L. Poole*, ed. H. W. C. Davis
(Oxford, 1927), pp. 153 ff. Wulfstan and Peter seem to have been together when
they received Lanfranc's letter: Wulfstan had administered Lichfield during the
vacancy (*Vita Wulfstani* ii. 1, ed. R. R. Darlington [Camden 3rd ser. xl, London,
1928], pp. 25–6); Peter had perhaps not yet left to take up his see. In short,
Lanfranc probably wrote to expedite the Orkney consecration as soon as he had
a second bishop to accompany Wulfstan.

ᵃLanfrancus gratia Dei sanctae Dorobernensis aecclesiae archi-

13 NVLv
ᵃ Lv *adds*: Epistola Lanfranci dorobernensis aecclesiae archiepiscopi ad
Wlstanum Wigornensem et ad Petrum Cestrensem episcopos anno ab incarnatione domini nostri Iesu Christi m. lxxiii Indictione XI

Most holy father, your son cries out to you! Your daughter rather, the church of York, as though running back to her mother's arms, makes filial entreaty to that church which in God's providence you govern, that out of the abundance of her mother's wealth her own indigence should be relieved, for her strength is failing her among these remote and barbarous peoples.[2]

A certain cleric[3] has come to us, whom Earl Paul[4] sent from the Orkneys with a sealed letter stating that he has granted to that cleric the office of bishop within his territory. Following the usage of his predecessors[5] the cleric asks that we should consecrate him bishop. It would be unjust for us to refuse him his just petition. We therefore ask you, father, to send us two bishops with the help of whose prayers we may perform this great sacrament in accordance with canon law. The suspicion that our brother and fellow bishop Remigius entertained not long ago can be utterly dismissed: that on this precedent I shall from now on seek jurisdiction over the bishop of Dorchester or the bishop of Worcester.[6] God is my witness that I shall never do this. If your holiness decides to accede to our request, we have firmly decided on York as the place and March 3rd as the date, as we hereby inform you.

May you have life and health and achieve spiritual gains throughout the land.

13

Lanfranc to Wulfstan, bishop of Worcester, and Peter, bishop of Chester[1]   *29 Aug. 1072–Feb. 1073*

Lanfranc, by the grace of God archbishop of the holy church of

---

[2] York is the sucking child returning to her mother's breast: 'ad maternum recurrens sinum . . . deliciarum'.   [3] Ralph (1073–1100): Watt, *Fasti*, p. 248.

[4] Earl Paul had assisted the Norwegian forces at Stamford Bridge: *A.S. Chron.* D s.a. 1066; *Flor. Wig.* i. 226–7. He returned to rule in Orkney until c. 1090: *Orkneyinga Saga* xxxiii–xxxiv, trans. A. B. Taylor (Edinburgh, 1938), pp. 190–3.

[5] The only previous bishop of the Orkneys known to have recognized York is Henry (?–? 1035): Watt, *Fasti*, p. 247.

[6] The sees of Worcester, Dorchester and Lichfield had just been assigned to the province of Canterbury (no. 3, lines 111–17). Dorchester however had its own dispute with the *diocese* of York over the control of Lindsey and Leicester: see further no. 7, n. 8. Lanfranc played doubly safe, in not sending Remigius to York and in reminding the bishops whom he did send to preserve his letter as a legal precedent (no. 13, lines 17–22).

---

13 [1] The transfer of the see of Lichfield to Chester was confirmed by the council of London in 1075 (no. 11, *can.* 3); 'Cestrensi' here is either a declaration of intent or a retrospective correction (cf. no. 3, lines 57–8).

episcopus uenerabilibus fratribus Wlfstano Wigorniensi et Petro
Cestrensi episcopis salutem.

Insinuauit nobis uenerabilis frater noster Thomas Eboracensis
5 archiepiscopus[2] aduenisse de Orchadum insulis ad se quendam
clericum, quem in episcopatu[b] ipsius terrae precipiente et in-
sinuante Paulo comite testatur esse electum. Et quia ex antiquo
more sui iuris est prefatarum insularum presules consecrare,[3]
petit a me ut mittam sibi de nostris suffraganeis duos qui tantae
10 rei sacramentum cum eo ualeant celebrare. Rogantes itaque
precipimus et precipientes rogamus quatinus omni excusatione
summota illuc eatis, et ex nostro precepto secum quod iustum
est in tantae[c] rei misterio compleatis. Non enim decet ut[d] qui
sacrandus in hanc terram uenit, et cum omni humilitate sacrari
15 se postulat, inopia adiutorum a tanto regno non sacratus abscedat.
Terminum huius consecrationis lator uobis praesentium indicabit.[4]
Et ne forte solliciti sitis, putantes quod uel ipse uel successores
f. 16 eius hac oc/casione super aecclesias uestras ius prelationis quandoque conentur arripere,[5] litteras quas ipse michi transmisit
20 fraternitati uestrae sollicitudinem de futuro gerens curaui transmittere. Quas et has quas uobis transmitto in archiuis aecclesiarum
uestrarum[6] ob memoriam futurorum seruatum iri praecipio.

14

Lanfranc to John, archbishop of Rouen
29 Aug. 1070–July 1077

The first of five letters to Archbishop John (nos. 14–17, 41): the limiting dates
are Lanfranc's consecration and the stroke that John suffered two years before
his death (Orderic, *Hist. Eccles.* iii. 16–19). In this letter Lanfranc is answering
criticism of his activity in a sphere new to him but long familiar to Archbishop
John. See further Introduction, pp. 8–9.

Domino merito sanctitatis insigniter efferendo Iohanni Normannorum archiepiscopo L. indignus uocari episcopus bene ceptis
meliora conectere.

Gratias ago colendae benignitati uestrae quia non solum presens
5 praesentem me indeficienti amore propter Deum[a] dilexistis,

    ᵇ episcopatum Lv   ᶜ tanto Lv   ᵈ et Lv

14 NVR
ᵃ propter Deum *om.* R

Canterbury, greets his reverend brothers Wulfstan, bishop of Worcester, and Peter, bishop of Chester.

Our reverend brother Thomas, archbishop of York, has informed us that[2] a certain cleric has come to him from the Orkney Isles, who has been (the archbishop assures us) elected bishop of that country at the command of Earl Paul, from whom this information comes. Because it has long been the prerogative of York to consecrate bishops for these isles,[3] he asks me to send him two of our suffragans to assist him in celebrating this great sacrament. We therefore require and direct you to go there as a matter of the first priority and on our directive to assist him in the due performance of so important a ceremony. For it is not right that a candidate for consecration who comes to this country and desires in all humility to be consecrated should depart unconsecrated from a great kingdom like ours for lack of clergy to assist the archbishop. The messenger who brings you this letter will tell you the time and place of the consecration.[4] And in case you are apprehensive that either this archbishop or his successors may try to use this as a pretext at some time or another to seize jurisdiction over your churches,[5] with an eye to the future, my brothers, I have made a point of sending you the letter which the archbishop himself sent to me. I advise you to keep both that and the letter I send you now in the archives of your churches[6] as a record for your successors.

14

Lanfranc to John, archbishop of Rouen
29 Aug. 1070–July 1077

To the lord John, archbishop of the Normans, a man who deserves to be singled out for his holiness, Lanfranc, unworthy of the name of bishop, wishes that he may add better achievement to what has been well begun.

I thank and honour your goodness that not only cherished me with an unfailing love in the Lord when we were together, but even in

[2] This sentence and the next are based on Archbishop Thomas's letter: no. 12, lines 12–19.

[3] Thomas's 'concessisse . . . antecessorum suorum' is hardened to 'electum . . . sui iuris': no. 12, lines 14–15.

[4] Cf. no. 12, lines 24–5.

[5] Cf. no. 12, lines 19–23.

[6] The Worcester copy is no doubt the immediate source of Lv.

uerum etiam absens pro absente paternam uos curam gerere
salubri admonitione euidenter ostenditis. Absit autem a me longe-
que a sensibus meis hunc errorem semper[b] auertat diuina cle-
mentia, ut molestum michi sit si quis respectu salutis meae
10 uitaeque aeternae contemplatione de anima mea sollicitudinem
gerat: si ea quae de actibus meis sibi displicent pietate motus
indicare non differat; si aliter me corrigere non potest, uerbis
quoque obiurgare praesentem aut litteris increpare absentem
non neglegat. Sed amicus potius a me iustus existimabitur qui
15 in misericordia corripit me et increpat; hostis autem peccator
qui oleo prauae adulationis caput meum aut inpinguat[1] aut
inpinguare laborat.

    Quicquid uero sanctitas uestra de stola scripsit multum michi
19 placuit, nec unquam displicuit. Sed quod subiunxit, quia ad
f. 16ᵛ dedicandam aecclesiam episcopus processurus sacris / uestibus
ex institutione episcopalis ordinis debeat esse indutus, atque in
expositione ipsarum sacrarum uestium casulam posuit, ualde
stupui, quia tale aliquid me unquam uidisse meminisse non
potui. Diuersos enim diuersarum prouinciarum praesules aecclesias
25 dedicare sepe conspexi, omnibusque quae ab eis acta[c] sunt quantam[d] potui curam adhibui. Qui etsi in nonnullis dissimilia egerunt,
omnes tamen cappis induti usque ad celebrationem missae debita
seruitia sine casula expleuerunt.[2] Denique sanctus Leo Romanae
sedis summus antistes Romericensem me praesente aecclesiam
30 dedicauit,[3] cunctaque quae ante missam fieri ordo poposcerat[e]
sine casula consummauit.

    Porro quod in dandis ordinibus soli subdiacono dari manipulum
perhibuistis,[4] ubi hoc acceperitis rogo me uestris litteris instruatis.
A quibusdam enim id fieri audio, sed utrum id fieri sacris auctori-
35 tatibus precipiatur meminisse non ualeo. Plerique autumant
manipulum commune esse ornamentum omnium ordinum, sicut
albam et amictum. Nam et in coenobiis monachorum etiam laici,

---

    [b] *om.* R   [c] facta R   [d] quantum N; quantam N¹   [e] depo-
poscerat R

14 [1] Ps. 140: 5.
    [2] Lanfranc is expounding the standard practice of the Western Church:
PRG i. 82–9, with references. As the ceremony consisted of (i) the elaborate
processions, aspersions and transfer of relics which established the building as
a church and (ii) the first Mass, so the bishop wore a non-eucharistic vestment,
the *cope*, for the first part and a specifically eucharistic vestment, the *chasuble*,
for the second. Lanfranc's opinion here is borne out by a late tenth-century

my absence by salutary criticism gives unmistakable proof of your fatherly concern. Be it far from me—may God's mercy ever defend me from any tendency to this error!—to feel resentment when anyone shows concern for my soul's welfare and its hope of eternal life: if there is anything in my conduct he disapproves of, his affection makes him quick to point it out; and he takes the trouble to rebuke me personally or send me a letter of criticism when I am elsewhere, if he cannot correct me in any other way. I shall always think him the true friend who 'smites me in mercy and reproves me' and him the sinful foe who anoints my head with the oil of false flattery,[1] or tries to do so.

With everything that your holiness wrote about the stole I was in complete agreement, nor did I ever dispute it. But what you said next I found quite extraordinary: that when he dedicates a church the bishop shall put on the sacred vestments belonging to his episcopal rank at the beginning of the ceremony, and that in enumerating these sacred vestments you included the chasuble. I cannot remember ever having seen anything like that. I have often watched various bishops of different provinces dedicating churches, and I have observed most scrupulously all that they did. In some respects their practice differed; but they all performed the appointed ceremonies in copes, without a chasuble, until they began the Mass.[2] I was present when St. Leo himself, supreme bishop of the Roman see, dedicated the church of Remiremont:[3] everything which the rite had prescribed up to the Mass he completed without a chasuble.

On another point, you took the view that when holy orders are conferred the maniple is given only to the subdeacon.[4] Please send me a note of where you found this ruling. I hear that it is the practice in some quarters, but I cannot recall whether it is prescribed in canon law. It is widely held that the maniple is an ornament common to all orders, like the alb and amice. There is the

pontifical from Christ Church, London, B.L., Cotton Claudius A. III f. 63ᵛ: 'Inde reuertatur pontifex in sacrarium cum ordinibus suis et induant se uestimentis aliis sollempnibus . . .', after which the cantor begins Mass (D. H. Turner, *The Claudius Pontificals* [London, 1971: Henry Bradshaw Soc. xcvii], p. 53).

[3] 14 Nov. 1049: G. Durand, *L'Église S. Pierre des Dames de Remiremont* (Épinal, 1929), i. 66–7, with references.

[4] Cf. John's own instructions on the vestments to be worn at the Eucharist: 'ceterique ministri sacris uestibus iuxta ordinem induantur, scilicet alba stola et dalmatica diaconus; alba et tunica et manipulo subdiaconus . . .', *De Officiis Ecclesiasticis*, ed. R. Delamare (Paris, 1923), p. 9. The maniple is an oblong towel carried over the arm, normally at the Eucharist and occasionally in other circumstances.

cum albis induuntur, ex antiqua patrum institutione solent ferre
manipulum.[5] In nostris episcopalis ordinis codicibus, quos ex
40 diuersis regionibus multos habemus,[f] de ordinando subdiacono
inter cetera sic[g] scriptum habetur: 'Postea uero accipiat ab
archidiacono urceolum *cum aquamanili*, ac manutergium.'[6] In
f. 17 quibusdam sic, 'cum / aqua manile'; in aliis ita, 'cum aquae
manili'.[7] Vrceolus quid sit liquido patet. Est enim uas superius,
45 unde lauandis manibus aqua infunditur. *Aqua manile* siue *aquae
manile* Italici unam partem dicunt, uocaturque lingua eorum uas
inferius, in quod manibus infusa aqua delabitur. Quod si fortasse
sic distinguendum putatis, 'urceolum cum aqua' et postea '*manile*
ac manutergium', quatinus *manile* esse manipulum intelligatis,
50 cur inter urceolum ac manutergium ponatur manipulus, et cur
cum cetera ornamenta ab episcopis dentur[h] dari ab archidiacono
manipulus iubeatur? In qua scriptura siue seculari siue diuina
sic uocatum manipulum reppereritis[i] posco sanctam paternitatem
uestram ut indicare michi competenti diligentia studeatis. In
55 Cartaginiensi concilio quarto omne huius rei ambiguum excluditur,
ubi sic legitur: 'Subdiaconus cum ordinatur, quia manus im-
positionem non accipit, patenam de manu episcopi accipiat
uacuam et calicem uacuum. De manu uero archidiaconi accipiat
urceolum cum aqua et aquamanile ac manutergium.'[8] Item
60 Ysodorus, in epistola *De sacris ordinibus*: 'Ad subdiaconum',
inquit, 'pertinet calicem et patenam ad altare Christi deferre et
leuitis tradere eisque ministrare, urceolum quoque et aquaemanile
et manutergium tenere, episcopo presbitero et leuitis pro lauandis
f. 17ᵛ ante altare manibus / aquam prebere.'[9]

---

[f] VR *add* et   [g] sicut V   [h] dantur VR (dentur V¹)   [i] reperitis R

[5] The laymen here are presumably lay *conversi* (cf. *Constitutions*, caps.
64, 73: *conversi* in albs). The tradition to which Lanfranc refers was broadly
Cluniac: see E. Martène and U. Durand, *Thesaurus Novus Anecdotorum*
(Paris, 1717), v. 1610AB and further references in J. Braun, *Die liturgische
Gewandung im Occident und Orient* (Freiburg im Breisgau 1907), pp. 522–3.

[6] *PRG* i. 22; M. Andrieu, *Le Pontifical romain du XIIᵉ siècle* (Vatican, 1938:
Studi e Testi 86), p. 128. The root of the problem, which Lanfranc detects, is the
changing meaning of 'aquamanile'. Originally an aquamanile was a basin, as in
Italian usage (lines 45–7) it remained. In northern Europe it was coming to
mean a ewer or jug, as in modern nomenclature for Romanesque metalwork:
cf. H. Swarzenski, *Monuments of Romanesque Art*, 2nd edn. (London, 1967),
nos. 262, 470–1, 473. Thus the subdeacon received two empty jugs ('urceolum
cum aquamanili') and no basin. Worse still, 'aquamanile' was divided into
'urceolum cum *aqua*' and a new word '*manile*', which *faute de mieux* was held

further point that in monastic houses even laymen, when they are
vested in albs, according to the ancient practice of our founders
normally carry a maniple.[5] In our own pontificals, of which we
have many from different parts of the world, the text for the ordination of a subdeacon includes the following: 'Then he shall receive
from the archdeacon a ewer *with a basin* and a towel.'[6] Some read
'a basin with water'; others 'with a basin of water'.[7] It is quite clear
what a ewer is. It is the vessel from which the water is poured from
above in washing the hands. *A basin with water* or *a basin of water*
the Italians treat as one word; in their language it means the vessel
held underneath, into which the water that has been poured over
the hands runs down. If on the other hand you think that the text
should be divided like this, 'a ewer with water' and then 'a *manile*
and a towel', taking *manile* to be a maniple, why is the maniple
grouped between the ewer and towel and why, since the other liturgical objects are conferred by bishops, is the archdeacon directed
to confer the maniple? I should be grateful, holy father, if you
would let me know very specifically in what text, whether sacred
or profane, you found the maniple so described. All uncertainty in
this matter is removed in the Fourth Council of Carthage, where
we read: 'When a subdeacon is ordained, because he does not
receive the laying-on of hands, let him receive at the hand of the
bishop an empty paten and an empty chalice. At the hand of the
archdeacon let him receive a ewer with water and a basin and a
towel.'[8] Again, Isidore says, in his letter *On holy orders*: 'It is for
the subdeacon to bring to Christ's altar the chalice and paten and
give them to the officiating clergy whom he serves; he must also
hold the ewer, the basin and the towel and bring water to the
bishop, the priest and their assistants for washing their hands
before the altar.'[9]

to be a maniple; on that rendering the subdeacon received one jug containing
water and two towels. In this way a eucharistic vestment (the maniple) was
added to the non-eucharistic objects conferred by the archdeacon: see further V.
Leroquais, *Les Pontificaux manuscrits des bibliothèques de France* (Paris, 1937) i,
pp. lix–lx.

    [7] Lanfranc's standard text here, 'urceolum cum aquamanili ac manutergium',
agrees with *PRG* i. 22, line 9; his first variant is found in the Christ Church
pontifical already quoted, MS London B.L., Cotton Claudius A. III f. 42
(ed. Turner, p. 34: see note 2 above); his second agrees with Isidore, *De
ecclesiasticis officiis* II. x (*PL* lxxxiii. 791A).

    [8] IV Carthage, *can.* 5 (Hinschius, p. 303): rectius *Statuta Ecclesiae Antiqua*
93, ed. C. Munier, *Concilia Galliae a. 314–a. 506* (C.C.S.L. 148, 1963), p. 182,
with references. The passage also appears in *PRG* and Andrieu, *Pontifical
romain*, loc. cit.

    [9] *Ep. ad Leudefridum Episcopum*: *PL* lxxxiii. 895B. Cf. R. E. Reynolds in
Visigothic Spain: New Approaches, ed. E. James (Oxford, 1980) ch. 10.

65   Omnipotens Dominus uitam uestram intus exteriusque tueatur,
augeatque in uobis auctamque conseruet dilectionem qua me
quondam diligere solebatis, quatinus de me quantum ad uos
quidem^j pertinet quae credenda sunt credatis, proculque ab
auribus uestris linguas detrahentium pastorali semper auctoritate
70 repellatis.

15

Lanfranc to John, archbishop of Rouen
                                   29 Aug. 1070–July 1077

Dating limits as no. 14; but Lanfranc's long delay in writing (lines 4–18) and the
possible reference to the insane monk of Christ Church (lines 27–9) suggest
that this is the latest of the five letters.

Domino merito sanctitatis insigniter honorando Normannorum
archiepiscopo Io. frater L. fidele seruitium aeternamque salutem
cum orationibus.

Quod paternitatem uestram quam teste Deo multo amore diligo
5   multa ueneratione suscipio^a longa temporis intercapedine litteris
uisitare supersedi, rogo multumque rogo ne sinistra a me id
factum esse intentione interpretemini, neque existimetis fuisse
causam aut radicem cuiuslibet rancoris uel odii. Hoc potius hac
in parte conicite quod rei ueritas habet, quod experientia uestra
10 multis referentibus quibus miserabilis uitae meae status notus^b
est cognoscere ualet. Tot enim tantisque huius mundi impedi-
mentis nescio quo occulto Dei iudicio incessanter subiaceo, tot
animi rancores tam ex propriis quam ex alienis negotiis sine inter-
missione sustineo, tot calamitates ex consideratione presentium
15 uenturas in futuro conicio,^1 ut perraro dictandi seu scribendi
facultas detur, aut siquando datur, uel desunt qui perferant, uel
personae tam idoneae sunt ut per eas litteras mitti iniuriam
f. 18 putent. Ego tamen et ea quae uobis accidunt / cum promissione
seruitii et auxilii mei scire desidero, et ea quae michi eueniunt
20 cognosci a uobis humiliter peto. Et hoc oro ut concors caritas
caraque concordia quae inter nos hactenus mansit omnibus diebus

---

^j hoc quod R

---

15 NV
^a suspicio N   ^b motus V

May almighty God preserve your life within and without, and increase in you and make steadfast the love with which you used to cherish me, so that in what concerns yourself you may believe of me what is true and by your authority as bishop drive all slanderous reports far out of earshot.

15

Lanfranc to John, archbishop of Rouen
29 Aug. 1070–July 1077

To the lord John, archbishop of the Normans, a man who deserves to be honoured for his holiness, his brother Lanfranc sends loyal service and prayers for his eternal welfare.

If for a long space of time I have omitted to visit you with a letter, father, for whom God knows I feel warm affection and deep reverence, I do most earnestly beg you not to conclude that I have done so out of ill will, nor consider my silence a cause or ground for any kind of hostility. Draw the conclusion rather (which is the truth of the matter) that you have the experience to infer from the reports of many witnesses of the wretched life I lead: I am for ever enmeshed—by what hidden judgement of God I know not—in so many of the world's great snares; I have constantly to endure so many wrangles both on my own behalf and in other men's affairs; when I contemplate the disasters of this present time I foresee so many still to come.[1] So it is very seldom that I have the opportunity to compose a letter or to write one down; or if I do, either there are no messengers or the men available are individuals of such status that they think it beneath their dignity to carry a letter. For my part I both desire to have news of your affairs, adding my assurance of service and aid, and humbly wish that you should be informed of my own circumstances. It is my prayer too that the loving concord that has existed between us until now may continue

15 [1] Cf. Lanfranc's *cri de cœur* to Alexander II: no. 1, lines 21–9.

uitae nostrae inuiolata permaneat, nec eam quaelibet detrahentium
lingua quolibet modo aut infirmare aut propulsare preualeat.²
Quod aliter ratum esse non poterit, nisi amatores discordiae aut
25 nostris exhortationibus ad amorem concordiae conuertantur, aut
persistentes in sua stulticia a nostris colloquiis penitus arceantur.

   De iuuene cuius euentum usque ad aures uestras fama uulgauit
l.itor presentium, qui uidit et interfuit, qualiter gestum sit uobis
ueraciter enarrabit.³

16

Lanfranc to John, archbishop of Rouen   *autumn 1073*

Written soon after the St. Ouen riot of 24 Aug. 1073. The archbishop's jurisdiction over the monastery of St. Ouen at Rouen was symbolized by his right
to celebrate Mass at the high altar on the patronal feastday (24 Aug.). In 1073,
when Archbishop John arrived to celebrate, he was set upon and thrown out of
the church: *Acta Archiepiscoporum Rothomagensium*, ed. J. Mabillon, *Vetera
Analecta* (Paris, 1723), pp. 224–6. Lanfranc forwarded the case to William the
Conqueror (lines 22–5), who gave judgement for the archbishop: Lemarignier,
Privilèges, pp. 155–6, with references. See Introduction, pp. 8–9 and no. 17
below.

Domino sanctae Rotomagensis aecclesiae archiepiscopo Io. frater L.
indignus antistes fidele seruitium cum orationibus.

Visis litteris uestris quibus temerariam superbiam[a] superbamque
temeritatem miserrimorum hominum aduersus Deum et ponti-
5 ficale fastigium presumptam significare studuistis, et dolui sicut
dolere debui, et tamen in ipso dolore non gaudere non potui.
Dolui quia id euenit celsitudini uestrae quod a temporibus
paganorum nulli legitur euenisse episcoporum. Gauisus uero
sum, quia spurcissima uita eorum quae multas regiones fetore
10 suae infamiae iam aspersit hac[b] occasione publicata est, cognitum-
que euidenter quales coram Deo sunt, qui abiecto diuino humano-
f. 18ᵛ que timore tantum nefas in conspectu hominum / moliti sunt.
Et nunc sanctitas uestra omnem rancorem de corde abiciat, non
plus aequo et bono pro hac re doleat, omnem intentionem qualiter
15 haec nequicia ad honorem Dei sanctaeque aecclesiae puniatur
intendat. Et quidem quantum ad illos spectat dolendum uobis
est, quia filii uestri erant si filii esse uellent. Quantum uero ad

16 NV
   ᵃ superbiam *om.* V   ᵇ hac *om.* V

unbroken all the days of our life, and that no slanderous report may succeed by any means in weakening it or driving it away.[2] This cannot be achieved unless the lovers of discord are either brought to love concord by our encouragement or entirely excluded from our company if they persist in their folly.

As for the young monk, rumours of whose experience have reached you, the man who brings this letter witnessed the affair himself; he will tell you what actually happened.[3]

16

Lanfranc to John, archbishop of Rouen   *autumn 1073*

To the lord John, archbishop of the holy church of Rouen, his brother Lanfranc, an unworthy prelate, sends loyal service and his prayers.

When I read your letter, in which you gave a vivid account of the proud and audacious attack made by the vilest of men on God and the archbishop's honour, certainly I was grieved as there was call to grieve, yet even in my grief I could not but rejoice. I grieved that your excellency has suffered what we do not read that any bishop has suffered since pagan times. At the same time I rejoiced that these men's filthy life, which has already contaminated many lands with the stench of its dishonour, has in this way become public knowledge and that it is clearly understood how such men appear before God who, reverencing neither God nor man, have been responsible for such an impious deed in the sight of men. Let your holiness now put all personal resentment out of your mind; grieve over this affair no more than is right and proper; direct all your efforts to punishing this wickedness in a way that does honour to God and his holy Church. As for the men themselves, you must grieve for them, for they were your sons, had they wished to be so. But you on your part should 'rejoice and leap for joy' as you wait

---

[2] Cf. no. 14, lines 66–70.

[3] If Lanfranc is referring to the monk Ægelward, who went mad while serving at the altar, this letter must be dated to 1076–19 Mar. 1077: i.e. after the appointment of Prior Henry and before Gundulf's consecration as bishop of Rochester. See Osbern, *Miracula S. Dunstani* 19, in *Memorials of St. Dunstan*, ed. W. Stubbs (R.S., 1874), pp. 144–50 and *Vita Gundulfi* ii (*PL* clix. 818c–19A).

uos, 'gaudendum potius et exultandum' expectantibus uobis
beatitudinem apostolis repromissam; quia uos oderunt 'et ex-
20 probrauerunt et eiecerunt tanquam malum propter filium hominis',[1]
quem uos amatis et honoratis et ad cuius amorem et honorem
illos trahere uolebatis. Litteras domino nostro regi transmittere
dispono, quales oportet et quales debeo. Et credo miserante Deo
quia sicut tempora eius obscurata[c] sunt immanitate tantae ne-
25 quiciae, sic enitescent competentis seueritate uindictae.[2]

Omnipotens Dominus uitam uestram custodiat, et contra
omnes emulos dextera[d] sua protegente defendat, diligende pater
et omni laude colende.

17

Lanfranc to John, archbishop of Rouen   *autumn 1073*

A letter recapitulating no. 16: see note 5.

Zelo Dei et amore iusticiae praecellenti sanctae Rotomagensis
aecclesiae archiepiscopo Io. L. indignus antistes seruitium cum[a]
orationibus[a].

Quando Robertum Beccensis coenobii[b] monachum[1] cum litteris
5 ad uos transmisi, adhuc nullas paternitatis uestrae epistolas suscepi.
Post abscessum eius capellanus Hugonis unam detulit, alteram
uero laicus quidam, qui interrogatus a me quis esset seruientem[2]
f. 19 regine se esse respondit. Vtrarumque sententia / una fuit; in
utrisque enucleate ostendistis[c] officium uestri ordinis, uidelicet
10 contra emulos patientiam et innocentiam uestram, perditissi-
maeque[d] congregationis horribilem puniendamque temeritatem.
In utroque laudandus in utroque benedictus Deus, quia et uos
eius gratia fecistis quod respectu episcopalis dignitatis facere
debuistis, et illi econtra iusto ipsius iudicio 'traditi in reprobum
15 sensum'[3] hoc fecerunt, quod nec quolibet impulsu uel qualibet
iniuria prouocati facere debuerunt—certissimum prauitatis suae

---

  [c] obscura V   [d] dextra V

---

17 NV
[a-a] et orationes V   [b] ecclesie V   [c] ostenditis V   [d] -que *om.* V

for the blessedness that was promised as a reward to the Apostles; for 'men have hated and reproached you and cast you out as evil for the Son of Man's sake',[1] whom you love and honour and whom you wished to lead those men to love and honour too. I am arranging to send the necessary letter to our lord the king, as is my duty. I am confident that in God's mercy as his reign has been overshadowed by such heinous wickedness so it shall be illumined by a correspondingly severe punishment.[2]

May the Lord almighty guard your life and defend you against all enemies with the shield of his right arm, my beloved father and most esteemed lord.

17

Lanfranc to John, archbishop of Rouen   *autumn 1073*

To John, archbishop of the holy church of Rouen, preeminent in devotion to God and the love of justice, Lanfranc, an unworthy prelate, sends his service and prayers.

When I sent you Robert the monk of Bec[1] with a letter, father, I had not then received any communication from you. After he left, Hugh's chaplain brought one and a layman another; when I asked him who he was, he said he was in the queen's service.[2] The tenor of both letters was the same: in each you displayed clearly your duty as a bishop—long-suffering towards your enemies and your own blamelessness—and the appalling insolence, which cannot go unpunished, of that most abandoned collection of monks. God be praised and blessed on both counts: you by his grace have done your duty in maintaining episcopal authority, whereas they, by his righteous judgement 'being given up to their own depraved reason',[3] have done what they should not have been incited to do

---

16 [1] Luke 6: 22–3.

  [2] The king's sentence, that the monks who had led the riot should be distributed among different monastic prisons—Fécamp, St. Wandrille, Jumièges— is recorded in the *Annals* from St. Étienne, Caen, ed. A. Duchesne, *Historiae Normannorum Scriptores Antiqui* (Paris, 1619), pp. 1017–18.

17 [1] Robert of Bec is mentioned in several of Anselm's letters, notably as the messenger who brought Lanfranc an advance copy of the *Monologion* (*Anselmi Epp.* 74). He is no doubt the monk 'R' of no. 18.

  [2] The layman may have been a knight in the queen's household; for the range of meaning that *serviens* had at this time see M. Chibnall, 'Mercenaries and the *familia regis* under Henry I', *History* lxii (1977), 18–19.

  [3] Rom. 1: 28.

iis^e qui eos non nouerant prebentes indicium, quo luce clarius
omnibus innotescat quales in conspectu Dei eos esse ab omni
populo existimari oportet.^f De hac re litteras domino nostro
20 regi mitto, eumque ut decet ad uindictam tanti facinoris prout
possum rogo et moneo. Quas iampridem transmisissem sed
legatum reperire non potui; et homo episcopi Walchelini,⁴ qui
alias uobis detulit,⁵ ut eas expectaret impetrare non potui.

De Rodberto et eius somniatore et monacho a communi sepul-
25 tura prohibito quicquid mandastis laudo, et quicquid de his rebus
sentitis ego quoque in omnibus et per omnia uobiscum sentio.
Non est enim credendum uisionem illam esse a Deo quae monachos
prohibet a monasterio cui ad seruiendum Deo se deuouerunt, et
in quo de oboedientia et conuersione morum suorum et stabilitate
30 sua professionem fecerunt, cum propheta dicat, 'Vouete et reddite.'⁶
Et Dominus de malis pastoribus loquens non ait 'Fugite eos, /
f. 19^v recedite de locis quibus praesunt',⁷ sed 'Super cathedram Moysi
sederunt scribae et Pharisei;⁸ quae dicunt facite, quae autem
faciunt, facere nolite.'⁹ Et beatus Benedictus in *Regula Mona-*
35 *chorum*: 'Praeceptis', inquit, 'abbatis in omnibus oboedire, etiamsi
ipse quod absit aliter agat.'⁹

De monacho fulgure interfecto, uir sapiens apertissima sententia
omnem ambiguitatis nodum soluit dicens, 'Iustus quacunque
morte preoccupatus fuerit, anima eius in refrigerio erit.'¹⁰ Denique
40 aecclesia Christi alios mortuos a suae communionis consortio non
repellit, nisi eos tantum quibus uiuentibus canonica censura
communicare contempsit.

Omnipotens Dominus uitam uestram custodiat, quia multum
utilis est inter cetera ad confutandas garrulorum ineptias.

ᵉ is V   ᶠ oporteat V

---

⁴ Walchelin, bishop of Winchester (1070–98).
⁵ We may postulate the following sequence: (1) Lanfranc to John, via Robert
the monk; (2) John to Lanfranc, via Hugh's chaplain; (3) Lanfranc to John, via
Walchelin's servant = no. 16; (4) John to Lanfranc, via the layman; (5) Lanfranc
to John = no. 17. The third and fourth letters crossed.
⁶ Ps. 75:12. This advice on monastic stability confirms the view that Lanfranc
is not the author of the letter *Indicatum est mihi* (App. B. ii).
⁷ Cf. Num. 16: 26.
⁸ Matt. 23: 2.
⁹ 'Praeceptis abbatis in omnibus oboedire, etiam si ipse aliter, quod absit,
agat, memores illud dominicum praeceptum: *Quae dicunt, facite, quae autem
faciunt, facere nolite*' (cf. Matt. 23: 3): *Regula Benedicti* iv. 61, ed. R. Hanslik
(C.S.E.L. lxxv, 1960), p. 33.

by any provocation whatever or by any wrong they had suffered. To those who did not know them they give indisputable proof of their wickedness, by which it is made clearer than daylight to everyone how the whole of society must reckon them to stand in the sight of God. I am sending a letter on the subject to our lord the king, and I am requesting and advising to the best of my ability that he, as is appropriate, punish such a fearful outrage. I should already have sent that letter, but I could not find a messenger and I could not prevail on Bishop Walchelin's[4] servant, who brought you the other letter,[5] to wait for that one as well.

In the case of Robert and his visionary and the monk who was excluded from the community's burial ground I approve whatever instructions you have given, and whatever your judgement in the affair I too share it entirely in all respects. We cannot believe that that vision is from God if it turns monks away from the monastery to which they have pledged themselves for God's service, and in which they have professed obedience, the reform of their life and their stability. As the prophet says, 'Vow, and pay your vow.'[6] The Lord himself, speaking of the evil shepherds, does not say, 'Flee them; depart from the houses which they rule',[7] but rather 'The scribes and the Pharisees have sat in Moses' seat.[8] Do what they say, but beware of acting as they act.'[9] St. Benedict too says in the *Rule for Monks*: 'Obey the commands of the abbot in all respects, even if he himself does otherwise—may that never happen!'[9]

As to the monk who was killed by lightning, a wise man has unravelled the whole tangle of uncertainty with a perfectly plain ruling; he says, 'Whatever death overtakes the just man, his soul will be in peace.'[10] In short the Church of Christ does not turn away any of the dead from the fellowship of her communion, except only those whom she has by a legal judgement excluded from communion while they were still alive.

May the Lord almighty guard your life, for it is of great value too in silencing the idiocies of frivolous men.

[10] Wisd. 4: 7; cf. no. 49, lines 13–41.

18

Lanfranc to Anselm, prior of Bec   c. *winter 1073*

Lanfranc's reply to *Anselmi Epp.* 25, written soon after the arrival of Lanfranc
the younger at Bec (professed before 1 Nov. 1073: see no. 19). This letter
is the first of a 'monastic' group (nos. 18–21), which contrasts sharply with the
high politics and sometimes inflated style of the correspondence with the
archbishops of York and Rouen.

Domino patri fratri amico Ans. L. peccator perpetuam a Deo
salutem.

Quid michi expediat beatitudo uestra optime nouit. In Anglorum
enim terram[a] ueniens siue Romam proficiscens omnia sanctitati
5 uestrae reseraui quae reseranda esse tunc temporis pro mearum
rerum necessitate iudicaui. Sic ergo orate, sic ab amicis ac familiaribus uestris oratum iri deposcite, quatinus omnipotens Deus
aut ad meliorem fructum me perducat aut de ergastulo huius
carnis[1] animam meam in sui sancti nominis confessione educat.
10 Tot enim tantisque tribulationibus terra ista in qua sumus cotidie
f. 20 quatitur, tot adulteriis aliisque spurciciis inquinatur, ut / nullus
fere hominum ordo sit qui uel animae suae consulat, uel proficiendi
in Deum salutarem doctrinam saltem audire concupiscat.[2]

Litteras quas per domnum .R.[3] transmisistis laetus suscepi
15 laetior legi, cum quanto autem gaudio adhuc eas relegendo
recolo et recolendo relego litteris explicare non possum: pro eo
uidelicet quod (sicut in eis scriptum est) dulcissimum michi
fratris mei filium[4] quem sicut animam meam diligo cum ingenti
laeticia suscepistis, quod maiorem erga uos mei amoris fiduciam
20 ex hac occasione concepistis, et precipue ac super omnia quod
onus prioratus quod inportabile antea uidebatur ex eius aduentu
leuigatum uobis perhibuistis.[5] (De quo breuem ueracemque
sententiam uobis dico: si inter paganos etiam ipse uiueret, plus
ceteris paganis ego ipsos diligerem, et prodesset eis siquid in hoc
25 seculo possiderem.) Quibus de rebus quantas possum Deo et
domno abbati uobisque omnibus gratias refero, quia quales uolo
tales uos erga me et omnes qui diliguntur a me semper esse comperio. Sed quia accedens ad seruitutem Dei et maxime id aetatis
homo multis uariisque temptationibus per temptatorum spirituum

18 NV
[a] terra NV

18

Lanfranc to Anselm, prior of Bec   c. *winter 1073*

To Anselm, his lord and father, brother and friend, the sinner
Lanfranc wishes God's eternal salvation.

You best know, blessed father, what is best for me. Whether I was
coming to England or setting out for Rome, I disclosed to your
holiness everything that I thought the needs of my situation required to be disclosed at that time. Pray then, and urge your friends
and household to pray, that almighty God will either guide me
forward to better success or bring my soul out of its fleshly prison[1]
in the faith of his holy name. This land of ours is daily shaken by
so many disasters, it is polluted with so much adultery and other
filthy behaviour that there is virtually no part of society in which
a man either thinks of his soul's welfare or desires even to listen
to the wholesome doctrine of his progress towards God.[2]

I was glad to receive the letter which you sent by Dom R.,[3] I
read it with greater gladness, but the joy that I feel even now in
reading it once more and reflecting on its meaning I cannot express
in a letter. I find written there that you have given a most joyful
welcome to my brother's son,[4] my own favourite, whom I love like
my own soul; you have thereby been more firmly assured of my
love for you; and in particular above all you declare that the burden
of the prior's office, which seemed intolerable before, has been
lightened for you by his arrival.[5] (To give you a brief and true
assessment of him: even were he to live among the heathen, I
should esteem those heathen more highly than the rest and whatever I possessed in this world would be at their disposal.) For this
I give all possible thanks to God and the lord abbot and to you all,
for I know very well that you always behave as I wish towards me
and all whom I love. But because he is a tyro in God's service, and
particularly because at that age a man is racked inwardly by many

---

18 [1] Cf. Jerome, *Epistulae* 22. 7. 4, ed. I. Hilberg (C.S.E.L. liv, 1910), p. 154:
'illud miserrimae carnis ergastulum'. Jerome in turn is quoting Exod. 6: 7.

[2] Lanfranc wrote in similar terms to Alexander II: 'tot aliorum in diuersis
personis perturbationes . . . ad haec tempora peruenisse' (no. 1, lines 23–7;
cf. no. 15, lines 11–15).

[3] Cf. no. 17, note 1.

[4] Lanfranc the younger, joint recipient of no. 19.

[5] Cf. *Anselmi Epp.* 25: 'In quo uestro actu . . . nuper leuigastis'.

30 suggestiones intrinsecus laniatur, multis diuersisque carnis titilla-
tionibus intus et exterius cruciatur, oportet ualde ut uestri eum
colloquii participem sepissime faciatis,[6] omnesque quorum doc-
f. 20ᵛ trina salubris ei esse potest colloqui cum eo quotiens / expedit
iubeatis. Discedenti ipsi a me rogando precepi et precipiendo
35 rogaui ne hoc anno aliquam uel in refectorio uel in capitulo aut in
monasterio lectionem legeret, quoadusque psalmorum scientiam
suique ordinis aliquem usum haberet. Hanc uoluntatem meam
omnino despexit et ut legeret suarum precum nimietate a uobis
extorsit. Pro qua re amarissimas litteras transmittere sibi dis-
40 posui, sed uisis aliis litteris uestris[7] conceptum aduersus eius
temeritatem mentis rancorem omisi.

19

Lanfranc to Lanfranc the younger and Wido

c. *winter 1073*

Lanfranc's rebuke to his nephew in this letter (lines 15–19) corresponds so
closely to no. 18, lines 34–40 that we may assume that both letters were
dispatched simultaneously. The two young men are 100th and 101st in the Bec
profession-list: A. A. Porée, *Histoire de l'Abbaye du Bec* (Évreux, 1901), i. 630.
(They were among the last monks to be admitted before the move to the new
church on 1 Nov. 1073.) Lanfranc the younger persevered at Bec for at least
ten years; Anselm was to speak of him as a model monk (*Anselmi Epp.* 39):
finally, however, he went as abbot to S. Wandrille in defiance of Anselm's
wishes (1089–90: *Anselmi Epp.* 137–8) and is heard of no more.

Dilectissimis fratribus L. et W. frater L. perpetuam a Deoᵃ
benedictionem.

Quia diuinitus ut credo uos dilexistisᵇ in seculo, rogo ut rogetis
Deum quatinus ipso cooperante uos diligatis in eo quod assumpsi-
5 stis sancto proposito. Alter alteri sit in tribulatione solatium, alter
ab alterius uita et doctrina sumat sanctae conuersationis exemplum. Humilitatem omnibus ostendite, linguas uestras ab omni
fraterna derogatione salubri censura compescite. Si quis cuiuslibet
fratris uitam Theodino dente[1] rodere delectatur, si correctus a
10 uobis emendare neglexerit, a uestro colloquio arceatur. Quicquid
alii de uobis dicant, laudantes fortasse et magnificantes quod

19 NV
ᵃ Domino V ᵇ dilexisti N

different temptations through the suggestions of evil spirits assail-
ing him and tormented by the itching of the flesh in many different
ways within and without, it is of the utmost importance that you
allow him to share as often as possible in your informal talk[6] and
that you direct all those whose teaching can do him good to con-
verse with him on every appropriate occasion. When he left me,
I enjoined him most urgently not to read any lesson in public this
year in the refectory, in the chapter-house or in the monastery
until he had learned the Psalter and gained some experience of his
own duties. He completely disregarded this wish of mine and by
his importunate entreaties extorted permission from you for such
reading. I decided to write to him about this in very severe terms,
but when I saw your other letter[7] the anger that I had felt at his
recalcitrance vanished.

19

Lanfranc to Lanfranc the younger and Wido

c. *winter 1073*

To his most beloved brethren L(anfranc) and W(ido) brother Lanfranc wishes God's eternal blessing.

Since I think that you showed a godly love for each other in the
world, I urge you to entreat God that with his help you may love
each other in this holy resolve that you have made. Comfort each
other in trouble; in your life and doctrine be a pattern to each other
of your holy calling. Show humility to all; curb your speech
strictly and well from all criticism of your fellow monks. If anyone
finds amusement in gnawing with Theon's tooth[1] at a brother's way
of life and shows no improvement after you have corrected him,
he must be banished from your company. Whatever others may

---

[6] For Anselm's 'colloquia', which ranged from the starting-point of the
Monologion to simple anecdotes and similes for edification, see Southern,
pp. 217–26; surviving fragments are edited by R. W. Southern and F. S. Schmitt,
Memorials of St Anselm (Auctores Britannici Medii Aevi, i, London, 1969).

[7] See no. 19, lines 15–19. Anselm's letter is not extant.

---

19 [1] Horace, *Epp.* I. xviii. 82: *rectius* 'Theonino', from the satirist Theon.

parentes possessiones carnalia oblectamenta pro Deo contempsi-
stis, uos semper introrsus ad conscientias uestras redite, peccatores
14 uos esse cognoscite, et peccatis uestris continuis orationibus /
f. 21 Deum propicium fore deposcite. Aduersum te carissime nepos
magnum mentis rancorem concepi, quia uidelicet transgressus es
praeceptum quod de hoc ordine primum tibi iniunxi; sed interueniente uenerando patre domno Anselmo,[2] cui sicut Deo oboedire
desidero, sincero tibi corde illam noxam indulgeo. Et moneo ne
20 tale aliquid amplius facias, quia quo impensius amicum diligo, eo
amplius maiorem contra eum iram pro parua etiam culpa concipio.

Omnipotens Dominus sua uos gratia protegat benedicat atque
ab omnibus peccatis clementer absoluat.

20

Lanfranc to Gilbert Crispin   c. *winter 1073*

Another letter concerning Lanfranc the younger and Wido, dispatched at
about the same time as nos. 18–19. By far the most likely recipient is Gilbert
Crispin, whose mother took a close interest in Bec (line 13) and who had himself
grown up in Bec from early childhood (lines 27–8).

Dilectissimo suo G. dilectissimus suus L. dilectionis ceptae
felicem perseuerantiam.

Fratres quos karissime frater litteris edocendos bonisque moribus
instruendos tibi precipue transmisi honeste et secundum uolunta-
5 tem meam tractari a te quorundam relatione cognoui. Pro qua re
gratias benignitati tuae refero, et ut ceptis insistas—si tamen
admonitione indiges—admonere te cupio. Karissimum michi
fratris mei filium (fratrem uidelicet tuum) caritati tuae commendo,
rogans sicut rogari a me oportet iocundissimum filium fratremque
10 meum, quatinus cum magna animi tui iocunditate eum diligas, et
ad uitam laudabilem pro uiribus tuis informare non desinas.
Fratrem tuum propterea dixi illum, quoniam reuera sic esse
uolo multumque rogo. Nam et uenerabilis mater tua, sicut michi
f. 21ᵛ relatum est, filium / suum eundem uocare dignatur; cum illa de
15 excellentissimo genere[1] iste humili loco sit natus, proculdubio
receptura ab eo mercedem suam qui dixit, 'Qui se humiliat
exaltabitur.'[2]

Crucem cum reliquiis fraternitatis tuae oculis dum missam

20 NV

say about you, if they perhaps praise and admire you for having disregarded family, wealth and the pleasures of this world for the sake of God, you must always turn inwards to your own consciences, know yourselves to be sinners and with ceaseless prayer entreat God's mercy for your sins. With you, dearest nephew, I was extremely displeased, for you disobeyed the first directive that I gave you on the monastic life; but at the mediation of our revered father Dom Anselm,[2] whom I strive to obey like God himself, I forgive you the offence from my heart. But I warn you not to do anything like that again, for the more dearly I love a friend the greater my anger against him for even a slight misdemeanour.

May the Lord almighty protect you by his grace, bless you and mercifully absolve you from all your sins.

20

Lanfranc to Gilbert Crispin   c. *winter 1073*

To his beloved G(ilbert) Lanfranc whom he loves wishes that their former love may continue to be fruitful.

Dearest brother, certain men have brought me the news that the brothers whom I consigned especially to you for their education and sound upbringing are receiving from you the excellent care that I should wish. Thank you for your generosity in this matter: I want to encourage you to persevere in the work you have begun, if indeed you need encouragement. I commend to your loving care my brother's son—your own brother—who is very dear to me, asking you (as it is right that I should), my dearest son and brother, to love him wholeheartedly and to spare no effort in training him in an exemplary way of life. I said that he was your brother because that indeed is what I desire and entreat that he should be. I am told that even your own honoured mother is gracious enough to call him her son. She is of the noblest lineage[1] and he born of humble rank: certainly she will receive her reward from Him who said: 'He who humbles himself shall be exalted.'[2]

I am sending you a cross with relics in it, brother, to look at as

[2] Cf. no. 18, n. 7.

---

20 [1] For Gilbert Crispin's mother Eva (died 1099), who was perhaps already in retirement at Bec, see J. Armitage Robinson, *Gilbert Crispin, abbot of Westminster* (Cambridge, 1911), pp. 14–16.

[2] Luke 14: 11.

celebras conspiciendam tibi transmitto, quam perpetuae amiciciae
20 monimentum inter te et ipsum esse desidero. Magno gaudio me
replesti, quia promissionem in puericia factam in iuuentute³
adhuc per diuinam misericordiam te seruare scripsisti. Quam si
ad finem illesam perduxeris, terribilem aliis iudicem proculdubio
cum magna securitate uidebis.

25   Omnipotens Dominus cordi tuo per Sancti Spiritus sui in-
spirationem inserere dignetur, quatinus in omni aetate tua sic
me diligas, sicut in puericia et adolescentia tua³ quondam diligere
me solebas; et ipse te benedicat atque ab omnibus peccatis propiciatus absoluat.

21

Lanfranc to G.   *1070–89*

There is no internal evidence for the date and no reason beyond proximity in the
collection to suggest that 'frater G.' here is Gilbert Crispin (no. 20). The letter
has been cited as evidence of Lanfranc's medical knowledge; but his argument
turns on self-examination and repentance: the herbal remedy is something of an
afterthought.

Dilectissimo fratri G. frater L. benedictionem a Deo et perpetuam
salutem.

Lectis litteris fraternitatis tuae multa te cognoui egritudine
laborare. Pro qua re ortor ne doleas, immo gaudeas tuoque
5 creatori qui de te curam habet indefessas gratias referas, sciens
scriptum esse: 'Libenter gloriabor in infirmitatibus meis.'¹ Et
alias: 'Flagellat Deus omnem filium quem recipit.'² Non enim te
in hoc seculo tantis flagellis attereret, nisi post hoc seculum sine
f. 22 flagello te esse disponeret. Tu ergo memento tui, / memorare
10 nouissima tua et confitere peccata tua. Hoc enim fatiens, aut
corporalem salutem a Deo consequeris aut mortem aliis metuendam
sine metu expectabis; quae uidelicet erit tibi finis malorum prin-
cipium uero bonorum.

     Mitto tibi dioprasium magnum quod ad hanc infirmitatem
15 ualde utile esse medici perhibent, de quo in modum siluestris
nucis tercia semper die accipies.³

21 NV

---

³ Gilbert was presented to Bec as a child *c.* 1055: Fauroux, pp. 33–4. Lanfranc

you celebrate Mass; it is my wish that it should be a token of per-
petual friendship between you and him. You gave me great joy
when you wrote that by God's mercy you were still keeping as a
man[3] the vow that you took as a boy. If you keep it intact until the
end, you will surely look with great confidence on the Judge who
is terrifying to other men.

May the Lord almighty graciously put into your heart by the
inspiration of his Holy Spirit to have such love for me throughout
your life as you had in years past when you were a boy and a youth;[3]
may he bless you and mercifully free you from all your sins.

21

Lanfranc to G.   *1070–89*

To his dearest brother G. brother Lanfranc wishes God's blessing
and eternal welfare.

When I read your letter, brother, I realized that you were suffering
from a serious illness. I urge you not to grieve over that but to
rejoice and to render unwearied thanks to your Creator for his care
for you, knowing that it is written, 'Most gladly will I glory in my
infirmities.'[1] And elsewhere: 'God scourgeth every son whom he
receiveth.'[2] He would not be scourging you so severely in this life
were he not intending that after this life you should be free from
scourging. So examine yourself, think on your last hours and confess your sins. If you do this, either you will receive physical health
from God or you will await death without fear, terrible as it is to
others; because for you it will be the end of evil and the beginning
of good.

I am sending you marrubium, which doctors reckon to be very
efficacious for this disease: you take a piece the size of a hazelnut
every three days.[3]

may have in mind here Isidore's reckoning of the six ages of man: 'infantia'
(0–7), 'pueritia' (7–14), 'adolescentia' (14–28), 'iuventus' (28–50), 'gravitas'
(50–70), 'senectus' (70+): *Etymologiae* xi. 2. 1–8; cf. J. de Ghellinck, 'Iuventus,
gravitas, senectus', in *Studia Mediaevalia in honorem R. J. Martin* (Bruges,
1948), pp. 39–59, with further references.

---

21 [1] 2 Cor. 12: 9.
   [2] Heb. 12: 6.
   [3] *Marrubium* or white horehound (Gk. πράσιον) was used *inter alia* as a
purgative and a cough mixture. A recommended dosage in the latter case was
(as here) 'per triduum': Marcellus, *De Medicamentis* xvi. 12, ed. G. Helmreich
(Leipzig, 1889: Teubner), p. 157.

Omnipotens Dominus custos tui semper existat, atque ab omnibus peccatis propiciatus absoluat.

22
Lanfranc to Baldwin, abbot of Bury St. Edmunds
1070–89

Baldwin was abbot of Bury throughout Lanfranc's archiepiscopate. Although this is the only letter in the collection addressed to him directly, he was one of Lanfranc's most valued colleagues in England; in particular he was his personal doctor (no. 44; cf. no. 41, lines 31–6). For the disputes between Bury St. Edmunds and the bishop of Thetford see nos. 42 and 47 below.

Lanfrancus diuina dignatione non suis meritis archiepiscopus abbati B. salutem cum orationibus.

Harum litterarum portitor iram uestram se dicit incurrisse, et propterea patriam in qua natus et conuersatus erat parentesque et amicos reliquisse. Et quia putauit quod pro me multum facere debeatis, nostris apud paternitatem uestram se petiit litteris adiuuari. Mota igitur nostris precibus uestra ei benignitas indulgeat, quatinus ipse amicum uestrum pro commissi sui uenia se petiuisse[a] cognoscat.[1]

23
Lanfranc to Thomas, archbishop of York
June 1072–28 May 1089

This letter is unlikely to be earlier than the summer of 1072: in the months before the council of Windsor Lanfranc could hardly speak of 'corporalis absentia seu quaelibet localis intercapedo' (line 6). Like no. 12 it is an excellent example of the archbishop of York turning for assistance to Canterbury.

[a]Dilectissimo fratri et amico Eboracensis aecclesiae archiepiscopo Tho. frater L.[b] perpetuam salutem cum orationibus.

[c]Illos quidem qui corporaliter tantum et propter terrena lucra se amant interualla locorum quo prolixiora sunt eo a mutuo amore

May the Lord almighty be your protector always; may he accept
your prayer and absolve you from all sins.

22

Lanfranc to Baldwin, abbot of Bury St. Edmunds
1070–89

Lanfranc, archbishop by divine favour and not his own merits,
sends prayerful greetings to Abbot Baldwin.

The man who brings this letter says that he has incurred your anger
and so has left his home, where he was born and brought up, and
his family and friends. Because he thought that for me you will do
much, he begged me to write to you, father, on his behalf. May our
intercession move you in your goodness to show him mercy, so that
he may know that the man to whom he has turned to find pardon
for his fault is indeed your friend.[1]

23

Lanfranc to Thomas, archbishop of York
June 1072–28 May 1089

To his much-loved brother and friend Thomas, archbishop of
York, Lanfranc his brother sends prayers for his eternal welfare.

Those whose affection is of this life only and dependent on
worldly reward are more thoroughly cut off from their mutual

22 [1] Cf. no. 54, lines 8–9.

5 impensius separant; eos uero quos sincera christianae religionis
caritas iungit corporalis absentia seu quaelibet localis intercapedo
f. 22ᵛ minime disiungit.[1] / Studeamus ergo fraterno inuicem amore
proficere, pro inuicem orare, alterius necessitatem propriam
deputare, quatinus in conspectu Dei atque hominum euidenter
10 appareat quod carnalis zelus quo animae uruntur uindicare in
nobis nichil preualeat.[c]

De iis autem qui uxores desponsatas causa fornicationis relinquere aliasque sibi coniungere uolunt—hoc enim uestra prudentia
a me requisiuit—dominus Iesus Christus quid[d] sentiendum sit
15 in euangelio secundum Marcum apertissime dicit: 'Quicunque
dimiserit uxorem suam et aliam duxerit adulterium committit
super eam. Et si uxor dimiserit uirum suum et alium duxerit,
mechatur.'[2] Item secundum Lucam: 'Omnis qui dimittit uxorem
suam et ducit alteram[e] mechatur. Et qui dimissam a uiro ducit
20 mechatur.'[3] Sunt etiam de hac re plurime sanctorum patrum
auctoritates, sed ubi sol lucet candelam ad proferendum lumen
proferri minime oportet.[4] In his uerbis dominicis luce clarius
liquet, quia uiuente uiro uel uxore extraneam copulam querere
nulli eorum licet. Eum uero qui mulierem quae uxor putatur
25 desponsasse se abnegat, aut euidentibus testimoniis seu quibuslibet
claris indiciis mentiri eum ostendite, aut inpresentiarum quoadusque res melius clarescat causam eius omittite.

24

Lanfranc to Herfast, bishop of Thetford
29 Aug. 1070–28 Aug. 1086

The dating depends on Lanfranc's consecration and the consecration of Herfast's
successor, Bishop William (A.L., p. 290). This is the first of four letters to
Herfast: nos. 24 and 43 relating to discipline within his diocese and nos. 42 and
47 relating to his dispute with Bury St. Edmunds and his personal shortcomings.
The first three legal quotations in this letter are 'starred' in Lanfranc's own
canon law book: Brooke, *English Church*, pp. 68–9.

Dilectissimo fratri et coepiscopo He. L. indignus antistes salutem
et amiciciam cum orationibus.

ᵈ qui V   ᵉ adulteram V

24 NV

love the greater the distance between them; but those who are
united in the pure love of Christians are in no way divided by
physical absence or any spatial separation.[1] Let us both endeavour
to grow in brotherly love for each other, to pray for each other and
each to consider the other's needs his own, so that it may be
plainly seen in the sight of God and man that the worldly emula-
tion which inflames men's minds has no power over us.

As for the men who wish to leave their wedded wives on grounds
of adultery and marry other women—the question on which you
wisely sought my advice—our Lord Jesus Christ says with the
utmost clarity in St Mark's gospel what our decision should be:
'Whosoever shall put away his wife and marry another, committeth
adultery against her. And if the wife shall put away her husband
and be married to another, she committeth adultery.'[2] Again, in
St Luke's gospel: 'Whosoever putteth away his wife and marrieth
another, committeth adultery; and whosoever marrieth her that
is put away from her husband committeth adultery.'[3] There are
also many patristic opinions on this subject; but where the sun is
shining we need not bring out a candle to give light.[4] In these
words of the Lord it is clearer than daylight that while the husband
or wife is alive neither is permitted to seek a union with anyone
else. But if a man denies that he has married the woman who is
thought to be his wife, you should either show that he is lying,
by reliable testimony or some kind of clear proof, or you should
drop his case for the moment until the position is better understood.

24

Lanfranc to Herfast, bishop of Thetford
29 Aug. 1070–28 Aug. 1086

To his well-beloved brother and colleague Herfast Lanfranc, an
unworthy bishop, sends friendly greetings and prayers.

23 [1] Cf. Augustine, *Epistolae* 147, ed. A. Goldbacher (C.S.E.L. xliv, 1904),
pp. 317–18: 'nulla locorum spatia tenent, nulla intercapedine separantur.'
   [2] Mark 10: 11–12; cf. no. 11, *can.* vi.
   [3] Luke 16: 18.
   [4] Cf. Cicero, *De Finibus* 4. 29, ed. T. Schiche (Leipzig, 1915: Teubner),
p. 132: 'in sole . . . lucernam adhibere nihil interest.'

De clerico quem ad nos misistis sanctarum Scripturarum testi-
f. 23 monio hoc sentimus, hoc tenendum / decernimus. Poenitentiam
5 prolixi temporis consideratis eius uiribus pro arbitrio uestro ei
iniungite, sacerdotii ordinem quod inordinate assumpsit ei
auferte, a ceteris ordinibus cessare iubete; quia in sacris canonibus
scriptum est: 'Qui aliena inuadit non exibit impunitus.'[1] Et Leo
papa ad Martianum: 'Propria perdit qui indebita concupiscit.'[2]
10 Siluerius ad Vigilium preuaricatorem: 'Sic enim decet fidem
sanctorum patrum in aecclesia seruari catholica, ut quod habuit
amittat qui improbabili temeritate quod non accepit assumpserit.'[3]
Quod si infra poenitentiae tempus carnis mundiciam digne
seruauerit, ceterarumque bonarum actionum sollicitus obseruator
15 extiterit, miserante Deo cuius misericordiae non est numerus[4]
experientia uestra indulgentiam ei praestare ualebit; ut sicut
beatus Gregorius et praefatus Leo in decretis suis concorditer
dicunt: 'Si poenitentia eius fuerit digna, sit etiam fructuosa.'[5]

25

Lanfranc to Manasses, archbishop of Rheims
29 Aug. 1070–1080

Archbishop Manasses (deposed 1080) is here asked to intervene in a claim made
by one of Lanfranc's vassals for loss of property in the diocese of Rheims. The
nature of his claim is uncertain: either (as I have assumed in the translation)
he was robbed of movables as he travelled through Rosnay or he is trying to
recover houses or land in Rosnay itself.

Domino in columnis aecclesiae[1] plurimum honorando Remensi
archiepiscopo M. peccator et indignus antistes L. salutem,
seruitium cum orationibus.

Lator harum litterarum regius ac noster homo magnam rerum
5 suarum apud Rosnacum[2] se asserit iniuriam pertulisse, et pro
ea re auribus summi pontificis lacrimabilem querimoniam in-
tulisse. Summus uero pontifex raptores ipsos nisi omnia sua ei
redderent terribiliter excommunicauit, et uobis ut ei de ipsis
9 raptoribus iusticiam faceretis sedis apostolicae litteras destinauit.[3]
f. 23ᵛ Et quamuis excellentia / uestra in talibus monitore non egeat, rogo

---

24 [1] *Decreta Eusebii* ii. 13: Hinschius, p. 238.
   [2] Leo the Great, *Ep. ad Martianum imperatorem*: Hinschius, p. 609.
   [3] Silverius, *Ep. ad Vigilium*: Hinschius, p. 628.

25 NV

In the matter of the clerk whom you sent to me, my judgement and directive in the light of holy Scripture is as follows. Impose on him a penance of long duration (having regard to his strength to bear it), take away from him the order of the priesthood, which he has irregularly assumed, and forbid him to exercise his other orders; for it is written in canon law: 'He who usurps what is not his own will not escape unpunished.'[1] And Pope Leo wrote to Martianus: 'The man who covets what is not due to him loses what is his by right.'[2] Silverius wrote to the apostate Vigilius: 'It is fitting that the faith of the holy Fathers be thus upheld within the catholic Church: namely that he who has the deplorable foolhardiness to take what he has not received loses what he did have.'[3] If throughout his time of penance he maintains physical chastity in a worthy manner and is punctilious in observing good behaviour in other respects, then by God's mercy (whose mercy is infinite)[4] a man of your experience will be free to treat him leniently, so that—as St Gregory and the afore-mentioned Leo are at one in saying in their decrees—'If his penance has been worthily performed, let it also be fruitful.'[5]

25

Lanfranc to Manasses, archbishop of Rheims

29 Aug. 1070–1080

To Manasses, lord archbishop of Rheims, a man greatly to be honoured among the pillars of the Church,[1] Lanfranc, a sinner and an unworthy bishop, sends his prayerful greetings and service.

The bearer of this letter is the king's vassal and our own. He declares that he has suffered serious damage to his property at Rosnay[2] and has brought a heart-rending complaint about the affair to the attention of the supreme pontiff. The supreme pontiff has solemnly excommunicated the robbers themselves if they fail to restore all his property to him, and dispatched to you an apostolic directive to see that he has just restitution from those same robbers.[3] Although in such matters your excellency needs

---

[4] Cf. Ps. 146: 5.
[5] *locum non inveni.*

25 [1] Cf. Gal. 2: 9.

[2] Presumably Rosnay (ct. Ville-en-Tardenois, arr. Rheims) 13 km due west of Rheims.

[3] No such papal letter survives, but Gregory VII condemns what are perhaps similar assaults in two letters to Manasses in 1074 (G.VII, *Reg.* ii. 5 and 32).

tamen multumque rogo ut ei benignitas uestra ita subueniat,
quatinus res suas quae iniuste ei ablatae[a] sunt sine diminutione
adquirat.

26

Lanfranc to Thomas, archbishop of York   June 1072–1081

Written presumably after the council of Windsor, May 1072 (cf. no. 23) and
certainly before the death of Robert, bishop of Séez (1081). As only a bishop
could assign penance (council of Windsor, 1070, *can.* xi), only a bishop could
grant remission.

Lanfrancus indignus antistes dilectissimo Eboracensi archiepiscopo Thomae salutem cum orationibus.

Robertus Sagiensis episcopus hunc poenitentem ad me misit, et
mandauit quod iste miserrimus tres homines Montem Sancti
5 Michaelis adeuntes tercia Pentecostes die[1] inuaserit et interfecerit.
Cui ex more poenitentia iniuncta commonitorias sibi litteras tradidit,[2] ut si quis episcopus pietate motus misericordiam ei uellet impendere, potestatem haberet quantum uellet ipsi ignoscere.[a] Huius
itaque rei testis eum ad uos mitto, quatinus hoc uerum esse sciatis
10 atque animae eius secundum quod uobis uisum fuerit consulatis.

27

Lanfranc to Peter, bishop of Chester
29 Aug. 1072–25 Dec. 1085

Although Peter was consecrated in 1072–3, his see was not formally transferred
to Chester until 1075 (no. 11, lines 48–9); on the other hand the title was current
by 1073 (no. 13, n. 1). Thus the only secure limits are Peter's consecration (29 Aug. 1072–Feb. 1073) and the nomination of his successor (25 Dec.
1085). Lanfranc is acting in response to a complaint by the abbot and community at Coventry (lines 9–10): he enjoins the bishop to restore the property
in dispute and rebukes him for neglecting his pastoral duty. The latter seems
an understatement indeed; but Peter's conduct, though reprehensible, was not
senseless. To establish himself in Chester he needed the secure base and income
that Coventry could provide; his successor was to find Coventry so indispensable
that he moved the see there formally in 1102. Strategic considerations apart,
it is quite possible that the abbot of Coventry had been rallying opposition to the
new bishop (note 1 below).

Lanfrancus gratia Dei archiepiscopus P. Cestrensi episcopo
salutem.

----

[a] oblatae V

26 NV
[a] ignoscere N[1]; ignosceret NV

27 NV

no guide, I do most urgently request you in your generosity so to assist him that he may obtain in full the property of which he was unjustly robbed.

26

Lanfranc to Thomas, archbishop of York   June 1072–1081

Lanfranc, an unworthy bishop, sends prayerful greetings to his beloved Thomas, archbishop of York.

Bishop Robert of Séez has sent me this penitent; he has explained that the wretched fellow attacked and killed three men who were on their way to Mont-Saint-Michel on the third day of Pentecost.[1] When as is customary he had imposed penance on him, he gave him a letter of attestation,[2] so that if any bishop should feel pity for him and wish to show him mercy, that bishop should have the power to remit him as much penance as he wished. In sending him to you I attest that this is the state of affairs, so that you may know that this is true and give him such spiritual counsel as seems good to you.

27

Lanfranc to Peter, bishop of Chester
                        29 Aug. 1072–25 Dec. 1085

Lanfranc, by the grace of God archbishop, greets Peter, bishop of Chester.

---

26 [1] The first Wednesday after Whitsun was an Ember Day: the men may have been bringing a customary payment to the monastery; cf. the council of Lille-bonne, *can.* 9 (Orderic, *Hist. Eccles.* iii. 28–9).
   [2] Cf. the sealed letter (from Leo IX as bishop of Toul) presented by the dancers of Kölbigk at the shrine of St. Edith in Wilton: Goscelin, *Vita Edithae* 16, ed. A. Wilmart, *Analecta Bollandiana*, lvi (1938), p. 287.

Litteras ante paucos dies tibi transmisi, et eas uix susceptas legere
despexisti, et cum magna indignatione sicut michi dictum est
5 supra quoddam sedile eas proiecisti. Nunc alias mitto mandans et
precipiens ex parte regis et nostra, quatinus ab omni grauamine
quod coenobio Couentreio inferre diceris omnino te subtrahas,
quicquid de ipso coenobio uel terris ipsius coenobii uiolenter
abstulisti sine mora restituas. Clamorem enim fecerunt ad me tam
10 abbas[1] quam monachi eius quod dormitorium eorum per uim
f. 24 introisti, / archas eorum fregisti, et equos et omnes proprietates
quas habebant rapuisti; insuper domos eorum destruxisti et
materias earum ad tuas uillas[2] asportari precepisti, in ipso quoque
coenobio cum familia tua consumens bona monachorum octo
15 dierum moram fecisti. Haec nec tui officii nec tuae potestatis esse
cognoscas. Immo magis oporteret te animabus eorum pastorali
discretione consulere, bonorumque morum sanctarumque actionum uerbis et operibus salubria exempla praebere.

28

Lanfranc to Adelelm, abbot of Abingdon   *1071–83*

Abbot Adelelm (1071–83) was English by name but a monk of Jumièges.
He was valiant in defence of the lands of Abingdon, in several cases with
Lanfranc's support, and a military leader in the Scottish expedition of 1072:
Chronicon Monasterii de Abingdon, ed. J. Stevenson (R.S., 1858), ii. 9; cf. 1–11.
Lanfranc shows extraordinary lenience here to the ultimate monastic mis-
demeanour; his closing admonition ('et paternum . . . ostendatis') suggests
that Adelelm too had been at fault.

Lanfrancus archiepiscopus dilecto filio et amico Adelelmo abbati
salutem et benedictionem.

Fratres isti ad me uenerunt accusantes se et dicentes in uos grauiter
peccasse, et sua culpa de monasterio recessisse. Ego uero stulticiam
5 illorum[a] eis audientibus multum adauxi, et satis duris atque ama-

28 NV
a eorum V

I wrote to you a few days ago: you were unwilling to accept my letter, scorned to read it and very disdainfully (as I am told) threw it onto a bench. Now I am sending another, instructing and directing you in the king's name and my own to desist completely from all the harassment which you are said to be practising on the monastery of Coventry and to restore forthwith everything pertaining to that house or its lands which you have removed by force. Both the abbot[1] and his monks have lodged a complaint with me that you forced an entry into their dormitory and broke into their strongboxes, and that you have robbed them of their horses and all their goods. Furthermore you pulled down their houses and ordered the materials of which these were built to be taken to your own residences;[2] finally you remained in that monastery with your retinue for eight days eating up the monks' provisions. You should be aware that it is neither your role as a bishop nor within your power to do these things. On the contrary you should have been giving them the spiritual advice of a discerning pastor and by your words and actions setting them edifying standards of a good life and godly conduct.

28

Lanfranc to Adelelm, abbot of Abingdon   *1071–83*

Archbishop Lanfranc sends greetings and his blessing to his beloved son and friend, Abbot Adelelm.

These monks have come to me as their own accusers, saying that they have sinned gravely against you and that they are to blame for having withdrawn from their monastery. For my part I expatiated to them at length on their folly, rebuking them in the

27 [1] The abbot was Leofwine, perhaps the deposed bishop of Lichfield (1053–70: no. 2, n. 2), but possibly 'Leofwine II', unknown except for his presence at the council of London, 1075 (no. 11, n. 16).
    [2] Sc. the 'hunting-lodges' or 'granges' in which a bishop stayed as he travelled round his estates. Lanfranc constructed such lodgings, at his own expense, for his circuit of the Christ Church lands: Eadmer, *H.N.*, p. 16, quoting Lanfranc's obit (Gibson, App. B, lines 30–4); Cf. no. 30, line 19.

rissimis uerbis eos prout decuit increpaui. Postea interrogati a me
si de cetero uellent emendare, responderunt se uelle et de hoc
quod egissent plurimum se dolere. Et precati sunt me quatinus
pro eis apud uos intercederem, et mea eos intercessione monasterio
10 unde exierant reconciliarem. Quapropter fraternitatem uestram
precor, si meis apud eam precibus locus existat,[b] ut pro amore
Dei et nostro quicquid in uos et contra ordinem deliquerunt
sincero corde remittatis, et in suis eos locis[1] in quibus ante culpam
erant suscipiatis, et paternum eis affectum ut Deus uobis misericors
15 sit de reliquo ostendatis. /

29

Lanfranc to Stigand, bishop of Chichester
29 Aug. 1070–29 Aug. 1087

The first of two letters to Stigand (nos. 29–30), neither closely datable. The
limits for both are Lanfranc's consecration and Stigand's death; here the likely
years for papal intervention are 1070–c.1080. The letter throws light both on
Lanfranc's use of a provincial synod to decide disciplinary disputes in other
sees (lines 6–8) and on his role as a *de facto* papal legate (cf. no. 7, lines 41–4).

f.24ᵛ Lanfrancus gratia Dei archiepiscopus dilectissimo fratri Stigando
episcopo salutem.

Misit michi litteras papa, in quibus precepit ut causam istius
mulieris quam aduersus eam habetis diligenter audiam, et interim
5 quietam et absolutam esse praecipiam.[1] Propterea mando uobis ut
pace uestra cum uiro suo maneat[2] quoadusque in unum conueniamus, et ipsam causam cum consilio episcoporum inter nos con-
feramus, et adiuuante diuina gratia salubri fine definiamus.

---

[b] existit N[1]V

---

29 NV

---

28 [1] i.e. their original order of seniority, according to the year in which each had
been professed as a monk.

harsh and bitter language that their condition merited. Then I
asked them if they desired to amend their life in the future; they
answered that they did and that they grieved deeply for what they
had done. They entreated me to intercede with you on their behalf
and to make their peace with the monastery which they had left.
In these circumstances I entreat you as a brother (if my entreaties
carry any weight with you) that out of love for God and for me you
forgive them wholeheartedly whatever injury they have done you
and whatever offence they have committed against their monastic
profession, and that you receive them back into the positions that
they held before their offence:[1] show them from now on such
fatherly love that God may show mercy to you.

29

Lanfranc to Stigand, bishop of Chichester
29 Aug. 1070–29 Aug. 1087

Lanfranc, by the grace of God archbishop, greets his well-beloved
brother, Bishop Stigand.

The pope has sent me a letter instructing me to give a thorough
hearing to the charge you are bringing against this woman and to
direct that meanwhile she should not be subject to any penalty or
duress.[1] My instructions then are that you acquiesce in her remaining with her husband[2] until we can meet together and discuss the
matter with the advice of our bishops and by the grace of God
reach a fair settlement.

---

29 [1] The papal letter is not extant. If, as would appear, either Stigand or the
unnamed woman had informed the pope in the first place, this is a rare instance
of an appeal to Rome: Brooke, *English Church*, p. 130.
  [2] The point at issue is the validity of the woman's marriage: cf. no. 11, *can.*
vi.

30

Lanfranc to Stigand, bishop of Chichester
29 Aug. 1070–29 Aug. 1087

Dating as no. 29, but likely to belong to the 1070s, when Lanfranc was still clarifying his jurisdiction: cf. no. 40 (spring 1076), in which Lanfranc plans to hold an ordination in Chichester. The archbishop held several estates in Sussex: F. R. H. Du Boulay, *The Lordship of Canterbury* (London, 1966), p. 45, with references; see particularly p. 376 (Tangmere). Lanfranc maintained that these estates, which lay within the diocese of Chichester, were subject to the *diocesan* jurisdiction of Canterbury; the jurisdiction of Chichester was limited to the distribution of chrism. See H. Mayr-Harting, *The 'Acta' of the Bishops of Chichester 1075–1207* (London, 1964: Canterbury and York Society), pp. 54–5, and for a recurrence of the dispute in the mid twelfth century *The Letters of John of Salisbury* i, ed. W. J. Millor, H. E. Butler and C. N. L. Brooke (N.M.T., 1955), no. 92. Several English sees, notably Durham, had external estates that were similarly withdrawn from the jurisdiction of the local bishop: Barlow, *English Church*, pp. 249–54, and id., *Durham Jurisdictional Peculiars* (Oxford, 1950), *passim*. In a comparable case (no. 51) Geoffrey of Coutances regarded a priest on a Coutances estate within the diocese of Bayeux as legally subject to the archdeacons of Bayeux. No. 30 is quoted in full by both Eadmer (*H.N.*, pp. 21–2) and V.L. (cap. 9).

Lanfrancus gratia Dei archiepiscopus dilectissimo fratri Stigando episcopo salutem.

Clerici uillarum nostrarum, qui[a] in uestra diocesi existunt, quaesti nobis sunt quod uestri archidiaconi repertis occasionibus
5 pecunias ab eis exquirunt;[1] et a quibusdam iam acceperunt. Meminisse debet fraternitas uestra quia contra morem antecessorum nostrorum atque uestrorum uobis concessimus eisque imperauimus, quatinus ad uestras synodos irent et ea quae ad christianae religionis noticiam prodesse possunt sine interpellatione
10 uel discussione aliqua a uobis audirent. Si quae in ipsis culpae inuenirentur, suspensa interim uindicta ad nostrum examen seruarentur, et nobis uel in miserendo uel in ulciscendo sicut semper consuetudo fuit obnoxii tenerentur. Mandamus itaque uobis ut male accepta sine dilatione reddi iubeatis, et ministris
15 uestris ne ulterius id presumant seruandae caritatis studio prohibeatis. Nos uero presbiteris nostris[b] qui extra Cantiam constituti sunt omnino precepimus ne ad uestram uel alicuius /
f. 25 episcopi sinodum amplius eant, nec uobis nec aliquibus ministris uestris pro qualibet culpa respondeant. Nos enim cum ad uillas

30 NV
[a] qui NV: ? *rectius* quae   [b] uestris V

30

Lanfranc to Stigand, bishop of Chichester
29 Aug. 1070–29 Aug. 1087

Lanfranc, by the grace of God archbishop, greets his dearest brother, Bishop Stigand.

The clergy of our estates who live within your diocese have complained to us that your archdeacons are finding pretexts to demand money from them;[1] already they have received it from some. You would do well to remember, my brother, that as a concession to you we directed these men to attend your synods, for which there is no precedent on your side or ours, and to receive guidance from you on Christian observance without any hindrance or supervision. If any faults were found in them, these men were to be presented to us for examination, and no penalties imposed in the interim; they were to come before us, as the custom has always been, for mercy or punishment. We therefore direct you to order the immediate return of the money wrongly received and to forbid your servants to make any further attempt of this kind, if they wish to retain our goodwill. For our part we have absolutely forbidden those of our priests who are stationed outside Kent ever again to attend your synod or that of any other bishop; they are not to be answerable to you or any of your servants for any fault whatsoever. When we ourselves come to visit our estates,

---

30 [1] Chichester had two archdeacons, but little is known of them at this early date: Mayr-Harting, op. cit., pp. 48–9. They were demanding fines for offences committed and perhaps also *synodalia*.

20 nostras ueniemus, quales ipsi uel in moribus uel in sui ordinis
    scientia sint pastorali auctoritate uestigare debemus. Crisma
    tantum a uobis accipiant, et ea quae antiquitus instituta sunt in
    crismatis acceptione persoluant.[2] Sicut nanque ea quae antiquitus
    usque ad nostra tempora antecessores nostri habuerunt sollerti
25 uigilantia cupimus illibata seruare, ita aliis debita aliqua quod
    absit usurpatione nolumus denegare.

31

Lanfranc to Roger, earl of Hereford   *1075*

Regesta, no. 78. The first of a series of letters (nos. 31–6: in chronological order)
concerning the revolt of 1075: the protagonists were Roger fitzOsbern, earl of
Hereford (1071–5), Ralph de Gael, earl of East Anglia (*c.* 1069–75) and Waltheof,
earl of Huntingdon (1065–75). Lanfranc regarded Earl Roger, son of a patron
of Bec (Fauroux, nos. 180–1, 189), as his special responsibility; Earl Ralph
was merely a traitor (nos. 34–5); Earl Waltheof—to whom no reference is made
in these surviving letters—he advised to seek the king's mercy, with fatal
results (*Gesta Regum*, ii. 313–14). Throughout the crisis William the Conqueror was abroad and Lanfranc, with the help of such magnates as Geoffrey
of Coutances and Odo of Bayeux, was acting in England on the king's behalf;
see further note 1.

Lanfrancus gratia Dei archiepiscopus dilectissimo filio et amico
R. comiti salutem et benedictionem.

Dominus noster Anglorum rex salutat uos et nos omnes sicut
fideles suos in quibus magnam fiduciam habet, et mandat ut
5   quantam possumus curam habeamus de castellis suis, ne quod
Deus auertat inimicis suis tradantur[1]. Propterea rogo uos sicut
rogare debeo carissimum filium[2] meum,[a] quem teste Deo toto
corde diligo et seruire desidero et cuius patrem sicut meam
animam dilexi, quatinus de hac re et de omni fidelitate domini
10 nostri regis talem curam geratis, ut a Deo et ab eo et omnibus
bonis hominibus laudem habeatis.[3] In memoria uestra semper
tenete qualiter gloriosus pater uester uixit, et quam fideliter
domino suo seruiuit, et cum quanta strenuitate multa adquisiuit
14 et adquisita magno honore retinuit.[4]
f. 25ᵛ   Item mandauit rex ne sui uicecomites aliqua / placita in uestris

31 NV
[a] *om.* V

it is for us by our pastoral authority to scrutinize the character of these men and their competence as priests. All that they may receive from you is chrism; and they may make those payments at the reception of the chrism that were instituted long ago.[2] On the one hand it is our desire by care and vigilance to maintain unimpaired the rights enjoyed by our predecessors from ancient times until the present day; on the other, we do not wish by any usurpation of rights (perish the thought) to deny to others what is their due.

31

Lanfranc to Roger, earl of Hereford   *1075*

Lanfranc, by the grace of God archbishop, greets his dearest son and friend Earl R(oger) and sends him his blessing.

Our lord the king of the English greets you and all of us as his faithful subjects in whom he places great trust, commanding us to do all in our power to prevent his castles from being handed over to his enemies:[1] may God avert such a disaster. I urge you then, as I must urge the dearest of my sons[2]—whom God knows I love wholeheartedly and long to serve, whose father too I loved like my own soul—to be so scrupulous in this matter and in all your duty as a vassal of our lord the king that you may have praise of God[3] and the king and all good men. Never forget your father's distinguished career: the faithful service he gave his lord, his zeal in winning great possessions and how honourably he held what he had won.[4]

On another point, the king has ordered his sheriffs not to

---

[2] Chrism (the mixture of oil and balm used for sacramental and quasi-sacramental purposes) was distributed annually by a cathedral or similarly ancient foundation to its dependent churches; conversely the reception of chrism, and the traditional payment made in return, was an acknowledgement of jurisdiction. See M. Brett, *The English Church under Henry I* (Oxford, 1975), pp. 164–6.

31 [1] A royal writ (not extant) which Lanfranc communicates to Earl Roger and no doubt other magnates who were directly concerned.

[2] The reiterated 'dilectissimo filio', 'carissimum filium' (no. 31), 'dilectissimo filio', 'dulcissime fili' (no. 32) culminate in Lanfranc's exercise of jurisdiction as 'pat(er) spiritual(is)' (no. 33, line 11). See further no. 33, n. 2.

[3] Cf. 1 Cor. 4: 5.

[4] William fitzOsbern, steward of Normandy (died 1071): see Orderic, *Hist. Eccles.* ii. 260–1, with references, 282–5.

terris teneant quoadusque ipse mare transeat, et inter uos et ipsos uicecomites per semetipsum causas uestras audiat.[5]

Libenter uellem uobiscum loqui. De qua re si uobis uoluntas est mandate michi ad quem locum possimus conuenire, et de 20 rebus uestris ac domini nostri regis colloquium habere. Ego uero paratus sum uenire uobis obuiam quocunque preceperitis.

Rogo ut harum litterarum portitori nomine Beringerio iusticiam faciatis de illis hominibus super quos clamorem facit pro equo suo, quem furto sibi ablatum dicit.

25 Omnipotens Dominus uos benedicat, et uitam uestram in omni bonitate disponat.

32

Lanfranc to Roger, earl of Hereford   *1075*

Regesta no. 79. A letter reinforcing no. 31; cf. no. 33, n. 2.

Lanfrancus gratia Dei archiepiscopus dilectissimo filio et amico R. comiti salutem et benedictionem.

Auditis de te quae audire nollem, doleo quantum dicere non possum. Neque enim deceret ut filius Willelmi comitis[1]—cuius 5 prudentia et bonitas et erga dominum suum et omnes amicos suos fidelitas multis terris innotuit—infidelis diceretur, et de periurio uel fraude aliqua infamiam pateretur. Immo conueniret potius ut filius tanti uiri imitator patris existeret, et omnis bonitatis et fidelitatis aliis exemplum preberet. Propterea rogo te dulcissime 10 fili et carissime amice quatinus propter Deum et honorem tuum si culpam de tali re habes, resipiscas; si uero non habes, manifestissimis documentis te non habere ostendas. Quicquid uero sit rogo ut ad me uenias, securus proculdubio quod neque in eundo f. 26 neque in redeundo per nos uel per regios / homines impedimenti 15 aliquid patieris.[2]

Omnipotens Dominus te benedicat.

32 NV

---

[5] Little is known of this dispute. In the decade after the Conquest some sheriffs were under baronial control rather than royal: e.g. in Shropshire under Roger of Montgomery and in the west midlands under William fitzOsbern. Roger no doubt wished to continue his father's jurisdiction (whether within Herefordshire as a palatine earldom or throughout all his estates is not clear);

hold any courts within your lands until he himself returns to England and can hear personally the matters in dispute between you and those sheriffs.[5]

I wish that I could speak to you in person. If that is your desire too, let me know where we can meet and discuss both your affairs and the interests of the king. For my part I am ready to meet you at whatever place you may name.

You are asked to see that Beringer, who brings you this letter, has a just settlement with those men whom he accuses of having stolen his horse.

The Lord almighty bless you and direct your whole life in righteousness.

32

Lanfranc to Roger, earl of Hereford   *1075*

Lanfranc, by the grace of God archbishop, greets his dearest son and friend, Earl R(oger) and sends him his blessing.

I grieve more than I can say at the unwelcome news I hear of you. It would not be right that a son of Earl William[1]—a man whose sagacity and integrity and loyalty to his lord and all his friends is renowned in many lands—should be called faithless and be exposed to the slur of perjury or any kind of deceit. On the contrary, the son of such a great man should follow his father's example and be for others a pattern of integrity and loyalty in all respects. I therefore beg you, as a son whom I cherish and the dearest of friends, for the sake of God and your own good name, if you are guilty of such conduct to return to your senses; and if you are not, to demonstrate this by the clearest possible evidence. In either case, come and see me: you have an unqualified assurance that you will not be hindered in any way by me or by the king's men either in making the journey or in returning home.[2]

The Lord almighty bless you.

and the king equally wished to introduce his 'own' sheriffs (*sui*: line 15). See further D. Walker, 'The *honours* of the earls of Hereford in the twelfth century', *Trans. Bristol and Gloucestershire Archaeological Soc.* lxxix (1960), 178; cf. J. F. A. Mason, 'The officers and clerks of the Norman earls of Shropshire', *Trans. Shropshire Archaeological Soc.* lvi (1960), 247.

32 [1] William fitzOsbern: see no. 31, n. 4.

[2] A necessary assurance: cf. the difficulties encountered by William of St. Carilef, notwithstanding his safe-conduct from the king: *De iniusta vexatione Willelmi episcopi*, in *Symeonis Monachi Opera*, ed. T. Arnold (R.S., 1882–5), i. 170–95.

33

Lanfranc to Roger, earl of Hereford   1075

Regesta no. 80. Written soon after nos. 31–2. Although 'Rod. comiti' (line 2: N only) points to Ralph, earl of Norfolk, it is clear that Lanfranc is addressing the recipient of nos. 31–2. The division into 33A and 33B, which has not been made in previous editions, is clearly marked in N (though not in V) with a rubricated capital at *Mandasti* and is in my judgement almost inescapable. In 33B Roger's obduracy has ceased and Lanfranc's tone is markedly more sympathetic; he now warns Roger to take no action as strongly as in 33A he urged him to act. These tactics were unsuccessful: when Roger surrendered to the king, he was imprisoned for life (Orderic, *Hist. Eccles.* ii. 318–19).

33A. Lanfrancus gratia Dei archiepiscopus dilectissimo[a] quondam filio et amico Rod.[b] comiti bene intelligere et salubrem de anima sua curam habere.

Doleo pro te quantum dici non potest, quia teste Deo te amabam
5 et te amare et tibi seruire toto corde desiderabam. Sed quia in-
stinctu demonis et consilio prauorum hominum ea molitus es
quae te moliri minime oportuerat, necessitate coactus mentem
mutaui, et dilectionem non in odium tantum quantum in rancorem
mentis[1] et iustam seueritatem conuerti. Legatis tamen et litteris
10 semel et iterum[2] te inuitaui ut ad me uenires, et consilium animae
tuae a me sicut a patre spirituali et amico sincero acciperes,
atque a stulto proposito quod conceperas consilio meliore desiste-
res. Tu uero id facere recusasti. Canonica igitur auctoritate te et
omnes adiutores tuos maledixi et excommunicaui atque a liminibus
15 sanctae aecclesiae et consortio fidelium separaui, et per totam
Anglicam terram hoc idem pastorali auctoritate fieri imperaui.[3]
Ab hoc uinculo anathematis absoluere te non possum nisi misericordiam domini mei regis requiras, sibique et aliis quorum res
iniuste predatus es iusticiam facias.

20 **33B.** Mandasti quod ad me uenire uelles. Hoc ego libentissime
uellem, nisi regalem iram pro hac re me incursurum metuerem.
Sed legato et litteris poenitudinem tuam et humilitatem et preces
f. 26ᵛ ei intimabo et te salua eius fidelitate prout melius potero / adiuuabo.
Interim rogo et moneo ut quiescas, nec aliquid coneris facere
25 unde maiorem eius iram incurras.

33 NV
[a] dilictissimo N   [b] .R. V

33

Lanfranc to Roger, earl of Hereford   *1075*

33A. Lanfranc, by the grace of God archbishop, to his one-time dearest son and friend Earl Roger: may he have sound judgement and some concern for his soul's welfare.

I grieve for you inexpressibly, for God knows I loved you and desired with all my heart to love and serve you. But because the devil's prompting and the advice of evil men have led you into an enterprise which under no circumstances should you have attempted, necessity has forced me to change my attitude and turn my affection not so much into hate as into bitterness[1] and the severity of justice. I have sent messengers, I have sent letters not once but a second time[2] inviting you to come to me: to receive counsel for your soul from me your father in God and true friend, and on better advice to abandon the foolish undertaking which you had planned. You would not do so. Therefore I have cursed and excommunicated you and all your adherents by my authority as archbishop; I have cut you off from the holy precincts of the Church and the assembly of the faithful, and by my pastoral authority I have commanded this to take effect throughout the whole land of England.[3] I can free you from this bond of anathema only if you seek my lord the king's mercy and if you render satisfaction to him and the other men whose property you have unjustly seized.

33B. You sent word that you wished to come and see me. Personally I should agree to this most willingly, did I not fear to incur the king's anger by so doing. But I shall inform him by both messenger and letter of your repentance and humble prayers for mercy, and I shall give you all the help that is compatible with my allegiance to him. For the moment I strongly advise you to lie low: take no initiative that may bring down his anger upon you more fiercely still.

33 [1] Cf. Ps. 108: 5 ('dilectionem . . . odium') and no. 19, line 16 ('mentis rancorem').

[2] For Lanfranc's canonical authorities see e.g. the council of Mileum, *can.* 24 (Hinschius, p. 319) and Gregory the Great, *Registrum* ii. 50 (ed. L. M. Hartmann [Berlin, 1895: *MGH Epistolae* I. i], p. 154). In failing to present himself Roger was *ipso facto* liable to excommunication; nos. 31–2 are the required summons 'semel et iterum'. The passage also echoes the liturgical form of excommunication: *PRG* i. 308–13.

[3] A practical exercise of primatial jurisdiction: cf. no. 47, lines 43–4.

34

Lanfranc to King William I
1075

Regesta no. 81: this letter and the next concern (no. 34, lines 6–8) the battle of *Fagaduna* near Cambridge and (no. 35) the siege of Norwich castle: Orderic, *Hist. Eccles.* ii. 316, with references. For the play on 'fidelis' throughout nos. 31–5 see Introduction, pp. 5–6.

Domino suo Anglorum regi Wil. fidelis suus L. fidele seruitium et fideles orationes.

Libenter uos uideremus sicut angelum Dei[1] sed hoc tempore nolumus uos mare transire, quia magnum dedecus nobis faceretis 5 si pro talibus periuris et latronibus uincendis ad nos ueniretis. Rodulfus comes, immo Rodulfus traditor, et totus exercitus eius in fugam uersi sunt, et nostri cum infinita multitudine Francigenarum et Anglorum eos insequuntur; et ante paucos dies, sicut michi mandauerunt principes nostri,[2] aut ipsi periuri de 10 terra uestra per mare fugient aut eos uiuos uel mortuos habebunt. Cetera per hunc monachum uobis mando, cui bene credere potestis, quia fidelitatem michi fecit.

Omnipotens Dominus uos benedicat.

35

Lanfranc to King William I
1075

Regesta no. 82. Written after the fall of Norwich castle. The siege had lasted three months: Orderic, *Hist. Eccles.* ii. 316. Earl Ralph had already departed to his Breton estates, which were beyond William the Conqueror's jurisdiction (Orderic, *Hist. Eccles.* ii. 318), leaving his wife in command at Norwich: *A.S. Chron.* DE s.a. 1075.

Gloriosissimo domino suo Anglorum regi W. fidelis suus L. fidele seruitium cum orationibus.

Gloria in excelsis Deo cuius misericordia regnum uestrum purgatum est spurcicia Britonum. Castrum Noruuich redditum est, et 5 Britones qui in eo erant et terras in Anglica terra habebant, concessa eis uita cum menbris,[1] iurauerunt quod infra quadraginta dies de regno uestro exirent, et amplius sine uestra licentia in illud

34 NV

35 NV

34

Lanfranc to King William I   *1075*

To his lord William, king of the English, Lanfranc as his loyal
vassal sends loyal service and loyally offers prayers.

We should welcome seeing you as we would God's angel,[1] yet we
do not want you to cross the sea at this moment; for you would
be offering us a grave insult were you to come to our assistance
in subduing such perjured brigands. Earl Ralph, or rather Ralph
the traitor, and his whole army have turned and fled; our forces
are pursuing them with a countless host of French and English
and within a few days (as our generals[2] have informed me) either
those oath-breakers will be fleeing from your land by sea or our
men will have them, alive or dead. Further details I send you
by the monk who is carrying this letter; you can believe all that
he says, for he has done fealty to me.

The Lord almighty bless you.

35

Lanfranc to King William I   *1075*

To his most glorious lord William, king of the English, Lanfranc
his loyal subject sends loyal service and his prayers.

Glory be to God on high, by whose mercy your kingdom has been
purged of its Breton dung. Norwich castle has been surrendered
and those Bretons in it who held lands in England have been
granted their lives and spared mutilation;[1] they have sworn for
their part to leave your kingdom within forty days and never to

---

34 [1] Cf. Gal. 4: 14.
 [2] Orderic (loc. cit.) names William of Warenne and Richard fitzGilbert
as the military leaders at *Fagaduna*. They were supported by Geoffrey, bishop of
Coutances and Odo, bishop of Bayeux: *Flor. Wig.* ii. 11.

35 [1] Contrast the mutilation of prisoners after the battle of *Fagaduna*, a few
months before: Orderic, *Hist. Eccles.* ii. 316. The council of London had just
agreed that ecclesiastics should not be party to judgements of death or mutilation (no. 11, *can.* ix); the Norwich garrison may have benefited by this ruling
when Lanfranc and/or Geoffrey of Coutances came to sentence them.

non introirent. Qui uero Rodulfo traditori et sociis eius sine
9 terra pro solidis seruierunt[2] ad hoc fatiendum unius mensis spacium
f. 27 multis precibus impetrauerunt. / In ipso castro remanserunt
episcopus Gausfridus, W. de Warenna, Rob. Malet et trecenti
loricati cum eis,[3] cum balistariis et artificibus machinarum[4]
multis. Omnis strepitus bellorum miserante Deo in Anglica terra
quieuit.
15   Omnipotens Dominus uos benedicat.

36

Lanfranc to Walcher, bishop of Durham
autumn–winter 1075

Regesta, no. 83. Written soon after the revolt of 1075 (nos. 31–5), before William
the Conqueror returned to England. The Danes (lines 9–10) were allies of Earl
Ralph, who arrived too late to help him. They did indeed plunder York:
A.S. Chron. D s.a. 1075.

Lanfrancus peccator et indignus antistes uenerabili fratri et
coepiscopo Walchero salutem.

Letatus sum in his quae dicta sunt michi[1] a uobis. Pacem uos
uestris litteris habere didicimus, quam procul a uobis esse multis
5 multorum relationibus territi credebamus. Nos uero, expulsis Bri-
tonibus et sedatis omnibus bellis, in tanta tranquillitate uiuimus ut
postquam rex mare transiit tranquillius nos uixisse nequaquam
meminerimus.[2] Res domini nostri regis in summa prosperitate
esse et eum ad presens ad nos transire certissime sciatis. Dani
10 ut rex nobis mandauit reuera ueniunt. Castrum itaque uestrum et
hominibus et armis et alimentis uigilanti cura muniri facite.[3]
Omnipotens autem Dominus ab omni malo[4] uos defendat.

---

[2] To judge by their treatment here, these are stipendiary knights who
expected to remain in the service of Ralph and his allies; they are not casual
mercenaries hired for the campaign. See further M. Chibnall, 'Mercenaries and
the *familia regis* under Henry I', *History* lxii (1977), 15–23, with references.

[3] Of the principals in the siege, whom only Lanfranc specifies, William of
Warenne had also taken part in *Fagaduna*: Orderic, loc. cit., with references.
The 'loricati' would be mounted knights in chain mail, such as appear in the
Bayeux Tapestry; they could both defend the castle and subdue the surrounding
country.

[4] Cf. William of Poitiers's account of the siege-towers built to capture

36 NV

enter it again without your permission. The landless mercenaries[2] who served Ralph the traitor and his associates begged for and were granted the same terms within the limit of one month. Bishop Geoffrey, William of Warenne and Robert Malet have remained in the castle itself with three hundred heavily-armed soldiers,[3] supported by a large force of slingers and siege engineers.[4] By God's mercy all the clamour of warfare has fallen silent in the land of England.

The Lord almighty bless you.

36

Lanfranc to Walcher, bishop of Durham
autumn–winter 1075

Lanfranc, a sinful man who is not worthy to be a bishop, sends greetings to his reverend brother and fellow bishop Walcher.

I was glad at the news you sent me.[1] Your letter told us that you have peace, which in our alarm at the many reports reaching us from many quarters we believed to be far from you. For our part, now that the Bretons are banished and all warfare is suppressed, we live in a tranquillity greater than we can recall ever experiencing since the king crossed the sea.[2] Be assured that our lord the king's affairs are prospering and that he himself is crossing to England without delay. The Danes are indeed coming, as the king told us. So fortify your castle with men, weapons and stores: be ready.[3]

May the Lord almighty preserve you from all evil.[4]

Brionne (1047–50): 'Victor mature insecutus arctam locauit obsidionem, castella, utrinque ad ripas fluminis bipartiti, opponens' (*Gesta Guillelmi Ducis* i. 9, ed. R. Foreville [Paris, 1952], p. 18). Note the size of Norwich castle within a decade of the Conquest: cf. J. Campbell, in *Historic Towns*, ed. M. D. Lobel, ii (London, 1975), Norwich, pp. 1–8.

---

36 [1] Ps. 121: 1.

[2] Cf. no. 35: 'Castrum Noruuich . . . introirent' and the concluding sentence 'Omnis strepitus . . . quieuit.'

[3] Lanfranc is said to have advised the king that all magnates, including bishops, should maintain a force of household knights against just such an eventuality: William of Malmesbury, *Vita Wulfstani* iii. 16, ed. R. R. Darlington (Camden 3rd ser., xl, London, 1928), p. 56.

[4] Ps. 120: 7.

37

Lanfranc to Remigius, bishop of Lincoln   ?*1075*

Another letter that concerns the king, and possibly also the 1075 revolt. *A.S. Chron.* DE s.a. 1075 refers to unnamed 'bishops and abbots' who supported Earl Ralph; in the second quarter of the twelfth century Henry of Huntingdon writes that Remigius had been accused of treason and cleared by the ordeal (vicariously undergone): *Historia Anglorum*, ed. T. Arnold (R.S., 1879), p. 212.

Lanfrancus gratia Dei archiepiscopus dilecto fratri et amico Remigio salutem.

Cum multi de te multa peruersa dicant, et perpauci sint qui uerbis detrahentium ingenita liberalitate contradicant, scias tamen
5 dominum nostrum regem nullius detrahentis contra te uerba recipere, sed potius contra omnes maledicos regali te auctoritate defendere. Itaque expedit tibi, si prope es et licitum habes, qua-
f. 27ᵛ tinus ad me uenias et ea quae pro sui prolixitate / breuiter scribi non possunt ore ad os audias.

38

Lanfranc to Pope Gregory VII   *summer 1080*

Nos. 38–9 are the reply to the legation of Hubert the subdeacon (cf. no. 3, lines 136–8), who presumably brought with him Gregory's letter to William the Conqueror dated 24 April 1080: G.VII, *Reg.* vii. 23. There Gregory makes several oblique references to William's feudal dependence, but clearly the legate said more. William was directed to do fealty to the pope and to be more punctilious in paying Peter's Pence; Lanfranc was directed to come to Rome without further delay. Gregory's initiative and the response from England have been much discussed. See Z. N. Brooke, 'Pope Gregory VII's demand for fealty from William the Conqueror', *E.H.R.* xxvi (1911), 225–38; H. E. J. Cowdrey, 'Pope Gregory VII and the Anglo-Norman Church and Kingdom', *Studi Gregoriani* ix (1972), 79–114; C. Morton, 'Pope Alexander II and the Norman Conquest', *Latomus*, xxxiv (1975), 371–5.

Reuerendo sanctae uniuersalis aecclesiae summo pastori Gregorio peccator et indignus antistes L., seruitium cum debita subiectione.

Litteras excellentiae uestrae per Hubertum sacri palatii uestri subdiaconum porrectas qua decuit humilitate suscepi. In quarum
5 fere omni contextu paterna me dulcedine reprehendere studuistis, quod in episcopali honore positus sanctam Romanam aecclesiam uosque ob eius reuerentiam minus diligam quam ante ipsius

37 NV

38 NV

37

Lanfranc to Remigius, bishop of Lincoln   *?1075*

Lanfranc, by the grace of God archbishop, sends greetings to his beloved brother and friend Remigius.

Although there are many who slander you freely and very few who speak out honestly against their disparaging words, be assured that our lord the king pays no attention to any disparagement of you, but rather by his royal authority defends you from all hostile criticism. That being so, if you are near and have permission to come, it is to your advantage to visit me and discuss personally matters which are too complicated to be summarized in a letter.

38

Lanfranc to Pope Gregory VII   *summer 1080*

To the reverend Gregory, the supreme pastor of the holy and universal Church, Lanfranc, a sinner and unworthy bishop, offers his service and due obedience.

I have received with fitting humility your Excellency's letter, brought by Hubert, a subdeacon of your holy court. Throughout almost its entire length you were concerned to rebuke me— gently, as a father—for showing less devotion to the holy Roman Church, and to yourself for the Church's sake, now that I am

honoris susceptionem diligere quondam solebam, presertim cum
apostolicae sedis auctoritate ad ipsius apicem honoris me peruenisse
10 non dubitem, nec quenquam dubitare existimem.[1] Et quidem
uenerande pater uerbis tuis calumniam ingerere nec uolo nec
debeo. Ego tamen teste conscientia mea in memetipso intelligere
non possum quod uel corporalis absentia uel locorum tanta intercapedo aut ipsa qualiscunque honorum sullimitas in hac parte
15 uindicare sibi quicquam preualeat, quin mens mea preceptis
uestris in omnibus et per omnia secundum canonum precepta
subiaceat. Et si praestante Deo praesens presenti loqui quandoque
ualerem, me amando creuisse uos uero (quod pace uestra dictum
sit) a pristino amore nonnulla ex parte defecisse non tam uerbis
20 quam rebus ipsis ostenderem.[2]

Verba legationis uestrae cum prefato legato uestro prout melius
potui domino meo regi suggessi; suasi sed non persuasi. Cur
f. 28 autem uoluntati uestrae omnifariam non assenserit / ipsemet[a]
uobis tam uerbis quam litteris innotescit.[3]

39

King William I to Pope Gregory VII   summer *1080*

For the date and circumstances see no. 38. Fealty was an innovation, but there
was solid precedent for Peter's Pence: J.L. 4757; cf. W. E. Lunt, *Financial
Relations of the Papacy with England to 1327* (Cambridge, Mass., 1939), pp. 3–34.
There William wisely took his stand, although it could be argued that he had
received his authority over England from Alexander II or even that Peter's
Pence itself was tribute-money: G.VII, *Reg.* vii. 23; William of Poitiers, *Gesta
Guillelmi Ducis* ii. 31, ed. R. Foreville, (Paris, 1952), p. 224; C. Erdmann,
Die Entstehung des Kreuzzugsgedankens (Stuttgart, 1935), pp. 172–3, with further
references.

Excellentissimo sanctae aecclesiae pastori GR. gratia Dei Anglorum rex et dux Normannorum W. salutem cum amicicia.

Hubertus legatus tuus[1] religiose pater ad me ueniens ex tua parte
me admonuit quatinus tibi et successoribus tuis fidelitatem
5 facerem, et de pecunia quam antecessores mei ad Romanam
aecclesiam mittere solebant melius cogitarem. Vnum admisi;
alterum non admisi. Fidelitatem facere nolui nec uolo, quia nec
ego promisi nec antecessores meos antecessoribus tuis id fecisse

---

ᵃ ipsimet V

39 NV

established in a bishopric than I showed formerly before I received that honour, the more so that I do not doubt that it was with the support of the apostolic see that I reached this pinnacle of honour; I think no one doubts that.[1] Honoured father, I neither desire to cast doubt on what you have said, nor have I the right to do so. But as my conscience is witness I cannot myself understand that either personal absence or the great distance separating us or even honours, however lofty, can have the least bearing on this question: my mind submits to your commands in all respects and in all matters according to canon law. If with God's help I were ever able to speak with you in person, I should demonstrate by events themselves as much as by words that my devotion has increased whereas you (if it may be said with respect) have declined somewhat from your original cordiality.[2]

I presented the text of your message and your above-mentioned legate with what skill I could to my lord the king; I commended it to him, but without success. Why he has not complied with your wishes in all respects the legate himself is explaining to you both orally and in a letter.[3]

39

King William I to Pope Gregory VII   *summer 1080*

To Gregory, the most exalted pastor of holy Church, William by the grace of God king of the English and duke of the Normans, sends greetings and the assurance of friendship.

Your legate Hubert,[1] who came to me, holy father, has on your behalf directed me to do fealty to you and your successors and to reconsider the money payment which my predecessors used to send to the Roman Church. The one proposition I have accepted; the other I have not. I have never desired to do fealty, nor do I desire it now; for I neither promised on my own behalf nor can I discover that my predecessors ever performed it to yours. As

---

38 [1] Cf. no. 1, lines 12–17; 31–32.
    [2] Lanfranc had visited Rome in 1071 (no. 3, n. 7); he never returned during Gregory VII's pontificate: see further G.VII, *Reg.* ix. 20.
    [3] i.e. no. 39.

39 [1] See no. 38.

comperio. Pecunia tribus ferme annis in Galliis me agente[2] neglegenter collecta est. Nunc uero diuina misericordia me in regnum meum reuerso quod collectum est per prefatum legatum mittitur, et quod reliquum est per legatos Lanfranci archiepiscopi fidelis nostri cum opportunum fuerit transmittetur.

Orate pro nobis et pro statu regni nostri, quia antecessores uestros dileximus et uos prae omnibus sincere diligere et oboedienter audire desideramus.

40

Lanfranc to Hugh, bishop-elect of London

spring 1076: before 5 Mar.

Hugh's predecessor, William, took part in the council of London (24 Dec. 1074–28 Aug. 1075; see no. 11, line 9); Hugh is already concerned with diocesan business: it is thus virtually certain that Lanfranc is writing in the spring of 1076 rather than in Jan.–Feb. 1075.

Lanfrancus diuina misericordia archiepiscopus dilecto fratri Londoniensi aecclesiae electo antistiti Hu. salutem.

In primis gratias ago quod meam sicut tuam desiderare salutem te asseris, quodque perfectum honeste uiuendi per meam qualemcunque doctrinam habiturum te esse confidis. Haec ex dilectione non modica procedere solent.

Ad interrogata tua breuia responsa remitto. De homine quem captum, et apud captores mortuum fuisse inuentum, scripsisti
f.28ᵛ absolute tibi ad presens respondere / non possum, quoadusque precedentes mortis eius causas diligentius audiam, et sic miserante Deo quid agi oporteat canonica auctoritate definiam. Interim iniunge eis aliquam poenitentiam usque dum conueniamus, et alterno colloquio quid postea facere debeant decernamus. De terris tuis[1] domino meo regi nichil adhuc locutus fui, quia de meis etiam rebus qualem uolui loquendi opportunitatem non habui. Goisfridus clericus qui apostasiae calumniam habet de episcopatu tuo recedat, aut formatas litteras ex parte sui episcopi sicut canones iubent ostendat.[2] Cicestrum sicut fraternitati tuae insinuaui uenies; et ibi sabbato ante *Laetare Ierusalem* cooperante Spiritu Sancto praesbiterii gradum recipies.[3]

40 NV

to the money, for almost three years it has been collected without due care, while I was engaged in France.[2] But now that by God's mercy I have returned to my kingdom, the sum already collected is being sent to you by the above-named legate and the balance will be conveyed, when the opportunity arises, by the legates of our faithful servant archbishop Lanfranc.

Pray for us and for the welfare of our kingdom, for we held your predecessors in great regard and it is our desire to show to you above all men unfeigned respect and obedient attention.

40

Lanfranc to Hugh, bishop-elect of London
spring 1076: before 5 Mar.

Lanfranc, by the mercy of God archbishop, greets his beloved brother Hugh, bishop-elect to the church of London.

First of all, thank you for declaring that you desire my welfare no less than your own, and for your confidence that you will find in whatever instruction I give you the pattern for an upright life. Such assurances spring from real affection.

Here are my brief answers to the matters on which you were asking advice. You wrote that a man who had been taken prisoner had been found dead in the hands of his captors. There I can give you no definitive reply at the moment, until I hear in more detail what factors caused his death; then by God's mercy I can give a canonical ruling on what is to be done. In the meantime impose some penance on them until we meet and reach a decision together on what they should do subsequently. I have not yet said anything to my lord the king about your lands[1] because I have not even had the opportunity I desired to speak of my own affairs. The clerk Geoffrey, who is accused of apostasy, must either leave your diocese or present a formal statement from his own bishop as canon law directs.[2] Come to Chichester, my brother, as I instructed you to do, and there on the Saturday before *Laetare* Sunday with the help of the Holy Spirit you will be ordained priest.[3]

---

[2] William spent much of 1076–9 campaigning in France: D. C. Douglas, *William the Conqueror* (London, 1964), pp. 401–7, with references.

---

40 [1] i.e. to arrange for Hugh to do homage for the temporalities of his see.

[2] Cf. the 'litterae commendaticiae' recently specified by the council of London (no. 11, *can*. iv).

[3] 5 Mar. 1076. Note that Hugh is so far only a deacon; we cannot assume that he was consecrated bishop on the same day. For his episcopal profession (whenever that was made) see Richter, no. 37.

41

Lanfranc to John, archbishop of Rouen
1 Apr. 1076–July 1077

Written after the council of Winchester, 1 Apr. 1076 (note 4 below) and before
John's incapacitating stroke (Orderic, *Hist. Eccles.* iii. 16–19) this letter is the
reply to a lost letter from Archbishop John (note 1). Both archbishops are concerned with clerical celibacy: but whereas John has attempted to impose it
across the board, on all clergy above the rank of subdeacon, Lanfranc's legislation affects secular canons only—and even they may keep their wives if they
renounce their prebends. See further note 2 below.

Venerabili sanctae Rotomagensis aecclesie archiepiscopo Io.
indignus antistes L. seruitium cum orationibus.

Litteras quas 'omnibus christianae religionis amatoribus'[1] amanda
paternitas uestra transmisit, quo tempore porrectae sunt, con-
5 gruum dare responsum michi non licuit. Nam et impeditum me
inuenerunt nec, si liceret, posset ea tempestate nuntius inueniri
qui ferret. Nunc uero[a] data opportunitate differre ultra non
debeo. Retulistis uobis a multis fuisse relatum quod ego quedam
uestra facta carpo, et maxime quod instituta sanctorum patrum de
10 seruanda clericorum castitate male uos intellexisse redarguo,
adiuncto quod aecclesiastice disciplinae moderamina non bene
f. 29 uos / tenere affirmo.[2] Meminisse debet beatitudo uestra presentes
uerbis absentes litteris nos sepe alterutrum monuisse esse multos
detestabili inuidia plenos, qui semper uelint nos inuicem dissidere,
15 quatinus hac occasione suas nequitias ualeant liberius exercere.
Quorum officii refert noua semper et inaudita fingere, leuiter et
incuriose prolata deterius exponere, bene et consulte dicta quantum in ipsis est in contrariam partem conuertere. Ego tamen teste
conscientia nullius eorum conscius sum, nec aliquid de laudabili
20 uita uestra uel dixisse uel dicenti assensum prebuisse me memini
quod in presentia uestra, si res ita exposceret, non posset cum
pacis uestrae securitate proferri.[3] Immo uestro aliorumque
uenerabilium patrum exemplo prouocatus per totam Anglicam
terram pastorali auctoritate prohibui, ne cuiuslibet ordinis quis-
25 quam canonicus uxorem accipiat nec sortito antea, si praesbiter
aut diaconus est, nisi prebenda carere uelit habere ulterius liceat.[4]

41 NV
[a] michi V

---

41 [1] The address of John's letter (now lost) to which Lanfranc is replying.
[2] Archbishop John's attempt to impose celibacy on all clergy above the rank

41

Lanfranc to John, archbishop of Rouen
1 Apr. 1076–July 1077

To the venerable John, archbishop of the holy church of Rouen, Lanfranc, an unworthy bishop, offers his service and prayers.

When the letter arrived, dear father, that you sent 'to all who hold dear the Christian life',[1] I was not at liberty to send an appropriate reply. For I had much to do when it arrived; and even had I been able to write, no messenger was then available to carry my letter. But now that the opportunity presents itself, I must delay no longer. You gave us to understand that you had received many reports of my criticizing certain aspects of your conduct: in particular maintaining that you have misunderstood the legislation of the holy Fathers that relates to clerical celibacy and asserting further that you have insufficient control of discipline in your church.[2] Holy father, you must not forget that we have often warned each other both personally and by letter that there are many men full of hateful envy who are always wanting to set us at variance, so that they may have freer scope for their own wickedness. It is characteristic of them always to be inventing extraordinary news, to interpret idle and casual remarks in a more damaging sense and so far as they can to pervert well-considered statements to the opposite meaning. But my conscience is witness that I have listened to none of these men; I do not recall either saying anything myself about your exemplary life nor agreeing with what anyone else said that could not, if the situation so required, be said in your presence without giving you offence.[3] On the contrary I have been spurred on by your example and that of other reverend fathers to prohibit by my pastoral authority any canon throughout the whole land of England, whatever his rule, from taking a wife; nor will a canon who is already installed, if he is a priest or a deacon, be permitted to have a wife from now on, if he wishes to keep his prebend.[4]

of subdeacon led to a riot in the council of Rouen, 1072: Orderic, *Hist. Eccles.* ii. 200–1. The legislation was repeated in the council of Lillebonne 1080, *can.* 3 (ibid. iii. 26–7). See further note 4.

[3] Cf. nos. 14, lines 65–70; 15, lines 6–8, 20–26.

[4] Winchester 1076, can. 2 (*Councils and Synods*, ad loc.): 'It is decreed that no canon shall have a wife. As to the priests who live in villages and townships, if they have wives they are not required to send them away; if they have none, they are now forbidden to marry. In future bishops shall take care not to ordain priests or deacons unless they have first made a declaration that they are unmarried.'

De Roberto quem pultrellum uocastis, quemque sine uestra
licentia mare transisse perhibuistis, certissime id sciatis quia
litteras uestro sigillo quod michi bene notum est signatas detulit,
30 in quibus (si uere fuerunt) sumopere me rogastis quatinus eum
cum honore susciperem, apud abbatem Balduinum in quantum
possem pro infirmitate sui corporis adiuuarem, de meis etiam
rebus sicut michi opportunum esset opem impenderem. Quae
34 omnia executus sum. Nam pro amore uestro honeste eum sus-
f. 29ᵛ cepi, / tribus septimanis mecum habui, abbati Baldeuuino precibus et promissionibus commendaui, reuertenti unde redire posset
denarios officiosa caritate impendi. Et miror ualde, si falsas litteras
porrexit, quonam modo tanti uiri sigillum ad persuadendam
falsitatem suam habere potuerit.⁵

40 De fide ab archidiaconis petita et data interrogantibus episcopis
Baiocensi et Constantiniensi hoc tantum respondi, me nec
legisse tale aliquid nec uidisse; uos tamen prudentem uirum esse
et strenue scire quid agatis quid omittatis, quid agendum quid
omittendum censeatis.⁶

45 De negotiis uestris cum domino nostro rege prout decuit et
oportuit nouiter sum locutus, et puto per misericordiam Dei quia
mordentibus uitam uestram aures excellentiae suae non est ultra
facile praebiturus.

Omnipotens Dominus uitam uestram ad honorem suae sanctae
50 ecclesiae incontaminatam custodiat.

42

Lanfranc to Herfast, bishop of Thetford

autumn 1070–?1081

The dating of nos. 42 and 47 probably depends on the royal diploma of 1081,
which concluded Herfast's attempt to exert jurisdiction over the abbey of Bury
St. Edmunds: see further no. 47. In no. 42 the bishop appears to have summoned to his own court clergy from within the liberty of Bury; in no. 47 he is
laying claim to Bury land. As William the Conqueror was overseas during much
of 1075 and 1076–9, the dating might reasonably be narrowed to 1075–81.

Lanfrancus archiepiscopus confratri et coepiscopo Herfasto salutem.

Meminisse debet caritas uestra quia rex dum nobiscum esset

42 NV

As to Robert, whom you called 'the colt' and who you said had crossed the sea without your permission, I assure you categorically that he brought a letter sealed with your seal, which I know well; in that letter (if it was genuine) you urged me to receive him honourably, to commend him as strongly as I could to Abbot Baldwin for the treatment of his physical infirmity and even to give him material help from my own resources as the occasion might arise. All this I have done. Out of affection for you I received him honourably; I kept him in my household for three weeks; I recommended him most earnestly to Abbot Baldwin; and when he returned I gave him a generous allowance for the journey home. I am greatly astonished if the letter he presented was a forgery—how could he have got hold of such a great man's seal to make his tale look true?[5]

As to the confession of faith that was required of the archdeacons and made by them, with the bishops of Bayeux and Coutances putting the questions, I had no comment except that I had never read of such a thing nor witnessed it: but you are a man of discretion and thoroughly understand what to do, what to leave undone, and what actions are to be approved and what condemned.[6]

I recently discussed your affairs as far as was right and fitting with our lord the king, and I think that by God's mercy he will not in the future lend his noble attention readily to the backbiters who seek to destroy you.

May the Lord almighty keep you in innocency of life to the honour of his holy Church.

42

Lanfranc to Herfast, bishop of Thetford
autumn 1070–?1081

Archbishop Lanfranc greets Herfast, his colleague and brother.

You may recall, my dear friend, that when the king was with us he

[5] The incident is otherwise unknown. For Abbot Baldwin's medical skill see no. 44, with references.

[6] As bishops had traditionally made a profession of faith and obedience to their metropolitan at their consecration (cf. no. 3, n. 5), so here the archdeacons of Bayeux (cf. no. 51) and Coutances are making a similar profession to their bishops on taking up office. As a man is not *ordained* archdeacon (as e.g. subdeacon, priest, bishop), the implied parallel is inappropriate. See further Introduction, p. 8.

precepit ut querimonia de clericis abbatis Balduini, quae inter
5 uos et ipsum abbatem uersabatur, sopita remaneret quoadusque
ipsemet causam ipsam audiret, uel a me si temporis opportunitas
se suggereret audiri preciperet. Sed quia priusquam id fieret mare
transiuit, uolo et rogo quatinus predictos clericos quos a uobis
excommunicatos didici absoluatis, et quietos ab omni inuectione
10 atque exactione ad presens dimittatis. Post paucos etenim dies
f. 30 ad partes uestras / uenturi sumus,[1] et utriusque partis assertiones
diligenti cura audiemus, et tam prolixae querimoniae in quantum
salua fidelitate regis fieri poterit finem legittimum imponemus.

43

Lanfranc to Herfast, bishop of Thetford
c. 1076–28 Aug. 1086

The dating depends on the council of Winchester (1 Apr. 1076), which provided
for the celibacy of the diaconate (cf. no. 41, note 4), and the consecration of
Herfast's successor (28 Aug. 1086). Herfast had blundered doubly, in ordaining
the man directly to the diaconate (omitting the minor orders) and in failing to
exact an oath of celibacy from a prospective deacon. See further Introduction,
p. 8.

Lanfrancus gratia Dei non suis meritis archiepiscopus confratri et
coepiscopo Her. salutem.

Clericus iste nouiter ad me uenit, causam suae infelicitatis michi
dixit, dictam testimonio litterarum uestrarum ueram esse asseruit.
5 Testatus est se inordinate ordinatum, uidelicet cum nullius esset
ordinis a fraternitate uestra factum esse diaconum. Interrogatus a
me si uxorem haberet, uxorem se habere nec eam se uelle dimittere
respondit. Propterea tali pacto consulendum ei diuina fultus
auctoritate decerno. Diaconatum ei auferte; ad ceteros minores
10 ordines congruis eum temporibus promouete. Diaconatus uero
ordinem nunquam recipiat nisi caste uiuat, nisi se de reliquo
caste uicturum canonica attestatione promittat. Si uero celibem
uitam egerit, et acturum se omni tempore spondere uoluerit,
non quidem eum ad ordinem diaconatus iterum ordinabitis, sed
15 ipsum officium per textum sancti euangelii[1] uel in sinodo uel
in multorum clericorum conuentu reddetis.

43 NVLz

gave instructions that the lawsuit over Abbot Baldwin's clerks, in which you and the abbot were then engaged, should remain in suspense until he could hear the case himself or until he might instruct me to hear it, if a convenient opportunity were to arise. But before either step could be taken he went overseas; I therefore request and require that you lift the excommunication that I hear you have laid on the clergy concerned, and that you send them away at once unconditionally, without their having to pay any fine. In a few days I shall be coming to your part of the country myself;[1] I shall give a most careful hearing to the claims of both sides and bring this long-drawn-out dispute to as definitive a conclusion as is possible, saving our loyalty to the king.

43

Lanfranc to Herfast, bishop of Thetford
c. 1076–28 Aug. 1086

Lanfranc, archbishop not by his own merits but by the grace of God, sends greetings to Herfast, his brother and fellow bishop.

A clerk of yours has just come to me, telling of his unhappy circumstances and presenting your letter to confirm his story. He declared that he has been irregularly ordained, in that when he was not in orders at all you, my brother, made him a deacon. When I asked him if he had a wife, he answered that he did have one and was not willing to send her away. That being so it is my decision, for which I have full canonical support, that he be directed as follows. Take the diaconate from him; promote him to the other minor orders on appropriate occasions: but never let him recover his deacon's orders unless he is living chastely and makes a legal undertaking to continue to do so. Should he live a celibate life and be willing to promise to remain celibate always, you will not of course re-ordain him to the diaconate but restore that function by giving him a gospel-book,[1] either in a synod or in a large assembly of clergy.

---

42 [1] Lanfranc had some experience as a king's justice in East Anglia: Gibson, pp. 157–9, with references.

---

43 [1] The man had received a gospel-book (as appropriate to his liturgical function) when he was originally ordained deacon: *PRG* i. 27.

44

Lanfranc to Bishop O.   *Jan. 1071–1086*

The dating depends on Lanfranc's acquisition of Freckenham (line 3) and its eventual transfer to Rochester: D.B. ii. 381; *Textus Roffensis*, ff. 170ᵛ–6ᵛ, 216, ed. P. Sawyer (Copenhagen, 1962: *Early English MSS Facs.* XI); cf. William the Conqueror's obit (Gibson, p. 214, with references). If Bishop O. is identified with Odo of Bayeux, acting as king's justice in East Anglia, the limit is 1082, the year of his imprisonment. But Osbern, bishop of Exeter (1072–1103), and Osmund, bishop of Salisbury (1078–99), cannot be ruled out.

Lanfrancus indignus antistes O. digno antistiti salutem cum orationibus.

Ad Frachenam¹ uillam nostram quae coenobio sancti Edmundi proxima est ueni, in qua rege precipiente et corporis mei in-
5 firmitate urgente aliquam accipere medicinam disposui. Pro qua
f. 30ᵛ re / abbatem Balduinum² detineo, cui rex curandae huius egritu-dinis curam suo ore iniunxit, qui contra Ricardum³ ad hunc conuentum de quibusdam querelis placitum accepit. Sed abbate apud uos et apud eum de hoc itinere excusato, causam ipsam
10 dilatam esse uolo et rogo quoadusque alio tempore in unum conueniamus, et pari studio pariter ipsum negotium sine aliquo partium fauore definiamus.

Omnipotens Dominus uos benedicat, et in omnibus uestris negotiis promptus uobis auxiliator assistat.

45

Lanfranc to Walcher, bishop of Durham
18 Nov. 1071–14 May 1080

Lanfranc is writing at least seven days after Martinmas (11 Nov.) in an un-specified year of Walcher's episcopate (Mar. 1071–14 May 1080). That Walcher submitted several problems on which he required advice by a given feastday suggests that he planned to hold a diocesan synod. The priest in question may have belonged to the quasi-monastic community at Durham cathedral, which Walcher replaced with secular canons: Symeon of Durham, *Historia Dunel-mensis Ecclesiae* iii. 18 in *Symeonis Monachi Opera*, ed. T. Arnold (R.S., 1882), i. 106; cf. D. Knowles, *The Monastic Order in England*, 2nd edn. (Cambridge, 1963), pp. 166–8.

Lanfrancus indignus antistes uenerabili Dunelmensi episcopo Wal. salutem.

44 NV

___

45 NVLz

44

Lanfranc to Bishop O.   *Jan. 1071–1086*

Lanfranc, an unworthy bishop, sends prayerful greetings to O., a man worthy of the office.

I have come to our estate of Freckenham,[1] near St. Edmund's abbey, where on the king's orders and under pressure of ill health I have decided to undergo a regime. That is why I am detaining Abbot Baldwin,[2] to whom the king has personally commended my case, even though he has entered into a lawsuit with Richard[3] at this assembly over certain matters in dispute between them. But since the abbot has been excused this journey by both you and Richard himself, I urgently recommend that the case itself be deferred until we can all meet on another occasion and by our united efforts conclude the affair without partiality to anyone.

May the Lord almighty bless you and come quickly to your help to defend you in all your affairs.

45

Lanfranc to Walcher, bishop of Durham
18 Nov. 1071–14 May 1080

Lanfranc, an unworthy bishop, greets Walcher, the reverend bishop of Durham.

---

44 [1] Acquired by Lanfranc Jan. 1071: *Regesta* no. 47.
 [2] Baldwin, abbot of Bury St. Edmunds (1065–97/8), was renowned for his medical skill; he had been Edward the Confessor's doctor: *Annales S. Edmundi* s.a. 1065, ed. F. Liebermann, *Ungedruckte anglo-normannische Geschichtsquellen* (Strasburg, 1879), p. 129; *Miracula S. Edmundi*, 41–2, ibid., pp. 251–4.
 [3] Presumably Richard fitzGilbert of Clare, a local magnate who received two royal writs concerning the property of Bury: *Regesta* nos. 242, 258; cf. D. C. Douglas, *Feudal Documents from the Abbey of Bury St. Edmunds* (London, 1932), p. 56.

Et longe ab urbe[1] positum et multis huius seculi negotiis inuolutum
me uestrae litterae inuenerunt, ob quam causam petitionibus
5 uestris ex omni parte effectum prebere non licuit. Nec si licuisset,
commonitorium quod in festiuitate sancti Martini habere uoluistis
fieri potuisset: septima enim post praedicti sancti solennitatem
die uester ad me nuntius uenit.

   Porro[a] de illo presbitero de quo mandastis, quia in claustro
10 monachorum sine benedictione nutritus fuit, aliquid me uobis
mandasse recordari non possum. Canones tamen decretaque
sanctorum patrum eos qui uestem religionis aliquot diebus in
conspectu hominum deferunt ad seculum quocunque modo
postea redire non sinunt.[2] Qui si uobis obtemperare noluerit,
15 euangelica auctoritate utimini quae ait, 'Compelle intrare.'[3]

46

*Lanfranc to Reginald, abbot of S. Cyprien, Poitiers,
Sewinus the monk and canon Henry   4 Nov. 1073–1078*

Reginald was consecrated abbot of S. Cyprien 4 Nov. 1073 and Sewinus became
abbot of Chaise-Dieu in 1078; canon Henry has been identified with Henricus
de Ingla, Reginald's nephew. Within these dates the most likely occasion for
Lanfranc's letter is the synod of Poitiers (13–14 Jan. 1075), at which Berengar's
teaching was fiercely condemned. Reginald was a man of similar outlook and
experience to Lanfranc himself: he too had been 'magister . . . scholarum
famosus' (probably in Poitiers); he had become monk and claustral prior
of the new ascetic foundation of Chaise-Dieu; now he is back in public life
at the head of a great Poitevin monastery. He was one of the first readers
of the *Monologion* (*Anselmi Epp.* 83). See the twelfth-century S. Cyprien
cartulary ad loc. (ed. L. F. X. Rédet: *Archives historiques du Poitou* iii [Poitiers,
1874]) and a little-known epitaph: 'Hic requiescit uenerabilis pater nomine
Rainaldus, in pago Pictauensium ortus, magister prius scholarum famosus,
dein Case Dei monachus, ibique prior claustralis probatus, postremo in hoc
monasterio abbas ordinatus, quod rexit xxvi annis, vi mensibus, xviiii diebus,
migrans ad Christum x kalendas Junii, episcopo Pictauorum Petro, comite
Willelmo.' References in R. Somerville, 'The case against Berengar of Tours:
a new text', *Studi Gregoriani* ix (1972), 62–3 and P.-R. Gaussin, *L'Abbaye de la
Chaise-Dieu 1043–1518* (Paris, 1962), pp. 128–39. This letter is a rare and
instructive example of Lanfranc's theological method. First he establishes Hilary's
authority: he is recognized by the Fathers and in canon law. Then he quotes the
disputed opinion (lines 43–9) and sets it in its wider context (lines 50–76);
finally he isolates one sentence that sums up the difficulty (lines 48–9) and
construes that sentence (lines 82–9).

f. 31 Lanfrancus antistes dilectissimis fratribus Rainaldo Pictauorum

---

[a] Et longe—Porro *om.* Lz

46 NVA

I was far from the city and greatly preoccupied with worldly business when I received your letter,[1] so I could not fulfil your requests at all points. But even had I been able to, the advice which you wanted to have at Martinmas could not have been forthcoming: your messenger reached me seven days after that saint's festival.

As to the priest that you said had been brought up in a monastery without being professed as a monk, I cannot recall giving you any advice on the case. But the legislation and letters of the holy Fathers do not permit those who wear the monastic habit for several days in public to return subsequently to secular life on any pretext.[2] If the man will not obey you, use that Gospel precept which says, 'Compel them to come in.'[3]

46

Lanfranc to Reginald, abbot of S. Cyprien, Poitiers, Sewinus the monk and canon Henry

4 Nov. 1073–1078

Archbishop Lanfranc sends greetings to his dearest brothers

---

45 [1] Cf. no. 49, lines 4–6.
[2] VI Toledo, *can.* 6 (Hinschius, p. 378); cf. no. 53 below.
[3] Luke 14: 23.

urbis abbati et Seuuino monacho et Heinrico canonico
salutem.

Lectis litteris a uestra michi per hunc hominem fraternitate
5 transmissis, uoluntatem uestram intellexi si facultas detur[a]
ad me ueniendi. Id[b] commode fieri posse non arbitror.[c] Nam
et iter prolixum est, pericula multa terra marique, et ego tot
tantisque huius mundi negotiis obuolutus sum ut talibus studiis
dare michi operam hac tempestate non liceat. Si diuina pietas
10 expeditum me esse quandoque uoluerit, et doceri pariter et
docere promptus michi semper animus erit.

Porro quod scismaticus ille, Beringerium dico,[d] sicut uestra
epistola testata est, constanter asserit quia beatus Hilarius uestrae
urbis uestraeque gentis quondam episcopus in tractatu fidei
15 peruersa senserit, et in libro *De diuina Trinitate*[1] improbabiles
sententias de Domino Iesu Christo protulerit, mirari non debet
beatitudo uestra si is, qui de ipso capite tam multa et tam nefanda
credere et docere uerissimis relationibus infamatur, de ipsius
capitis membro tam perniciosa dicere traditus in reprobum
20 sensum[2] diuino iudicio permittatur. Reuera quisquis Ylario
alicuius hereseos notam imponit multos orthodoxos patres, qui
magnis eum laudibus extulerunt, eiusdem erroris macula inuoluit.
Gelasius papa in decretis suis omnes libros eius inter catholicas
f. 31ᵛ scripturas enumerat.[3] Eius auctoritas in sacris canonibus / decen-
25 tissime memoratur, recipitur et laudatur.[4] Sanctus Augustinus
in libro *De Trinitate* excellenti laude eum extollit et quaedam
ab eo de Patre et Filio et Spiritu Sancto obscure dicta enucleatius
exponit.[5] Beatus Ieronimus quantis eum[e] omnesque libros eius in
quibusdam scriptis suis preconiis effert epistolari breuitate com-
30 prehendi non potest,[6] uocans eum Romanorum luciferum,
aecclesiarum lucernam, lapidem preciosum ad quem mortalia
uix ascendunt, pulchro sermone aureoque ore[f] uniuersa loquentem.[7]

ᵃ daretur A   ᵇ quod A   ᶜ credo A   ᵈ Beringerium dico]
Beringerius A   ᵉ illum A   ᶠ *om.* VA

46 [1] Hilary, *De Trinitate*: *PL* x. 25–472 (see n. 9 below).
  [2] Cf. Rom. 1: 28.
  [3] Gelasius, *De recipiendis et non recipiendis libris*: Hinschius, p. 636.
  [4] Perhaps a confusion with Pope Hilary (461–8): Hinschius, pp. 630–2.
Hilary of Poitiers contributed one passage (*De Trinitate* viii. 13–14, 16: *PL*
x. 246A–7B, 249A) to the Paschasian catena of eucharistic proof-texts that passed
into canon law via Ivo of Chartres, *Decretum* ii. 4 (*PL* clxi. 138D–9C), but so far
as I am aware he is not quoted in Pseudo-Isidore.

Abbot Reginald of the city of Poitiers, Sewin the monk and canon Henry.

When I read the letter, my brothers, that you sent to me by this messenger, I understood it to be your wish to visit me, if that were possible. I do not consider that it would be opportune. The journey is long, there are many dangers by land and sea; and I myself am so involved with many of this world's great affairs that I cannot turn my attention at this time to such scholarly inquiries. If God in his goodness ever grants me release, I shall always be ready both to teach and to be taught.

As to that schismatic Berengar, who (as your letter relates) persists in maintaining that blessed Hilary, once bishop of your city and people, held erroneous views in discussing the faith and in his book *On the Divine Trinity*[1] put forward unsound propositions concerning the Lord Jesus Christ: your holiness should not be surprised if the man who, according to the most accurate reports, is a byword for believing and teaching so many blasphemies about the Head lapses into error,[2] and is permitted in God's wisdom to make such damaging statements about a member of that Head. The truth is that anyone who accuses Hilary of heresy of any kind tars with the same brush the many orthodox Fathers who have quoted him with great approval. Pope Gelasius in his decretal letters lists all his books as catholic texts.[3] In canon law his teaching is most respectfully recorded, accepted and commended.[4] St Augustine, in his book *On the Trinity*, exalts him with unqualified praise and explains more clearly some of his statements about the Father, the Son and the Holy Ghost which are hard to understand.[5] The praise that blessed Jerome accords to him and to all his books in some of his own writings cannot be encompassed in the brief space of a letter.[6] He calls him the morning star of the Romans, the lamp of the churches, a precious stone to which what is mortal can scarcely attain, his golden tongue uttering all things in elegant language.[7] Whenever other teachers of holy

---

[5] Augustine, *De Trinitate* vi. 10, ed. W. J. Mountain (C.C.S.L. 1, 1968), pp. 241–3.

[6] Jerome, *De uiris illustribus*, cap. 100 (*PL* xxiii. 699B–701A); cf. J. N. D. Kelly, *Jerome: his life, writings and controversies* (London, 1975), pp. 28, 95.

[7] See Hincmar of Rheims: 'Sed et de eo, ut notum est, a notissimo dicitur, "Hilarius episcopus Romanorum lucifer, ecclesiarum lucerna et pretiosa lampas, pulchro aureoque ore loquitur uniuersa" ' (*De Predestinatione*, c. 3; *PL* cxxv. 87A). Hincmar is quoting some authority—'a notissimo dicitur'—but not, it would appear, Jerome. I am much indebted to Canon Kelly for his assistance on this point.

Ceteri sacrae religionis doctores quicunque de eo aliquid locuti
sunt ab horum sententia in hac parte minime dissenserunt.[g]
35 Tutius igitur est lectori in difficillimis sanctorum patrum senten-
tiis, quas ingenii sui[h] imbecillitas capere non potest, interrogato[i]
quod nescit dicere se nescire quam pertinaci arrogantia et arro-
ganti[j] pertinacia,[k] non sine sua et aliorum perniciae fidei con-
traria definire; presertim si talis persona sit quae uel scientia
40 litterarum uel probitate morum uel potius utraque parte auctoritatis pondus prae se gerere uideatur.[8] Verba prefati doctoris, quae
prefatus inuersor in eius calumniam conatur inuertere, haec[l]
in uestris litteris repperi: 'Dei Filius hominem uerum secundum
similitudinem nostri hominis, non deficiens a se Deo, sumpsit.
45 In quo, quamuis aut ictus incideret aut uulnus discinderet,
afferrent quidem haec impetum passionis non tamen dolorem
passionis inferrent: ut telum aliquod[m] aut aquam perforans aut
f. 32 ignem / conpungens aut aera uulnerans.'[n] Et paulo post: 'Virtus
corporis sine sensu poenae uim poene in se deseuientis excepit.'[9]
50 Haec sine preiudicio melioris expositionis, consona ut putamus
sanctis patribus[o] astipulatione, sic exponuntur[p] a nobis: Dominus
Iesus Christus in eadem persona uerus homo et uerus Deus
secundum humanitatem quidem esuriuit, sitiuit, fatigatus est,
fleuit, appropinquante hora mortis 'pauere et tedere coepit.'[10]
55 Vnde et orauit dicens: 'Pater si fieri potest transeat[q] a me calix
iste.'[11] Plagas uirgarum uulnerumque discissiones ut homo similis
nobis sensit et doluit, ceterasque humanae naturae infirmitates
assumendo hominem preter peccatum assumpsit; secundum
diuinitatem uero, qua Patri et Spiritui Sancto per omnia aequalis
60 est, nichil horum sustinuit. Hoc uelle approbare nichil attinet,
cum apud omnes fideles haec semper sit fueritque sententia; et
sacra pagina huiusmodi documentis paene sit ubique referta. Et
tamen propter unitatem personae, in quam conficiendam Deus
et homo conuenerant, sepe quae hominis sunt assignantur Deo
65 et quae solius Dei sunt dicitur habere homo. Vt illud Apostoli:
'Si enim cognouissent, nunquam Dominum gloriae crucifixissent.'[12]
Non enim reuera, quantum ad ipsum spectat, Dominus gloriae
est crucifixus; sed propter assumptum hominem quod hominis

[g] recedunt A	[h] om. A	[i] interrogata VA	[j] arrogante NV
[k] pernicie N	[l] om. A	[m] aliquot N	[n] uerberans A
[o] sanctis patribus om. A		[p] exprimuntur A	[q] transferatur A

[8] Berengar himself was known not only for his learning but (at least in his

doctrine have mentioned him, in this respect they have not departed in the slightest from the opinion of these men. In these
very difficult passages of the holy Fathers which the reader's
intellect does not have the strength to grasp it is safer for him, when
he is asked something he does not know, to say that he does not
know, rather than in stubbornness and pride to give explanations
that are contrary to the faith, endangering himself and others.
This is particularly so if he is a man whose learning or whose
virtuous life, or even both, seem to give his authority additional
weight.[8] The words of that teacher, which that misinterpreter is
trying to turn against him, appear in your letter like this: 'The
Son of God took upon himself a real man, looking like us, while
not being any the less God. In this state, if a blow struck him or a
wound tore his flesh, he was aware of the impact of the suffering,
but he did not experience the pain—in the same way that a
weapon pierces water or pricks fire or wounds air.' And a little
further on: 'His body had the power to experience the force of the
torment that raged within him, without feeling the torment.'[9]
Until a better exposition of these passages is forthcoming, our
explanation, which we believe to be entirely compatible with
patristic teaching, is as follows. The Lord Jesus Christ, being in
the same person truly man and truly God, did as a man experience
hunger and thirst; he was tired, he wept and as the hour of his
death came near 'he began to be terrified and exhausted.'[10] That is
why he prayed, 'Father, if it is possible, let this cup pass from me.'[11]
He felt the blows of the rods and the wounds which tore him, and
he experienced the pain, as a man like us; and in becoming man he
took on the other weaknesses of human nature, except for sin.
But as God, whereby he is in all respects equal to the Father and
the Holy Ghost, he underwent none of these experiences. There is
no need to prove this, for it is and always has been the position
of all the faithful; holy writ too is full of such texts virtually
throughout. But because the person, to make whom God and man
had united, is one, the qualities of the man are often attributed to
God and the man is said to have qualities that belong to God
alone. For instance the Apostle says, 'Had they recognized him,
they would never have crucified the Lord of glory.'[12] In fact the
Lord of glory was not crucified qua Lord of glory; but because

later years) for his asceticism; he died as a hermit on the island of S. Côme near
Tours: J. Mabillon, *Vetera Analecta* (Paris, 1723), p. 515.

  [9] Hilary, *De Trinitate* x. 25: *PL* x. 361A–2A (not quoted by Augustine).
  [10] Mark 14: 33.
  [11] Matt. 26: 39. For 'transferatur' (A) cf. Mark 14: 36 and Luke 22: 42.
  [12] 1 Cor. 2: 8.

fuit dicitur pertulisse Deus. Et ipse Dominus in euangelio:
70 'Nemo ascendit in caelum nisi qui descendit de caelo, Filius
f. 32ᵛ hominis qui est in caelo.'¹³ Et rursus / id quod Dei erat homini
est assignatum: neque enim homo in terra degens in caelo tunc
esse poterat. Sed quia Vnigenitus Patris ita in mundum uenit ut
tamen a paterno sinu nunquam discederet, quod solius diuinitatis
75 erat loquens in terra assumpto homini propter unitatem personae
tribuebat. Hoc locutionis modo superius dictum est quia homini
assumpto a Filio Dei ictus et uulnera impetum passionis afferrent,
non tamen dolorem passionis inferrent. Et hoc suppositis simili-
tudinibus declaratur: ut si telum aquam perforet et cetera quae
80 sequuntur.¹⁴ Ac si diceret: 'Homo assumptus impetum passionis et
uim doloris sensit; Deus assumens non sensit.' Et hoc paulo post
declarat dicens:¹⁵ *Virtus corporis*, id est diuinitas assumens ipsum
corpus, *sine sensu poenae*, quantum ad ipsam pertinet, *uim poene
in se*, id est in carne assumpta, *deseuientis excepit.* Quod si *uirtus*
85 *corporis* magis 'robur ipsius corporis' hoc in loco intelligenda est,
eadem sententia in ceteris manet, ut sit sensus: *Virtus corporis
sine sensu poenae*, quantum ad assumentem diuinitatem, *uim
poenae in se deseuientis excepit*, quantum ad assumptam humanitatem. Et hoc locutionis genere reuera et salua christianae religionis
90 fide dici potest, quia Christus siue corpus Christi siue caro
Christi in cruce patiebatur et non patiebatur, dolebat et non
dolebat, moriebatur et non moriebatur, et in hunc modum multa
f. 33 numeroque carentia. Alioquin / si praefatus doctor contra usitatis-
simam aecclesiae fidem, contra euangelicam auctoritatem, contra
95 omnium sanctorum patrum definitionem carnem Christi insensi-
bilem et doloris expertem intelligi uoluisset, assumptum a Filio
Dei hominem 'similem nobis'¹⁶ in praefata sententia minime retu-
lisset. Quae enim similitudo sensibili et insensibili, dolentis et
doloris experti? Retulit autem. Non igitur intelligi uoluit. Obsecro
100 uigilate omnibus modis, quia scismatici et fautores eorum circa
uos et intra uos sunt. Opponite eis scutum timoris Dei,ʳ im-
petentes eos iaculis diuinorum eloquiorum.¹⁷

ʳ Domini V

---

¹³ John 3: 13.
¹⁴ See lines 45–8 above.
¹⁵ See lines 48–9 above.
¹⁶ i.e. 'secundum similitudinem nostri hominis' (lines 43–4).

he had become man God is said to have suffered what he experienced as man. The Lord himself says in the Gospel, 'No one has ascended into heaven but him who came down from heaven, the Son of Man who is in heaven.'[13] There again what was a quality of God is attributed to the man: a man living on earth could not at the same time be in heaven. But because the only-begotten of the Father came into the world in such a manner that he never left the Father's bosom, when he was speaking on earth he used to ascribe to his manhood what belonged only to his divine nature, because the two were united in one person. This is the sense in which it was said above that the blows and wounds transmitted the impact of suffering to the man that the Son of God had become, but did not inflict the pain. It is expressed in the metaphors that are subjoined: like a weapon piercing water and the other instances that follow.[14] It is as though he were to say, 'The man that God became felt the impact of suffering and the intense pain: God who became man did not.' He expresses this a little further on, when he says:[15] *The power of his body*, that is the divine nature taking on that body, *without feeling the torment*, so far as refers to that divine nature, *experienced the force of the torment* that *raged within him*, that is within the flesh taken on by God. If in this passage the phrase, *the power of his body*, is to be understood rather as the strength of the body itself, the text is in other respects unchanged; it means: *The power of his body, without feeling the torment* qua God, *experienced* qua man *the force of the torment that raged within him*. In this sense it can truly be said, without endangering Christian belief, that Christ—or the body of Christ or the flesh of Christ—suffered on the cross and yet did not suffer; he experienced pain and yet he did not; he died and yet did not die, and so on infinitely in this way. If on the contrary that doctor had wished it to be understood—contrary to the customary and established faith of the Church, contrary to the authority of the Gospels and contrary to the consensus of all the holy Fathers—that Christ's flesh was impassive and not subject to pain, then in the passage quoted he would never have asserted that the Son of God became a man 'like us'.[16] How can the feeling be like the unfeeling or the man who feels pain be like him who does not? But he did assert it. Hence that was not the meaning he wished to convey. I entreat you to exercise all possible vigilance, for schismatics and their fellow-travellers are around you and among you. Hold them off with the shield of the fear of God and attack them with the darts of holy Scripture.[17]

[17] Cf. Eph. 6: 16–17.

Adminiculamini nobis, memores nostri in orationibus uestris. Omnipotens Dominus det uobis bene agere, et feliciter quo
105 tenditis peruenire.

47

Lanfranc to Herfast, bishop of Thetford

autumn 1070–?1081

The dispute between Bishop Herfast and Baldwin, abbot of Bury St. Edmunds, whatever forms it took (cf. no. 42) turned essentially on Herfast's attempt to assert jurisdiction over an exempt abbey. The papal privilege which Baldwin secured in 1071 (J.L. 4692; cf. no. 3, n. 7) specified that the abbot could appeal directly to the archbishop of Canterbury as 'primate'; and Gregory VII directed Lanfranc so to intervene (G.VII, *Reg.* i. 31: 20 Nov. 1073). But the definitive settlement was reached not in an ecclesiastical court but by the king's justices. See the disputed diploma of 1081: D. C. Douglas, *Feudal Documents relating to the Abbey of Bury St. Edmunds* (London, 1932), nos. 7–8 and pp. xxxii–xxxiv, lxiii, with references; F. E. Harmer, *Anglo-Saxon Writs* (Manchester, 1952), pp. 141–5. Lanfranc was unwilling to undermine diocesan jurisdiction, even though Baldwin was a personal friend and Herfast a disedifying bishop. What he does emphasize is the duty of Thetford to recognize the metropolitan authority of Canterbury, passing from there to the comprehensive dictum that 'per misericordiam Dei totam hanc quam uocant Britannicam insulam unam unius nostrae aecclesiae constet esse parrochiam' (lines 43–4): cf. Brooke, *English Church*, pp. 130–1.

Lanfrancus Dei misericordia non suis meritis sanctae Dorobernensis aecclesiae archiepiscopus HE. episcopo humiliter sapere et sobrie intelligere.

Berardus abbatis Balduini clericus et famulus nostras de
5 negotio suo litteras tibi detulit. Quas ut ipse postea michi testatus est procaciter irrisisti, satis uilia multumque indigna de me multis audientibus protulisti, pro me de eadem re nichil te facturum plurimis contestationibus affirmasti. De his alio tempore atque alio loco sermo erit.
10   Veruntamen ad presens precipio tibi ne in[a] rebus sancti Eadmundi aliquid appetas, nisi id ab antecessoribus tuis appetitum fuisse certis documentis ostendas; prefatum Berardum quiaetum et inconcussum dimittas, quoadusque res in nostram audientiam /
f. 33ᵛ ueniat finemque congruum canonica auctoritate nostrique iudicii
15 definitione recipiat.

47 NV
[a] V *adds* his

Give us the support of remembering us in your prayers. May the Lord almighty enable you to act rightly and auspiciously to reach your journey's end.

47

Lanfranc to Herfast, bishop of Thetford

autumn 1070–?1081

Lanfranc by the mercy of God, not his own merits, archbishop of the holy church of Canterbury, wishes that Bishop Herfast may be humble in wisdom and of sober understanding.

Abbot Baldwin's clerk and servant Berard brought you our letter about his affairs. As he himself affirmed to me later, you made a coarse joke about it; you uttered cheap and unworthy remarks about me in the hearing of many; and you declared with many an oath that you would give me no assistance in that matter. There will be another time and another place to speak of these things.

But my immediate instructions are these: that you lay no claim to the property of St. Edmund unless you can give indisputable proof that it was claimed by your predecessors and that you discharge the aforesaid Berard without any fine or threat of punishment, until the case comes into our own court and can be rightly concluded according to canon law and our own ruling as judge.

Postpositis aleis—ut maiora taceam—ludisque secularibus
quibus per totam diem uacare diceris, diuinas litteras lege,
decretisque Romanorum pontificum sacrisque canonibus precipue
studium impende. Ibi quippe inuenies quod nescis; perlectis
20 illis friuolum duces unde aecclesiasticam disciplinam effugere te
confidis. In decretis sic legitur:[1] 'Metropolitani sui unaquaeque
prouincia in omnibus rebus ordinationem semper expectet.'[2]
In Niceno concilio: 'Firmitas omnium quae geruntur per unamquamque prouinciam metropolitano tribuatur episcopo.'[3] In
25 Antiocheno: 'Per unamquamque prouintiam episcopos conuenit
nosse metropolitanum episcopum totius prouintiae sollicitudinem
gerere. Propter quod ad metropolem omnes undique qui negotia
uidentur habere concurrant. Vnde placuit eum et honore prae-
cellere.'[4] Et in Toletanis conciliis: 'Sic enim iustum est ut inde
30 unusquisque sumat regulas disciplinae, unde consecrationis honorem accepit; ut iuxta maiorum decreta sedes quae unicuique
sacerdotalis mater est dignitatis sit aecclesiasticae magistra
rationis.' Et paulo post: 'Quisquis autem horum decretorum
uiolator extiterit, sex mensibus communione priuatus apud metro-
35 politanum sub poenitentiae censura permaneat corrigendus.'[5]
Sunt alia plurima de excellentia et potestate primatum atque
archiepiscoporum tam in prefatis scripturis quam in aliis ortho-
f. 34 doxorum patrum autenticis libris; / quae si studiosus legeres lecta
memoriae commendares, nichil inconueniens contra tuam matrem
40 aecclesiam sentires, quod dixisse diceris non dixisses immo dictum
ab aliis salubri inuectione reprehenderes. Nec sobrius quisquam
putauerit hoc esse in aliena parrochia aliquid temere presumere,
cum per misericordiam Dei totam hanc quam uocant Britannicam
insulam unam unius nostrae aecclesiae constet esse parrochiam.

45 Hermannum monachum,[6] cuius uita multis reprehensionibus
obnoxia perhibetur, a consortio tuo tuaeque domus penitus
remoue. Volo enim ut in regulari monasterio regulariter uiuat
aut, si hoc renuit, de regno Anglorum abscedat.

---

47 [1] All five quotations which follow are 'starred' in Lanfranc's own canon
law manuscript: Brooke, *English Church*, pp. 68–9.

[2] Boniface I, *Ep. to Hilary, bishop of Narbonne*: Hinschius, p. 556.

[3] Cf. Council of Nicaea, *can.* 4: *PL* lxvii. 42B.

[4] Cf. Council of Antioch, *can.* 9: ibid. 62c.

[5] XI Toledo, *can.* 3 (Hinschius, p. 408).

[6] Possibly Hermann 'the archdeacon', author of the *Miracula Sancti Edmundi*.

Give up the dicing (to mention nothing worse) and the world's amusements, in which you are said to idle away the entire day: read Scripture and above all set yourself to master the decrees of the Roman pontiffs and the canons of the holy councils. There you will discover what you do not know; when you study these, you will consider the argument trivial on which you are relying to evade the discipline of the Church. In the papal decrees we read as follows:[1] 'Let every province always look to its own metropolitan for direction in all its affairs.'[2] In the council of Nicaea: 'Control of all that takes place in any given province shall be assigned to the metropolitan bishop.'[3] In the council of Antioch: 'In any given province the bishops must recognize that the metropolitan bishop has charge of the whole province. That being so, all those throughout the province who have business to transact shall meet in the metropolis. Hence it has been resolved that the metropolitan bishop also enjoys greatest honour.'[4] In the councils of Toledo too: 'Thus it is right that every man look to the bishop from whom he received the honour of consecration for direction in his manner of life. So according to the decrees of our fathers that see which is a man's mother in the priesthood shall instruct him in his conduct as a churchman.' And a little further on: 'Anyone infringing these decrees shall spend six months with his metropolitan bishop, excluded from communion, under a penitential regime.'[5] There are many other passages relating to the status and power of primates and archbishops both in the canon law just quoted and in the other authentic writings of the orthodox Fathers. Were you to read these attentively and reflect on what you had read, you would hold no opinion that was at variance with your mother church; you would not have said what you are said to have said: indeed were others to say it, you would check them with a salutary rebuke. No reasonable man can think that I am rashly encroaching on a jurisdiction that is not mine, for by God's mercy it is agreed that this whole island called Britain is within the undivided jurisdiction of our one church.

Banish the monk Hermann,[6] whose life is notorious for its many faults, from your society and your household completely. It is my wish that he live according to a rule in an observant monastery, or—if he refuses to do this—that he depart from the kingdom of England.

If so, he had perhaps strayed from some continental monastery in search of preferment; the author of the *Miracula* entered Bury St. Edmunds only after Herfast's death: F. Liebermann, *Ungedruckte anglo-normannische Geschichts-quellen* (Strasburg, 1879), pp. 225–8.

48

Lanfranc to Odo, abbot of Chertsey   c. *1084–28 May 1089*

The dating depends on Odo's installation and Lanfranc's death. Little is known of Odo; lines 12–15 suggest that Lanfranc had not met him. As Odo's predecessor, Wulfwold, had held Chertsey and Bath in plurality for many years, Gregory (who is otherwise unknown) may have been seeking a more observant house and equally been regarded by Lanfranc as the key to reform in Chertsey itself.

Lanfrancus archiepiscopus O. abbati salutem.

Fratrem Gregorium monachum tuum uolentem mare transire prohibuimus, et ad monasterium suum ei redire praecepimus et precipiendo compulimus. Tu non bene egisti quod ipsi uagandi[1]
5 extra patriam licentiam concessisti. In hoc satis euidenter apparet qualis pastor existas, et qua sollicitudine gubernare commissas tibi animas scias. Mandamus igitur et precipimus et precipiendo rogamus quatinus cum honore eum recipias, et de cetero sicut filio tuo paternam ei caritatem impendas. Credimus
10 enim per misericordiam Dei, si sollicitus tui ordinis esse uolueris, quod consilium et auxilium tam in causis spiritualibus quam in secularibus per eum habere ualebis. Laetificauit me multum quod
f. 34ᵛ timorem Dei te habere et bonum / hominem esse perhibuit, sed tamen pro simplicitate tua neglegentem te esse nostri ordinis
15 negare non potuit.

49

Lanfranc to Domnall Ua h-Énna, bishop of Munster, and his colleagues   *29 Aug. 1080–28 Aug. 1081*

A.L. date this letter to Lanfranc's eleventh year in office: it is certainly later than the initiative to Toirrdelbach Ua Briain prompted by Gregory VII (no. 10; cf. no. 8). Domnall was the leading Irish prelate of the day, and his inquiry shows the isolation of the Irish clergy proper as distinct from the Norse enclave in Dublin. As Toirrdelbach laid the foundations for the synods of Muirchertach his successor, so Domnall was a precursor of Malachy of Armagh and the 'reform'-minded native clergy of the twelfth century. Having answered Domnall's immediate inquiry (lines 13–41) Lanfranc turns from those who have never received communion to the Eucharist itself. Here he draws on his own treatise *De corpore et sanguine Domini*, expounding the meaning and effect of the sacrament (p. 158 n. 11) and citing two familiar proof-texts (pp. 158–9 nn. 12 and 15). The proof-texts lead to the condemnation of Lanfranc's old opponent, Berengar of Tours and those of his persuasion (p. 158 n. 13).

Lanfrancus indignus sanctae Cantuariensis aecclesiae antistes

48 NV

49 NVCcCpLv

48

Lanfranc to Odo, abbot of Chertsey   c. *1084–28 May 1089*

Archbishop Lanfranc greets Abbot O.

We have forbidden brother Gregory, your monk, to cross the sea as he wished to do; we have directed him to return to his own monastery and constrained him to obey. For your part, you acted unwisely in giving him permission to travel around[1] outside his own country. It is clear enough from this affair what kind of pastor you are and how conscientiously you guide the souls that are committed to your care. We therefore enjoin and direct you to receive him as a monk in good standing, and for the future to show him the fatherly love that you would to a son. It is our conviction that if you desire to take your own monastic profession seriously, you will by God's mercy find him a source of advice and help both in spiritual affairs and in secular. I rejoiced greatly that he assured me that you were a God-fearing and good man; but he could not deny that through your inexperience you are failing to live up to our monastic profession.

49

Lanfranc to Domnall Ua h-Énna, bishop of Munster, and his colleagues   *29 Aug. 1080–28 Aug. 1081*

Lanfranc, unworthy archbishop of the holy church of Canterbury

---

48 [1] Cf. St. Benedict's condemnation of unstable monks: 'semper uagi et numquam stabiles et propriis uoluntatibus et guilae inlecebris seruientes': *Benedicti Regula* i. 10–11, ed. R. Hanslik (C.S.E.L. lxxv, 1960), pp. 18–19.

uenerando Hiberniae episcopo D.[a] et iis qui sibi litteras trans-
miserunt salutem et benedictionem.

In itinere positi et a ciuitate in qua nobis sedes episcopalis est
5 longe sepositi eramus, quando litteras uestras nuntio uestro
deferente suscepimus.[1] Quem cum rogassemus ut saltem paucis
diebus nobiscum maneret, quatinus perquisitis libris congruum
pro captu nostro ad consulta uestra responsum uobis referret,
peticioni nostrae effectum negauit, et se diutius non posse morari
10 multis assertionibus allegauit. Itaque dulcissimam nobis fraternitatem uestram paterna caritate monemus ut[b] indignum uobis[c]
sit quod de tanta re tam breuiter respondemus.

Reuera et procul pulsa omni ambiguitate sciatis neque transmarinas aecclesias neque nos Anglos[2] hanc de infantibus tenere
15 sententiam quam putatis. Credimus enim generaliter omnes omnibus aetatibus plurimum expedire tam uiuentes[d] quam morientes
Dominici corporis et sanguinis perceptione sese munire. Nec
tamen, si prius quam corpus Christi et sanguinem sumant con-
tingat baptizatos statim de hoc seculo ire, ullatenus credimus eos
20 —quod Deus auertat—propter hoc in aeternum perire.[3] Alioquin
Veritas non esset uerax quae dicit: 'Qui crediderit et baptizatus
fuerit, saluus erit.'[4] Et per prophetam:[e] 'Effundam super uos
f. 35 aquam / mundam, et mundabimini ab omnibus inquinamentis
uestris.'[5] Quod de baptismo esse dictum omnes huius sententiae
25 expositores concorditer asseuerant. Et Petrus apostolus: 'Et uos
nunc similis formae saluos facit baptisma.'[6] Et Paulus apostolus: 'Quotquot in Christo baptizati estis, Christum induistis.'[7]
Christum est enim induere, habitatorem Deum per remissionem
peccatorum in se habere. Nam sententia illa quam Dominus in
30 euangelio dicit: 'Nisi manducaueritis carnem Filii hominis et
biberitis eius sanguinem, non habebitis uitam in uobis',[8] quantum
ad comestionem oris non potest[f] generaliter dicta esse de omnibus.
Plerique etenim sanctorum martirum ante baptismum quoque

---

    [a] Donato Lv   [b] ne NCcCpLv   [c] V[1] *adds* non   [d] V *ends*
(*see p. 21*)   [e] CcCpLv *add* Et   [f] potes Cp

49 [1] Cf. no. 45, lines 3–4.
    [2] Contrast no. 2, lines 42–3: 'Ego tamen nouus Anglus etc.'
    [3] The practice of giving a child communion immediately after baptism
is attested for ninth-century Ireland by the Stowe Missal (*The Stowe Missal*,
ed. G. F. Warner, London, 1915: Henry Bradshaw Soc. xxxii. ii. 32; cf. F. J.
Byrne, 'The Stowe Missal' in *Great Books of Ireland: Thomas Davis Lectures*

sends greetings and his blessing to the reverend D(omnall),
bishop of Ireland, and to those who sent him the letter.

We were on a journey and far removed from the city in which we
have our episcopal see when we received the letter that your
messenger brought.[1] Although we asked him to stay with us for
at least a few days, so that when we had fully studied the literature
he could take you back the answer to your inquiries of which
we were capable, he refused to accede to our request, asserting
very volubly that he could not delay any longer. So we warn you,
dearest brethren, whom we love as a father, that the reply is
inadequate which we are giving you so briefly on so serious a
matter.

You may be assured that it is absolutely beyond question that
neither the continental churches nor we English[2] hold the view
that you think we hold concerning infants. We do all universally
believe that it is of great benefit to people of all ages to fortify
themselves by receiving the body and blood of the Lord during
their lives and when they are dying. But should it happen that
baptized infants leave this world at once, before they receive the
body and blood of Christ, we do not in any sense believe—God
forbid!—that on this account they are lost for eternity.[3] Were
that so, the Truth would be untrue in saying, 'He who has
believed and been baptized shall be saved.'[4] And according to the
prophet, 'I shall pour pure water upon you and you will be cleansed
from all your filthiness.'[5] All the commentators on this passage
are unanimous in maintaining that it refers to baptism. The
Apostle Peter says, 'Now baptism, which follows a similar pattern,
saves you also.'[6] The Apostle Paul says, 'As many of you as have
been baptized in Christ have put on Christ.'[7] To 'put on Christ'
is to have God dwelling in you through the remission of sins.
For that text which the Lord utters in the Gospel, 'Unless you
shall eat the flesh of the Son of Man and drink his blood, you
will not have life in you',[8] cannot be applied to all men universally in the sense of eating in the mouth. Many of the holy martyrs,

(Dublin, 1967), pp. 38–50). As usual Irish evidence for the eleventh century is
lacking. On the Continent the question was debated in the school of Laon *c.* 1100:
O. Lottin, *Psychologie et Morale aux XIIᵉ et XIIIᵉ siècle*, v (Gembloux, 1959),
no. 372.

    [4] Mark 16: 16. For the equation of Christ and Veritas (John 14: 6) cf.
L.D.C.S.D., cap. 3: D'Achery, p. 233 (*PL* cl. 412c).

    [5] Ezek. 36: 25; cf. Jerome, *In Hiezechielem* xi, lines 836–8, ed. F. Glorie
(C.C.S.L. lxxv, 1964), p. 506.

    [6] 1 Pet. 3: 21.   [7] Cf. Gal. 3: 27.

    [8] John 6: 54.

diuersis excruciati poenis de corpore migrauerunt. Eos tamen in
35 numero martirum computat et saluos credit aecclesia, per illud
testimonium Domini quo dicitur: 'Qui me confessus fuerit coram
hominibus, confitebor et ego eum coram Patre meo qui est in
caelo.'⁹ Infantem quoque non baptizatum, si morte imminente
urgeatur, a fideli laico si praesbiter desit baptizari posse canones
40 precipiunt; nec eum tamen si statim moriatur a consortio fidelium
seiungunt.¹⁰ Necesse est ergo predictam Domini sententiam sic
intelligi, quatinus fidelis quisque diuini misterii per intelligentiam
capax carnem Christi et sanguinem non solum ore corporis sed
etiam amore et suauitate cordis comedat et bibat: uidelicet amando
45 et in conscientia pura dulce habendo quod pro salute nostra
f. 35ᵛ Christus / carnem assumpsit, pependit resurrexit ascendit, et
imitando uestigia eius, et communicando passionibus ipsius in
quantum humana infirmitas patitur et diuina ei gratia largiri
dignatur.¹¹ Hoc est enim uere et salubriter carnem Christi com-
50 edere et sanguinem eius bibere. Quam sententiam in libro De
Doctrina Christiana beatus Augustinus exponens sic ait: 'Facinus
uel flagicium iubere uidetur. Figura ergo est precipiens passioni
dominicae communicandum esse, et suauiter atque utiliter in
memoria recondendum quod pro nobis caro eius uulnerata et
55 crucifixa sit.'¹² Figuram uocat figuratam locutionem; neque enim
negat ueritatem carnis et sanguinis Christi, quod plerisque scisma-
ticis uisum est et adhuc non cessat uideri.¹³ Et Dominus in euangelio: 'Qui manducat carnem meam et bibit sanguinem meum in
me manet et ego in eo.'¹⁴ Quod exponens beatus Augustinus ait:
60 'Hoc est nanque carnem Christi et sanguinem salubriter comedere
et bibere: in Christo manere et Christum in se manentem habere.'¹⁵
Nam et Iudas qui Dominum tradidit cum ceteris apostolis ore
accepit; sed quia corde non comedit iudicium sibi¹⁶ aeternae
damnationis accepit.
65 Quaestiones secularium litterarum nobis soluendas misistis, sed
episcopale propositum non decet operam dare huiusmodi studiis.

---

⁹ Cf. Matt. 10: 32 and Luke 12: 8.
¹⁰ Elvira, can. 38 (Hinschius, p. 341).
¹¹ Cf. L.D.C.S.D., cap. 17: D'Achery, pp. 243D–4A (PL cl. 429BC).
¹² Augustine, De Doctrina Christiana iii. 55, ed. G. M. Green (C.S.E.L. lxxx, 1963), pp. 93–4; cf. L.D.C.S.D., cap. 17 (PL cl. 429BC).
¹³ Lanfranc is writing more than a year after Berengar's final recantation (Feb. 1079), the text of which did reach England, but perhaps not in Lanfranc's lifetime: Brooke, English Church, pp. 231–3.

racked by various tortures, departed from the body without even being baptized. Yet the Church reckons them in the number of martyrs and believes them to be saved, following the Lord's assurance that 'He who shall confess me before men, him will I confess also before my Father who is in heaven.'[9] Again canon law directs that an unbaptized infant at the point of death can be baptized by a lay believer if no priest is available; nor does it cut him off from the community of the faithful if he dies immediately after.[10] Therefore the Lord's saying must be understood in this way. Let every believer who can understand that it is a divine mystery eat and drink the flesh and blood of Christ not only with his physical mouth but also with a tender and loving heart: that is to say, with love and in the purity of a good conscience rejoicing that Christ took on flesh for our salvation, hung on the cross, rose and ascended; and following Christ's example and sharing in his suffering so far as human weakness can bear it and divine grace deigns to allow him.[11] This is what it means to eat the flesh of Christ and drink his blood truly and unto salvation. Blessed Augustine expounds this text in his book *De Doctrina Christiana*, where he says, 'He seems to be ordering us to commit an outrage or an obscene act. It is therefore a figure of speech: we are directed to share in the Lord's suffering and to meditate tenderly and profitably on the fact that it was for us that his flesh was wounded and crucified.'[12] It is figurative speech that Augustine calls 'a figure'. He does not (as many schismatics have thought and have not yet ceased to think)[13] deny that the flesh and blood of Christ are really present. The Lord himself says in the Gospel, 'He who eats my flesh and drinks my blood dwells in me and I in him.'[14] Blessed Augustine expounds this text as follows: 'To eat and drink the flesh and blood of Christ unto salvation is to dwell in Christ and have Christ dwelling in you.'[15] Even Judas who betrayed the Lord, received in his mouth as the other Apostles did; but because he did not eat in his heart he received the judgement[16] of eternal damnation.

You also sent problems of profane learning for us to elucidate; but it does not befit a bishop's manner of life to be concerned with

---

[14] John 6: 57.
[15] Cf. Augustine, *Tractatus in Iohannem* xxvi. 18, ed. R. Willems (C.C.S.L. xxxvi, 1954), p. 268.
[16] Cf. 1 Cor. 11: 29.

Olim quidem iuuenilem aetatem in his detriuimus,[g] sed accedentes
ad pastoralem curam[17] abrenuntiandum eis decreuimus.

50

Lanfranc to Margaret, queen of Scotland   1070–89

This letter is an isolated survival of complex negotiations: (i) that Lanfranc
should be spiritual adviser to Queen Margaret—a relationship that her daughter
Matilda, Henry I's queen, endeavoured to maintain with Archbishop Anselm
(Southern, *Anselm*, pp. 191–3); (ii) that Christ Church should establish a
daughter-house in Dunfermline, the first regular Benedictine monastery in
Scotland. In a sense the two run parallel: archbishop to queen and community to community. Although Lanfranc's primatial jurisdiction is never
mentioned, these new arrangements could not but reinforce it; the metropolitan
jurisdiction of York was still only potential (no. 3, lines 111–17), and would in
any case be exercised through the diocesan clergy rather than through an alien
priory. In the long run however it was not the archbishops of Canterbury
who effected the modernization of the Scottish Church but monks from Durham
and the new international orders, particularly the Cistercians.

Lanfrancus indignus sanctae Cantuariensis aecclesiae antistes
gloriosae Scotorum rigine M. salutem et benedictionem.

f. 36   Explicare non potest / epistolaris breuitas quanta cor meum laetitia
perfudisti, perlectis litteris tuis quas michi Deo amabilis regina
5   misisti. O quanta iocunditate uerba profluunt quae diuino Spiritu
inspirata procedunt! Credo enim non a te sed per te dicta
esse quae scripseras. Reuera per os tuum locutus est ille qui
discipulis suis ait, 'Discite a me quia mitis sum et humilis
corde.'[1] De hac Christi disciplina processit quod regali stirpe
10   progenita, regaliter educata, nobili regi nobiliter copulata, me
hominem extraneum uilem ignobilem peccatis inuolutum in
patrem eligis, teque michi in filiam spiritualiter habendam pre-
caris.[2] Non sum quod putas, sed sim quia putas. Ne decepta
remaneas ora pro me, ut sim dignus pater orare Deum et exaudiri
15   pro te. Orationum et benefactorum sit inter nos commune com-
mercium. Parua quidem tribuo, sed multo maiora me recepturum
esse confido. Dehinc igitur sim pater tuus, et tu mea filia esto.

Mitto glorioso uiro tuo et tibi carissimum fratrem nostrum
domnum Goldeuuinum secundum petitionem tuam, alios quoque
20   duos fratres; quia quod de seruitio Dei et uestro fieri oportet
solus ipse per se explere non posset.[3] Et rogo multumque rogo

_____

[g] decreuimus CcLv   Lv *ends here with* Valete

_____

50 N

studies of that kind. Long ago in our youth we did devote our time to these matters, but when we came to pastoral responsibility[17] we decided to give them up altogether.

50

Lanfranc to Margaret, queen of Scotland   *1070–89*

Lanfranc, unworthy archbishop of the holy church of Canterbury, sends greetings and his blessing to Margaret, the glorious queen of the Scots.

In the brief span of a letter I cannot hope to unfold the joy with which you flooded my heart when I studied the letter that you sent me, o Queen beloved of God. With what holy cheer the words flow on which are uttered by the inspiration of the Holy Spirit! I am convinced that what you had written was said not by you but through you: by your mouth of a truth he spoke, who says to his disciples, 'Learn of me, for I am meek and lowly in heart.'[1] It is as a result of Christ's teaching here that you, who are born of a royal line, brought up as befits a queen and nobly wedded to a noble king, are choosing me as your father—a foreigner of neither birth nor worth, who is ensnared in sin: and you ask me to accept you as my spiritual daughter.[2] I am not what you think me to be; but may I be so because you think it. Do not continue under that misapprehension: pray for me that I may be a father fit to pray to God for you and have my prayers granted. Let there be a mutual exchange between us of prayers and good works. Those that I render are small indeed; but I am confident that I shall receive far greater benefits in return. From now on then may I be your father and be you my daughter.

I am sending your glorious husband and yourself our very dear brother Dom Goldwin as you asked me to, and two other brothers with him; for he could not accomplish single-handed what is required in God's service and your own.[3] I do most urgently

---

[17] It is uncertain whether Lanfranc reckons his 'pastoral care' from *c.* 1045 (prior of Bec) or from 1063 (abbot of St. Étienne, Caen) or even 1070 (archbishop of Canterbury).

50 [1] Matt. 11: 29.
  [2] Cf. the aristocratic Eva Crispin, who yet treats Lanfranc's nephew as her spiritual son (no. 20, lines 13–17).
  [3] For Queen Margaret's establishment of Holy Trinity, Dunfermline see G. W. S. Barrow, *The Kingdom of the Scots* (London, 1973), pp. 193–5, with references.

quatinus quod pro Deo et pro animabus uestris coepistis instanter
et efficaciter perficere studeatis. Et si possetis aut uelletis opus
uestrum per alios adimplere, multo desiderio uellemus hos fratres
nostros ad nos redire, quia ualde in officiis suis necessarii erant
aecclesiae nostrae. Fiat tamen uoluntas uestra, quia in omnibus
25 et per omnia desideramus oboedire uobis. /
f. 36ᵛ   Omnipotens Dominus uos benedicat, et ab omnibus peccatis
clementer absoluat.

51

Lanfranc to the archdeacons of Bayeux

1082–9 Sept. 1087

The concluding sentence (lines 21–2) and the fact that Lanfranc has been
asked to intervene at all imply a date during Bishop Odo's imprisonment.
The archdeacons of Bayeux active in the 1080s were Goscelin and Ralph (both
occ. *c.* 1075–82; 1092) and perhaps Bernard (occ. *c.* 1075–82): Rouen, Archives
Départementales Seine-Maritime 14 H. 160 (Goscelin, Ralph, Bernard) and
V. Bourrienne, *Antiquus Cartularius Ecclesiae Baiocensis* (Société de l'Histoire
de Normandie, Rouen–Paris, 1902), i. 30 (Goscelin, Ralph); I am indebted
here to the help of Dr David Bates. The letter as a whole is a good practical
illustration of the legal and pastoral responsibilities of an archdeacon.

Lanfrancus indignus antistes sanctae Baiocensis aecclesiae archidiaconis salutem.

Indicauit michi litteris suis Constantiensis episcopus¹ quendam
praesbiterum uillae suae in parrochia uestra sitae² manibus suis
5 fecisse homicidium, cum contra moriturum se defenderit et
patrem suum. Addidit quoque consilium meum super hac re uos
uelle habere: si uel nunquam uel post quantum temporis missam
homicidae liceat celebrare. Periculose fratres mei a me de hac re
uobis respondetur, cum reus reique uita a me penitus ignoretur.
10 Quam si aut propria experientia aut ueracium relatione cognitam
tenerem, multo tutius fraternitati uestrae de tanta re respondere
ualerem.ᵃ Vos igitur, quorum officii id interest, uitam eius per-
quirite: uidelicet quomodo uixerit, quomodo uiuat, si humiliter
poeniteat, si doleat, si lugeat, maxime si castitatem sui corporis de
15 reliquo seruare disponat eamque usque ad finem uitae suae ser-
uaturum³ se esse promittat.ᵇ Haec et huiusmodi alia poenitentis

51 NLz
ᵃ Quam si—ualerem *om.* Lz   ᵇ eamque—promittat *om.* Lz

entreat you to strive to complete the work that you have begun
for God and your souls' welfare as quickly and effectively as you
can. Should you be able to achieve it with the help of others, or
wish to do so, we most fervently desire that our own monks should
return to us, for in the positions they held they were really indispensable to our church. But let it be your decision: in all
respects we entirely desire to render you obedience.

May the Lord almighty bless you and mercifully free you from
all your sins.

51

Lanfranc to the archdeacons of Bayeux
1082–9 Sept. 1087

Lanfranc, an unworthy bishop, greets the archdeacons of the holy
church of Bayeux.

The bishop of Coutances[1] has told me in his letter that a certain
priest on an estate of his that lies within your jurisdiction[2] has
personally committed homicide in defending himself and his
father against the man who subsequently died. He added too that
you wish to have my advice on this point: after how long a time, if
ever, can a homicide be permitted to celebrate Mass. It is hazardous, my brothers, for me to give you an answer on this point when
I know nothing whatever about the guilty man or his manner of
life. If I could gain some knowledge of his life either by personal
interview or by a report from trustworthy witnesses, I should be
able to give you a ruling with much greater security, my brothers,
on so grave a question. So examine his life, for that is one of the
duties of your office: in other words, how he has lived in the past,
how he is living now, whether he is doing penance with humility,
whether he grieves and weeps, and above all whether he is deter-
mined to maintain physical chastity from now on and promises
that he will maintain it until the end of his life.[3] If you discern

---

[1] Geoffrey de Montbray: see J. Le Patourel, 'Geoffrey of Montbray, bishop
of Coutances (1049–1093)', *E.H.R.* lix (1944), 129–61.

[2] i.e. an estate that formed part of the endowments of Coutances but lay
within the diocese of Bayeux; cf. similar estates held by Canterbury within the
diocese of Chichester (no. 30).

[3] See Introduction, p. 8.

indicia si in eo esse deprehenderitis, peracta poenitentia licentiam celebrandi missam dare ei potestis.[c] Alioquin periculosum uobis et illi perniciosum erit,[d] si pollutis manibus corpus Christi et
20 sanguinem sanctificare presumpserit.

Omnipotens Dominus uos benedicat, et de pastore uestro desideratam uobis laeticiam tribuat.

52

Lanfranc to Hu(go Candidus)
25 June 1080–25 May 1085

The limiting dates are the election of the antipope Clement III and the death of Gregory VII; Lanfranc's reference to Henry IV's military success (lines 11–12) suggests that he is writing after Clement's consecration in Rome (24 Mar. 1084). The recipient is traditionally identified as Hugo Candidus, cardinal priest of San Clemente, who—like Ermenfrid of Sion (no. 1, n. 1)—had gone over to the emperor; this is a reasonable conjecture for which there is no further evidence either way. Certainly 'Hu' speaks for Clement III, who himself wrote to Lanfranc on three occasions: F. Liebermann, 'Lanfranc and the antipope', *E.H.R.* xvi (1901), 328–32. None of these letters met with any response: from the election of Clement III until the consecration of Archbishop Anselm (4 Dec. 1093) England neither maintained relations with Gregory VII and his successors nor recognized Clement III; nos. 38–9 above are the last known communication with Gregory.

Lanfrancus Hu.[1]

f. 37 Litteras tuas quas michi per portitorem mearum / misisti suscepi et legi, et displicuerunt michi quaedam quae in eis inueni. Non probo quod papam Gregorium uituperas, quod Hildebrandum
5 eum uocas, quod legatos eius spinosulos nominas,[2] quod Clementem tot et tantis preconiis tam propere exaltas. Scriptum est enim non esse laudandum in uita sua hominem nec detrahendum proximo suo.[3] Adhuc incognitum est humano generi quales nunc sint et quales futuri sint in conspectu Dei. Credo tamen quod
10 gloriosus imperator sine magna ratione tantam rem non est aggressus patrare, nec sine magno Dei auxilio tantam potuit uictoriam consummare.[4] Non laudo ut in Anglicam terram uenias, nisi a rege Anglorum licentiam ueniendi prius accipias.[5] Nondum enim

---

[c] Lz *ends*   [d] V *begins (see p. 21)*

---

52 NV

in him these and other similar signs that he is penitent, you can give him permission to celebrate Mass when his penance is complete. But if not, it will be hazardous for you and disastrous for him if with unclean hands he dare to sanctify the body and blood of Christ.

May the Lord almighty bless you and grant you the joy that you long for in the matter of your bishop.

52

Lanfranc to Hu(go Candidus)

25 June 1080–25 May 1085

Lanfranc to Hu.[1]

I have received and read the letter which you sent me by the messenger who brought you mine: certain passages which I found in it displeased me. I disapprove of your attacks on Pope Gregory, calling him Hildebrand and labelling his legates 'thick-heads',[2] and your readiness to laud Clement with such a paean of praise. It is written that a man should not be praised in his lifetime, nor his neighbour slandered.[3] What men are like now in the sight of God and what they shall be like hereafter is still unknown to them. But it is my conviction that the glorious emperor did not undertake such a mighty achievement without good cause, nor could he have gained so notable a victory without great assistance from God.[4] I am not in favour of your coming to England unless you first get permission to come from the king of the English.[5] Our

52 [1] The shortest salutation in the collection, perhaps by scribal accident perhaps to avoid mutual recognition of titles.

[2] Cf. Jerome, *Epistulae* 69. 2. 5, ed. I. Hilberg (C.S.E.L. liv, 1910), p. 68: 'spinosulus noster'. This contemptuous term for an opponent in debate has already been noticed by Cardinal Humbert, who extends the metaphor thus Spinosulus is made to unfold the beginning, middle and end of his evil desig just as a hedgehog uncurls its head, feet and tail when dropped in water (*A versus Simoniacos* I. vii, ed. F. Thaner, *MGH, Libelli de Lite* i: Hanover 18 p. 111).   [3] Cf. Ecclus. 11: 30; Ps. 100

[4] Note that Henry IV, long excommunicate, is still 'gloriosus imperat it was difficult for William the Conqueror's clergy not to see victory in ba as a sign of divine approval.

[5] Hu. no doubt hoped to collect Peter's Pence, which was significant p revenue in this period: Liebermann, art. cit., p. 332; cf. no. 39 above.

insula nostra priorem refutauit, nec utrum huic oboedire debeat
15 sententiam promulgauit. Auditis utrinque causis, si ita contigerit,
perspicacius quid fieri oporteat peruideri ualebit.

53

Lanfranc to Gundulf, bishop of Rochester
                                    19 Mar. 1077–28 May 1089

The recipient is identified only in Lz; the other manuscripts have 'G'. Hence
Helen Clover preferred the identification with Bishop Geoffrey of Coutances,
acting as the king's justice somewhere in England. I have accepted Gundulf,
mainly because it is not a case for a king's justice, even though the king (as we
see) has been consulted. What strikes the eye are the Anglo-Saxon women
fleeing to convents in the early years of the Conquest; but the more common
and enduring situation was the young girl of good family, convent-educated,
who wished to leave and get married. Lanfranc's ruling was cited in just such
a case in 1100, when Matilda of Scotland, who had been living at Wilton,
wished to marry Henry I: Eadmer, *H.N.*, pp. 121–5; Southern, *Anselm*,
pp. 182–90.

Lanfrancus archiepiscopus uenerabili G.ᵃ episcopo salutem et
seruitium.

De sanctimonialibus de quibus dulcissima michi paternitas uestra
ad me litteras misit hoc uobis respondeo.ᵇ Sanctimoniales quae de
5 seruanda regula professionem fecerunt, uel quae quamuis adhuc
professae non sint ad altare tamen oblatae fuerunt,¹ secundum
mores et uitas earum ad seruandam regulam moneantur, in-
crepentur, constringantur. Quae uero nec professae nec oblatae
9 sunt, ad praesens sic dimittantur, donec uoluntates earum de
f. 37ᵛ seruando ordine / subtilius exquirantur. Quae uero non amore
religionis sed timore Francigenarum sicut uos dicitis ad monasterium confugerunt, si hoc firmo meliorum sanctimonialium
testimonio probare possunt, libera eis recedendi concedatur
potestas.ᶜ Et hoc est consilium regis et nostrum.
15   Omnipotens Dominusᵈ uitam uestram in beneplacito suo conseruet.

53 NVLz
   ᵃ Gundulfo Lz   ᵇ De sanctimonialibus—respondeo *om.* Lz   ᶜ Lz
ends   ᵈ Deus V

island has not yet repudiated the one nor decided whether to obey the other. When the case for both sides has been heard (if that should happen), it will be possible to see more clearly what is to be done.

53

Lanfranc to Gundulf, bishop of Rochester

19 Mar. 1077–28 May 1089

Archbishop Lanfranc sends his respectful greetings to the reverend Bishop G(undulf).

Concerning the nuns about whom you wrote to me, dearest father, I give you this reply. Nuns who have made profession that they will keep a rule or who, although not yet professed, have been presented at the altar,[1] are to be enjoined, exhorted and obliged to keep the rule in their manner of life. But those who have been neither professed nor presented at the altar are to be sent away at once without change of status, until their desire to remain in religion is examined more carefully. As to those who as you tell me fled to a monastery not for love of the religious life but for fear of the French, if they can prove that this was so by the unambiguous witness of nuns better than they, let them be granted unrestricted leave to depart. This is the king's policy and our own.

May the Lord almighty preserve your life according to his own good pleasure.

---

53 [1] i.e. a decision is required: either by the woman herself (taking vows when she is an adult) or by her parents (presenting her as an oblate when she is a child).

54

Lanfranc to Abbot W.   *1072–28 May 1089*

The dating limits are Serlo's election (1072: line 4) and Lanfranc's death. As Serlo found Gloucester very decayed and made it a model of 'religionis discretio' (*Gesta Pontificum*, pp. 292–3), we may assume that Lanfranc is writing some time after Serlo's arrival. Abbot W. cannot be securely identified. Given that his house was probably within reach of Gloucester, he may be Warin of Malmesbury (1070–*c*. 1091) or Walter of Evesham (1077–1104), Lanfranc's former chaplain. The implied laxity of Abbot W.'s house points to Warin as marginally the more likely.

Lanfrancus archiepiscopus carissimo amico suo abbati W. salutem.

Rogo te quantum rogare possum et debeo, quatinus huic fratri Rainaldo concedas licentiam conuersandi apud Gloecestram cum abbate Serlone per spatium unius anni. Expedit enim animae 5 suae ut hoc fiat. Huius nanque indicium hinc permaxime capio quod regularem locum petit—quamuis et monasterio tuo in quo nutritus est in nullo detrahat; sed cur hoc facere uelit rationabilem causam enarrat. Iterum rogo ne moleste feras quod ad me uenit, quod me amicum tuum pro necessitate sua expetiit.[1]

55

Lanfranc to Riwallon, abbot of New Minster

1082–88

Dated by the reference to Dom Godfrey the prior, who can only be the prior of Winchester cathedral (1082–1107; cf. *Gesta Pontificum*, pp. 172–3). Given that the bishop of Winchester has an interest (line 7), the obvious abbot within his diocese is Riwallon of New Minster (1072–88), the second monastic community in Winchester itself. Having blundered in his assessment of the unnamed monk, Lanfranc here gives the abbot and the local bishop (or his representative) full authority to settle the case.

Lanfrancus archiepiscopus abbati R. salutem.

Quod fratrem de quo michi scripsit fraternitas tua in monasterium recipiendum cum meis litteris tibi direxi, teste conscientia mea diuino id zelo et amore nostri ordinis feci. Neque enim gratia 5 uitandi scandali aliquid uolo uel rogare uel precipere quod aliquo modo in maius uel deterius scandalum ualeat prouenire. Loquere igitur cum episcopo[1] si forte adest et cum domno Godefrido

54 NV
---
55 NVH

54

Lanfranc to Abbot W.   *1072–28 May 1089*

Archbishop Lanfranc greets his well-beloved friend, Abbot W.

I urge you as wholeheartedly as I can and may to give brother Rainald (who brings this letter) leave to be a monk at Gloucester with Abbot Serlo for a period of one year. It is to his spiritual advantage to do so. I find particular evidence for this in his search for an observant monastery—although he is in no way criticizing your own monastery in which he was brought up; he gives a sound reason for wanting to take this step. Once again I urge you not to be offended that he has come to me, or rather that in his need he has sought me out as your friend.[1]

55

Lanfranc to Riwallon, abbot of New Minster

1082–88

Archbishop Lanfranc greets Abbot R(iwallon).

In sending you the monk about whom you wrote to me, my brother, with my letter recommending that he be admitted to your monastery, I do assure you on my conscience that I acted from a godly and zealous devotion to our monastic life. In order to avoid scandal I do not wish to give any directive or advice that may in any way cause the scandal to worsen or increase. Discuss the matter with the bishop,[1] should he be available, and with Dom

---

54 [1] Cf. no. 22: 'quatinus ipse amicum uestrum pro commissi sui uenia se petiuisse cognoscat'.

---

55 [1] Walchelin, bishop of Winchester (1070–98).

priore eius; et quicquid super hoc negotio inter uos consulueritis
f. 38 et consultum opere complendum decreueritis, in omnibus / et
10 per omnia michi quoque placere noueritis. Neque enim superbiam
nutrire uolo, quam procul ab omni genere hominum et precipue a
nostro ordine remotam esse desidero.

56

Lanfranc to S. 1086

The passage 'in illis comitatibus quorum exquirendorum tibi cura commissa est'
(lines 9–10) strongly suggests that Lanfranc is writing *à propos* of the Domesday Inquest. As it was only in Essex and Suffolk that all the Christ Church lands
were held by the monks rather than the archbishop, he is addressing an official
concerned with circuit VII (Norfolk, Essex, Suffolk): F. Barlow, 'Domesday
Book: a letter of Lanfranc', *E.H.R.* lxxviii (1963), 284–9. The identification of
S. is more difficult; two possible candidates are Suain, sheriff of Essex and Samson, the future bishop of Worcester: see respectively Barlow, loc. cit., and V. H.
Galbraith, 'Notes on the career of Samson, bishop of Worcester (1096–1112)',
E.H.R. lxxxii (1967), 86–101.

Lanfrancus indignus antistes dilecto et fideli amico suo S. salutem
et benedictionem.

Gratias ago benignae sollicitudini tuae et sollicitae benignitati
tuae, quia amiciciam quam[a] a primordio mutuae cognitionis michi
5 promisisti re ipsa cum opportunitas se ingessit semper demon-
strare studuisti. Et nunc precor multumque precor, quamuis non
tantopere precibus indigeas, quatinus de praesenti negotio tantum
rebus nostris ualeas, quantum ualere fuerit tibi desuper data
facultas. Scias autem in illis comitatibus quorum exquirendorum
10 tibi cura commissa est me nichil in dominio habere, sed omnes in
illis partibus nostrae aecclesiae terras ad uictum monachorum per
omnia pertinere.[1] Frater noster qui has tibi litteras portat multa
laudanda de te michi retulit, quorum pluralitas et epistolaris
breuitas ea nunc enumerari non sinit. Sed omnipotens Deus cuius
15 memoriam nichil subterfugit[2] sicut nouit multipliciter tibi
rependat, et ab omni opere malo pius[b] auxiliator te incessanter
defendat.

56 NVH
[a] *om.* V   [b] prius V

Godfrey his prior; and whatever decision you jointly reach on this affair and decide to implement, be assured that it has my full assent in all respects. I have no desire to encourage pride: I long for it to be removed from every class of men, and from our monastic life above all.

56

Lanfranc to S.   1086

Lanfranc, an unworthy bishop, greets his dear and loyal friend S. and sends him his blessing.

I am most grateful for your thoughtfulness and goodwill, in that from the outset of our acquaintance you have assured me of your friendship and whenever the occasion offered you have always been ready to prove it in practice. Now once more I pray and beseech you—though you have no need of so many prayers— to act as effectively on our behalf in this present business as the opportunity to do so is given you from on high. I confirm that in those counties in which you have been assigned the duty of making an inquest I have no demesne land; all the lands of our church in those parts are entirely given over to providing food for the monks.[1] The brother who is bringing you this letter has told me a great deal in your favour, too much to be set out here within the brief limits of a letter. May almighty God, whose memory nothing escapes,[2] recompense you according to his knowledge many times over and be your vigilant helper at all times to defend you from every evil machination.

---

56 [1] *Domesday Book* ii. 8; 372–3. No mention is made of Little Stambridge (Essex: one hide), a monastic manor that contributed to the upkeep of the archbishop's knights: F. R. H. du Boulay, *The Lordship of Canterbury* (London, 1966), pp. 46, 81–3.

[2] A wry contrast with the officials who were drawing up Domesday Book.

57

Lanfranc to Abbot Thurstan   *1070–73 or 1083*

The possible recipients of this letter are the abbots of Ely (?1066–72/3), Glastonbury (*c.* 1077/8–1096+) and Pershore (1085–7). Although Pershore may be discounted, Ely and Glastonbury both have a claim. Thurstan of Ely was involved in the Fenland resistance of 1069–72: *Liber Eliensis* ii. 100–12, ed. E. O. Blake (Camden 3rd ser., xcii, London, 1962), pp. liv–lvii, 169–95, with references. Thurstan of Glastonbury faced a monastic riot in 1083: Orderic, *Hist. Eccles.* ii. 270–1, with references. Certainly the king had a more direct interest in the political resistance at Ely than in the internal disturbances at Glastonbury.

Lanfrancus indignus antistes abbati Turstino salutem.

Consilium meum tibi breuiter intimandum rogasti, et ego illud tibi paucis intimare curaui. Roga Deum ut meminerit tui et misereatur tibi, et hoc instanter tam per te quam per amicos tuos; nos
5 uero hoc agimus in quantum possumus. Domino nostro regi offer
f. 38ᵛ rectitudinem per amicos / et perᵃ fideles internuntios. Si spreuerit, noli multum inde esse tristis neque sollicitus. Visitabit enim Deus plebem suam[1] cum expedire decreuerit.

Misericordia Dei tecum sit.

58

Lanfranc to Abbot G.   *1070–89*

Abbot G. has not been identified. The tone of the letter probably excludes Gilbert Crispin, abbot of Westminster (*c.* 1085–1117/18: cf. no. 20 above) and the circumstances of his appointment certainly exclude Guy, abbot of St Augustine's, Canterbury (1087–93: cf. A.L., pp. 290–2). The remaining candidates are Gausbert, abbot of Battle (*c.* 1076–95), Geoffrey, abbot of Tavistock (*c.* 1082–*c.* 1088), Gunter, abbot of Thorney (1085–1112), Geoffrey, abbot of Westminster (occ. 1072) and—perhaps the most likely—Galannus, abbot of Winchcombe (1066–75+).

Lanfrancus indignus antistes uenerabili abbati G. salutem et benedictionem.

Gratias quantas possum paternitati uestrae ago, quod presentes et absentes nobis et de nobis bona dicitis, meliora obtatis, utrumque
5 uerbis et litteris confirmatis. Et reuera sciatis me eandem circa uos

57 NV
ᵃ *om.* V
___
58 NV

57

Lanfranc to Abbot Thurstan   *1070–73 or 1083*

Lanfranc, an unworthy bishop, greets Abbot Thurstan.

You asked me to give you my advice in brief; that is what in a few words I have endeavoured to give you. Pray God to be mindful of you and have mercy on you; do so urgently both yourself and through your friends: we personally are offering such prayers as we can. Offer satisfaction to our lord the king through your friends and through loyal intermediaries. If he will not listen, do not be too dejected or anxious on that account: God will come to the help of his own people[1] when he deems it right to do so.

God have mercy on you.

58

Lanfranc to Abbot G.   *1070–89*

Lanfranc, an unworthy bishop, sends greetings and his blessing to the reverend Abbot G.

I thank you most heartily, father, that whether present or absent you say favourable things to me and about me and expect better, and that you confirm these expressions both by the spoken word and in writing. Indeed you may be assured that I have the same

57 [1] Cf. Luke 7: 16.

uoluntatem habere, et uobis et uestris sinceram dilectionem in
omnibus et per omnia exhibere. Quod de domno Vrricio mandastis
gratanter accipio, sed contra preceptum regis nil rogare et nil
iubere praesumo. Sed rogo multumque rogo quatinus propter
10 Deum et propter amorem meum et quia ipse dignus est eum
diligatis, honeste tractetis, paternum ei affectum sicut prudentia
uestra iudicauerit impendatis. Pro iusticia nanque persecutionem
patitur,[1] et cum superna uoluntas fuerit in gaudium sibi et laetitiam
conuertetur.[2] Misertus est tamen ei Dominus quod inter uos eum
15 uoluit esse, et putantes nocere sicut Domino placuit plurimum
profuere.

59

Lanfranc to Maurice, bishop of London
5 Apr. 1086–28 May 1089

The extreme dates are Maurice's consecration and Lanfranc's death. Nothing
further is known of the dispute between the abbess of SS. Mary and Ethelburga,
Barking and her prioress. The abbess was still Ælfgyva until at least 7 Mar.
1087: see *Studia Monastica* vii (1965), 437–44, 387. Barking was a non-exempt
house within the diocese of London; we do not know why Bishop Maurice
was so reluctant to intervene.

Lanfrancus archiepiscopus dilecto amico suo M. episcopo salutem.

Sicut in aliis litteris in his quoque rogamus et monemus et
pastorali auctoritate precipimus, quatinus si uobis oportunum est
Bercinge eatis, et auditis utrinque querelis abbatissam esse abba-
5 tissam et priorem esse priorem iubeatis. Vtraque in suo ordine sit
f. 39 sicut / oportet, et sicut beati Benedicti *Regula* iubet.[1] Maior
precipiat, minor oboediat, si tamen ea praeceperit quae congruis rationibus conueniant et quibus sacrae auctoritates minime
contradicant. Vtraeque quae Dei sunt et quae seculi sunt seruata
10 suorum ordinum dignitate communi consilio agant, sanctimoniales
et clerici et laici tam intus quam extra eis seruiant et oboediant.
Quaecunque illarum hanc constitutionem nostram praetergressa
fuerit uestra annitente instantia corripiatur, et ne conceptam
praesumptionem adimpleat competenti seueritate compescatur.
15 Quod si discordia in tantum partes armauerit ut earum sententia
in unam concordiam conuenire non possit, res nobis innotescat,
ut cuius culpa fuerit regulari districtioni subiaceat.

59 NVH

goodwill towards you and that I display in all respects and in every way I can an unfeigned love for you and your monks. I am pleased to receive your recommendation about Dom Ulric, but I cannot take the responsibility for giving any directive or order that is contrary to the king's instructions. But I do most earnestly beg you for God's sake, and because I love him and because of his own merits, to cherish him, treat him well and show him such fatherly affection as you think wise. He is suffering persecution for righteousness' sake,[1] and when God wills it will be changed for him into joy and gladness.[2] In placing him among you the Lord has shown him mercy and those who wish to injure him have, as it has pleased the Lord, acted to his great advantage.

59

Lanfranc to Maurice, bishop of London
5 Apr. 1086–28 May 1089

Archbishop Lanfranc sends greetings to his dear friend Bishop Maurice.

As in previous letters we again enjoin, require and by our pastoral authority direct that if you have the opportunity you go to Barking and, when you have heard both sides of the dispute, order the abbess to be an abbess and the prioress a prioress. Let each behave as befits her station and as the *Rule of St. Benedict* commands.[1] Let her who is senior give directions and her who is junior obey, so long as these directions are reasonable and do not in any way conflict with canon law. Let each of the ladies do God's work and the world's by mutual consultation in a way appropriate to her station; and let the nuns, clergy and laity both within the convent and beyond serve and obey them. If either of them violates our ruling, you shall sternly rebuke her and with due severity restrain her from continuing in her obstinacy. But if the parties are so at loggerheads that they cannot achieve concord, let us know, so that the offender may be subjected to the discipline of the Rule.

58 [1] Matt. 5: 10.
   [2] Cf. Ps. 50: 10.

59 [1] *Benedicti Regula* ii (abbot) and lxv (prior), ed. R. Hanslik (C.S.E.L. lxxv, 1960), pp. 19–27, 152–5.

60

Lanfranc to Abbot T.   *1070–89*

None of the principals here has been identified. Abbot T. may be any of the abbots Thurstan (Ely, Glastonbury, Pershore) noted in no. 57 or Theodwine of Ely (?1073–5/6) or Turold of Peterborough (1070–98): Glastonbury and Peterborough seem the most likely. (The very reading 'abbati T.' is open to question: perhaps the scribe of N wrote not 'T' but lower-case 'r'. In that case Riwallon of New Minster is the leading candidate; cf. no. 55 above.) As the case was heard in London and this letter immediately follows Lanfranc's letter to Bishop Maurice (no. 59), Godwin and Lifgiva may have belonged to the diocese of London. On the other hand, the case may have come from another diocese to a provincial synod held in London: e.g. in 1075 or 1077–8 (A.L., p. 289).

Lanfrancus archiepiscopus dilectissimo amico suo abbati T.ᵃ salutem.

Causam Goduini et Lifgiuae adulterae suae optime noui, et reuera Lundoniae coram me eam uestigari precepi. Auditaque
5 utriusque partis assertione in adulteros sententiam diximus, et iuste eos esse excommunicatos communi consensu decreuimus. Propterea nichil aliud restat, nisi quod fraternitas tua adulteram de cimiterio eici precipiat, quousque uel corruptor eius uel aliquis pro ea quod iustum est episcopo¹ faciat. Libenter facerem quod tibi
10 posse placere intelligerem, et multum doleo quod de praesenti negotio uoluntatem tuam implere non ualeo.

61

Lanfranc to William, abbot of S. Étienne, Caen
                                    autumn 1070

Given the recipient's close association with Bec, it is reasonable to identify him as William 'Bona Anima', monk of Bec and Lanfranc's successor as abbot of S. Étienne. The departing prior (lines 5–6) is thus Gundulf, who is going to join Lanfranc in Canterbury (autumn 1070). Ernost (line 11) was indeed chosen as the next prior; when he in turn went to England to be bishop of Rochester (cons. 29 Aug. 1075–spring 1076), he was succeeded by Helgot (pre-1078–92; cf. *Anselmi Epp.* 29, 48).

Dulcissimo patri W. L., quondam dulcissimus et utinam nunc

---

60 NV
ᵃ N *arguably reads* r

---

61 NV

60

Lanfranc to Abbot T.   *1070–89*

Archbishop Lanfranc greets his beloved friend Abbot T.

I am fully informed about the case of Godwin and his mistress Lifgiva; indeed I ordered it to be examined in my presence at London. When we had heard a statement by both parties, we gave sentence against the adulterers and with general assent decreed that they were justly excommunicate. So there is nothing further to do except for you, my brother, to order the adulteress to be cast out from the burial-ground until either the man who ruined her or someone on her behalf makes a settlement with the bishop.[1] I would gladly do what I know would meet with your approval, and greatly regret that in this particular affair I am unable to comply with your wishes.

61

Lanfranc to William, abbot of S. Étienne, Caen
autumn 1070

To William his dearest father, Lanfranc—once dearest to him

---

60 [1] Abbot T.'s diocesan: i.e. *either* the bishop of Dorchester (if Ely or Peterborough) *or* the bishop of Wells (if Glastonbury) *or* the bishop of Worcester (if Pershore).

f.39ᵛ saltem / dulcis, quicquid in hoc seculo et in futuro honestius
et melius.

In litteris quas nuper transmisistis hoc precipue inter cetera
5 posuistis et rogastis, ut amoto eo qui nunc presidet de substituendo
aecclesiae uestrae priore uobis consulerem, consultaque sub cele-
ritate rescriberem. Quam rem fratribus qui mecum sunt ostendi,
michique consulere uolenti quatinus ipsi quoque consulerent
obnixe rogaui. Communis omnium sententia fuit: ut si aliquo
10 secundum Deum modo efficere ualeatis, summum aecclesiae
uestrae priorem domnum Ernostum constituatis.¹ Quod si ipse
rennuerit aut fortasse domnus abbas² huic rei consensum prebere
noluerit, ordinate quem concors fratrum electio ordinandum esse
decreuerit. Si uero hoc uobis consilium displicuerit, capite illud
15 quod sanum sapienti displicere non poterit: uidelicet ut idᵃ agatis
quod ex ore domni abbatis Herluini domnique Anselmi agendum
esse cognoueritis. Nam et ego ut peccator homo diuini consilii
ignarus existo, et ipsi utrique ut credimus spiritu Dei pleni sunt
et secum habent qui in huiusmodiᵇ negociis apud Deum adiuuare
20 eos ualent.

Diuina maiestas uenerande pater iocundeque frater te benedicat,
atqueᶜ ab omnibus peccatis prorsus absoluat. Vale.

ᵃ *om.* V   ᵇ huius mundi V   ᶜ *om.* V

and still, he trusts, at least dear—wishes whatever is most worthy and good in this world and the next.

In the letter which you have just sent me you made this request more urgently than the others: that when the man who is now in charge is removed I should advise you on whom to put in his place as prior of your church, and that I should send you that advice with all due speed. I put the question to the brothers who are with me here, urgently requiring that as I desired to give advice they in turn should advise me. We were all in agreement that if with God's help you can by any means bring it about you should make Dom Ernost the chief prior of your church.[1] If he declines, or if the lord abbot[2] should withhold his consent, let the appointment be decided by the unanimous choice of the brethren. If this advice is unacceptable to you, take that advice which can be unacceptable to no reasonable and judicious man: act according to the advice you receive personally from the lord abbot Herluin and from Dom Anselm. For I am a sinful man who has no understanding of God's counsel, whereas both of them are, we believe, filled with the spirit of God and have men with them who in affairs of this kind can give them support in their prayers to God.

May the divine majesty bless you, the father I revere and the brother in whom I rejoice, and set you wholly free from all sins. Farewell.

61 [1] Ernost is 69th in the Bec profession-roll: A. A. Porée, *Histoire de l'abbaye du Bec* (Évreux, 1901), i. 629. He appears briefly in *Anselmi Epp.* 25 and Robert of Torigny, *Chronicle* s.a. 1089, ed. L. Delisle (Rouen, 1872–3: *Société de l'histoire de Normandie*), i. 73.

[2] i.e. Herluin, abbot of Bec.

APPENDIX A

BIBLIOGRAPHY

i. *Editions*

1605   Rome   C. Baronius, *Annales Ecclesiastici* vol. xi. s.a. 1070: nos. 3, 1, 6, 2; s.a. 1071: no. 7; s.a. 1072: nos. 3, 4, 5; s.a. 1073: no. 8; s.a. 1075: no. 11; s.a. 1079: nos. 38, 39; s.a. 1088: no. 46; s.a. 1089: nos. 9, 10.
Reprinted Mainz 1606, Antwerp 1608, Cologne 1609, etc.

1613   London   J. Ussher, *Gravissimae Quaestionis de Christianarum Ecclesiarum . . . Statu Historica Explicatio*, p. 182: no. 39.
Reprinted *Whole Works* (Dublin, 1864), ii. 200.

1623   London   J. Selden, *Eadmeri Monachi Cantuariensis Historiae Novorum libri vi*, p. 164: no. 39; pp. 201–2: nos. 12, 13.

1626   Douai   C. Reyner, *Apostolatus Benedictinorum in Anglia*, Appendix p. 211: letter to Prior Henry (App. B).

1632   Dublin   J. Ussher, *Veterum Epistolarum Hibernicarum Sylloge*, pp. 68–75: letter from Dublin (App. B), nos. 9–10, 49.
Reprinted Dublin, 1864: *Whole Works* iv. 488–97.

1648   Paris   L. d'Achery, *Beati Lanfranci Cantuariensis archiepiscopi . . . opera omnia*, pp. 12–14: nos. 3, 11; pp. 299–376: nos. 1–2, 4–10, 12–49, 52–61.
Reprinted Venice, 1745, pp. 219–67.

1671   Paris   Ph. Labbé and G. Cossart, *Sacrosancta Concilia ad regiam editionem exacta* ix. 1211A–24E: nos. 3, 4, 26, 23, 14, 43, 47, 40, 45, 30, 53, 49, 33, 60, Indicatum est mihi (spuria); x. 306B–7A: no. 8; 346D–50D: no. 11.

1714   Paris   J. Hardouin, *Acta Conciliorum et Epistolae Decretales ac Constitutiones Summorum Pontificum* VI. i. 1173–88: nos. 3, 4, 26, 23, 14, 43, 47, 40, 45, 30, 53, 49, 33, 60, Indicatum est mihi (spuria); ibid., cols. 1555–60: no. 11.

1737 London   D. Wilkins, *Concilia Magnae Britanniae et Hiberniae* i. 324–9: nos. 3, 7, 4, J.L. 4761 (App. B), letter to Prior Henry (App. B); ibid., i. 361–5, 368: nos. 49, 12–13, 11, 30.

1775 Venice   J.-D. Mansi, *Sacrorum Conciliorum Nova et Amplissima Collectio* xx. 19–34: nos. 3, 4, 26, 23, 14, 43, 47, 40, 45, 30, 53, 49, 33, 60, Indicatum est mihi (spuria); ibid., xx. 449–56: no. 11.

1844 Oxford/   J. A. Giles, *Beati Lanfranci Opera* i. 19–80: nos.
      Paris   1–2, 4–10, 12–61; ibid., 85–6: letter to Prior Henry (App. B); see further App. B (d).

1854 Paris   J.-P. Migne, *Patrologiae cursus completus series latina* cl. 515–624: nos. 1–2, 4–6, 9–10, 12–61; ibid., 443C–5D: letter to Prior Henry (App. B); ibid., cxlvi. 1365: no. 7; cxlviii. 643: no. 8.

1902 Leipzig   H. Boehmer, *Die Fälschungen Erzbischof Lanfranks von Canterbury*, pp. 165–73: nos. 3, 4.

1951 London/   D. Knowles, *The Monastic Constitutions of*
      Edinburgh   *Lanfranc*, N.M.T., pp. 1–3: letter to Prior Henry (App. B).
    Reprinted Siegburg, 1967: *Corpus Consuetudinum Monasticarum*, ed. K. Hallinger, iii. 3–4.

1963 London   F. Barlow, 'Domesday Book: a letter of Lanfranc', *E.H.R.* lxxviii. 289: no. 56.

ii. *Translations and Calendar*

1844 Oxford/   J. A. Giles, *Beati Lanfranci Opera* i, pp. xiv–xvi:
      Paris   no. 1.

1862 London   W. F. Hook, *Lives of the Archbishops of Canterbury*, ii, pp. 122–4: no. 1; pp. 136–57: nos. 34, 39, 38, 52, letter from Dublin (App. B), 50, 13, 43, 47, 30.

1913 Oxford   H. W. C. Davis and R. J. Whitwell, *Regesta Regum Anglo-Normannorum* i, nos. 64–5, 78–83, 280: calendars nos. 3, 31–6, 27.

1926 Oxford   A. J. Macdonald, *Lanfranc: A Study of His Life, Work, and Writing, passim*: nos. 1, 47, 57, 48, J.L. 4761 (App. B), 19, 20, 50, 13, 31–6, 38, 52–3; fragments—18, 21, 16, 17, 41, 15.
    Reprinted Oxford, 1944.

1929	New York	J. F. Kenney, *The Sources for the Early History of Ireland: Ecclesiastical,* nos. 635–8: letter from Dublin (App. B), nos. 9–10, 49; i.e. as Ussher (1632), with summary in English. Reprinted New York, 1966.
1951	London/ Edinburgh	D. Knowles, *The Monastic Constitutions of Lanfranc,* N.M.T., pp. 1–3: letter to Prior Henry (App. B).
1953	London	D. C. Douglas, *English Historical Documents* ii. 636–49: nos. 1, 50, 47, 30, 13, 39, 38, 52. Reprinted London, 1961; 1968.

iii. *Secondary literature*

For a bibliography of Lanfranc's works as a whole see Gibson, Appendix D. Studies specifically of the Letters are:

1913	Tamworth	R. White, *The 'Epistolae Lanfranci' proved a forgery:* nos. 1–61. (A deservedly obscure publication, which proves nothing.)
1958	London	R. W. Southern, 'The Canterbury Forgeries', *E.H.R.* lxxiii. 193–226: no. 4.
1963	London	F. Barlow, 'Domesday Book: a letter of Lanfranc', ibid., lxxviii. 284–9: no. 56.
1967	London	V. H. Galbraith, 'Notes on the Career of Samson, Bishop of Worcester (1096–1112)', ibid., lxxxii. 86–101: no. 56.
1967	Lille	H. Clover, 'Alexander II's Letter *Accepimus a quibusdam* and its Relationship with the Canterbury Forgeries', in *La Normandie bénédictine,* ed. G.-U. Langé, pp. 417–42: no. 4.

APPENDIX B

EPISTOLAE VAGANTES AND SPURIA[1]

(a) LANFRANC to Prior Henry

Mittimus uobis nostri ordinis	*Constitutions*, pp. 3-4 (1st edn., N.M.T., 1951, pp. 1-3)	1079/89

(b) PAPAL LETTERS TO LANFRANC

Nicholas II

Satis desideratam[2]	J.L. 4446	1059-61

Alexander II

Quisquis diuina[3]	J.L. 4644	14 Jan. 1068
Gratias omnipotenti[2]	J.L. 4669	1063-70
Accepimus a quibusdam[4]	J.L. 4761	1071-3
Peruenit ad aures[5]	J.L. 4762	1071-3

Gregory VII[6]

Non minima ammiratione	J.L. 4803: G.VII, *Reg.* i. 31	20 Nov. 1073
Quod ex illo tempore	J.L. 5121: G.VII, *Reg.* vi. 30	25 Mar. 1079
Saepe fraternitatem tuam	J.L. 5228: G.VII, *Reg.* ix. 20	May-June 1082

[1] The handlist that follows gives the principal manuscripts and printed editions, without attempting either to be exhaustive or to say how the manuscripts and the printed editions are related. See further Gibson, App. A and D ad loc.

[2] MS. Cambridge, Trinity Coll., B. 16. 44 pp. 211 and 405.

[3] MS. Paris, B.N., nouv. acq. lat. 1406: J.L. 4644.

[4] MSS. London, B.L., Cotton Cleopatra E. I f. 52ra-va; Harley 633 f. 59ra-va; Durham, Cath. Lib., B. IV. 18 f. 70^r-v; Cambridge, Univ. Lib., Kk. 4. 6 f. 278rb-va: D'Achery 4.

[5] MSS. London, B.L., Harley 633 ff. 58vb-9ra; Cambridge, Univ. Lib., Kk. 4. 6 f. 278ra-rb: J.L. 4762, printed by H. Wharton, *Anglia Sacra* (London, 1691), i. 322, cf. 320.

[6] MS. Vatican, Archives, Registrum Vaticanum 2 ff. 20^v-1, 167^r-v, 225^r-v: J.L. 4803 (D'Achery 20), 5121, 5228.

Clement III (antipope)[1]

Fraternitati tuae	*c.* 1085–6
Nouerit caritas tua	1088–9
Benedictus sit Deus	*c.* 1086–9

Urban II

Non latere credimus[2]	J.L. 5351	10 Apr. 1088

(*c*) OTHER LETTERS TO LANFRANC

Anselm[3]

As prior	*Anselmi Epp.* 1, 14, 23, 25, 27, 32, 39, 49, 57, 66, 72, 77	1070–78
	prefatory letter to the *Monologion* (Schmitt i. 5–6)	1077
As abbot	*Anselmi Epp.* 89, 90, 103, 124	1078–89

Berengar of Tours

Peruenit ad me, frater Lanfrance[4]	*PL* cl. 63CD	1049

Clergy and people of Dublin

Vestrae paternitati est cognitum[5]	*PL* cl. 534C–5A	1074

(*d*) SPURIA

Two letters and a charter have been wrongly ascribed to Lanfranc:

1. *Letter to Ralph, abbot of S. Vito, Verdun*

inc: Indicatum est mihi quia de tuo monasterio recedere uis . . .

---

[1] Cambridge, Trinity Coll., B. 16. 44 pp. 405–6: printed by F. Liebermann, 'Lanfranc and the Antipope', *E.H.R.* xvi (1901), 328–32.

[2] MS. London, B.L., Cotton Claudius E. V f. 245ra–rb (Lc): J.L. 5351.

[3] MS. London, B.L., Cotton Nero A. VII ff. 41–112^v (see p. 16 above) and others: Schmitt iii. 94, with references.

[4] MSS. Brussels, Bibliothèque Royale, 4399–4402 f. 62 and Paris, B.N., lat. 1858 f. 107^r–v: critical edition by R. B. C. Huygens, 'Textes latins du xie au xiiie siècle', *Studi Medievali* viii (Spoleto, 1967), 451–9.

[5] MS. London, B.L., Cotton Cleopatra E. I f. 28rb (Le): D'Achery 36. The letter petitions Lanfranc to consecrate Patrick, bishop of Dublin; see further A. Gwynn, *The Writings of Bishop Patrick 1074–1084* (Dublin, 1955: *Scriptores Latini Hiberniae* i), p. 2.

MSS: Brussels, Bibl. Roy., 302 f. 110ᵛ (s. xiii); Cambridge, Trinity Coll., O. 7. 9 ff. 175ᵛ–6 (s. xii: Buildwas, O. Cist.); London, B.L., Harley 3098 ff. 66ᵛ–7 (s. xii¹: English); Paris, Bibl. Arsenal, 391 f. 12 (s. xiii: St. Victor), 539 f. 203ᵛ (4 Oct. 1469: Ste Croix, Namur);¹ Rouen, Bibl. Mun., 115 f. 100ᵛ (s. xii: French).

D'Achery 60; Giles 66.

A discussion of monastic stability that fits uneasily with Lanfranc's known opinions. The manuscript tradition is entirely separate from that of Lanfranc's letters. See further G. Morin, 'Rainaud l'ermite et Ives de Chartres: un épisode de la crise du cénobitisme au xıᵉ–xııᵉ siècle', *Revue Bénédictine* xl (1928), 109–10; Gibson, p. 243. It is hoped to discuss the text and influence of this letter more fully elsewhere.

2. Letter from L. to I.

inc. Quotiescunque necessariis . . .

MS: Brussels, Bibl. Roy., 10615–729 (s. xii: S. Matthias, Trier).

J. A. Giles, *Anecdota Bedae Lanfranci et aliorum* (London, 1851: Caxton Society vii), pp. 79–83.

Giles assumed, on no discernible evidence, that the 'L.' of the salutation should be expanded to 'Lanfrancus'.

3. Charter in favour of St Mary's, Southwark

inc. Concedimus et presentis carte pagina confirmamus . . .

MS: London, B.L., Cotton Nero C. III f. 188 (original: 1139–47).

Giles 67; *PL* cl, no. 63 (from Giles).

Here Giles has attributed to Lanfranc an original charter of Archbishop Theobald (in which 'Teobaldus' is abbreviated to 'T.'): see further A. Saltman, *Theobald, Archbishop of Canterbury* (London, 1956), no. 252; Gibson, p. 207. For other charters, genuine and spurious, see Gibson, pp. 206–7.

¹ C. Samaran and R. Marichal, *Catalogue des manuscrits en écriture latine portant des indications de date, de lieu ou de copiste* i (1959), p. 97.

APPENDIX C

CONCORDANCE WITH THE
ACTA LANFRANCI

The *Acta Lanfranci* are based on material preserved in Christ Church, much of which is still extant.[1] The compiler certainly used Lanfranc's letters; in year 7 they lead him into chronological error.[2] Equally it is clear from the following table that his staple documents were the episcopal professions to Canterbury and the records of councils.[3] In what follows 'abb.' = abbot, 'bp.' = bishop.

Acta Lanfranci	*Letters*	*Other documents*
1. Aug. 1070–Aug. 1071	no. 3, lines 1–50	
2. Aug. 1071–Aug. 1072	no. 3, lines 51–80	council of Winchester;[4] profession of Osbern, bp. Exeter (Richter no. 35); profession of Scotland, abb. St Augustine's, Canterbury[5]
3. Aug. 1072–Aug. 1073	Nil	profession of Peter, bp. Lichfield (not extant); plea on Penenden Heath[6]
4. Aug. 1073–Aug. 1074	nos. 9–10	profession of Patrick, bp. Dublin (Richter no. 36)

[1] *Acta Lanfranci*, in *Two of the Saxon Chronicles Parallel*, ed. C. Plummer and J. Earle (Oxford, 1892–9), i. 287–92.   [2] See Introduction, p. 11.

[3] See respectively Richter and *Councils and Synods*; for a brief hand-list see Gibson, pp. 211–12.

[4] Easter 1072: Osbern of Exeter, who was consecrated 'post dies paucos', witnesses the council of Windsor (Whitsun 1072) as bishop. See further *Councils and Synods* ad loc.

[5] C. Eveleigh Woodruff, 'Some early professions of canonical obedience to the see of Canterbury by heads of religious houses', *Archaeologia Cantiana* xxxvii (1925), 60.

[6] J. Le Patourel, 'The reports of the trial on Penenden Heath', in *Studies in Medieval History presented to F. M. Powicke*, ed. R. W. Hunt and others (Oxford, 1948), pp. 15–26. See further D. R. Bates, 'The land pleas of William I's reign: Penenden Heath revisited', *Bull. Inst. Hist. Res.* li (1978), 1–19.

Acta Lanfranci	*Letters*	*Other documents*
5. Aug. 1074–Aug. 1075	no. 11	= council of London
6. Aug. 1075–Aug. 1076	Nil	profession of Ernost, bp. Rochester (Richter no. 38); council of Winchester; Ernost's obit[1]
7. Aug. 1076–Aug. 1077	nos. 12–13	profession of Gundulf, bp. Rochester (Richter no. 39)
8. Aug. 1077–Aug. 1078	Nil	council of London
9. Aug. 1078–Aug. 1079	Nil	Nil
10. Aug. 1079–Aug. 1080	Nil	Nil
11. Aug. 1080–Aug. 1081	no. 49	council of Gloucester; consecration of William, bp. Durham[2]
12. Aug. 1081–Aug. 1082	Nil	Nil
13. Aug. 1082–Aug. 1083	Nil	Nil
14. Aug. 1083–Aug. 1084	Nil	Nil
15. Aug. 1084–Aug. 1085	Nil	Nil
16. Aug. 1085–Aug. 1086	Nil	profession of Donngus, bp. Dublin (Richter no. 42) council of Gloucester; professions of Robert, bp. Chester (Richter no. 45), William, bp. Elmham (Richter no. 43) and Maurice, bp. London (Richter no. 44)
17. Aug. 1086–Aug. 1087	Nil	Nil
18. Aug. 1087–Aug. 1088	Nil	coronation of William Rufus;[3] professions of Geoffrey, bp. Chichester (Richter no. 46), Guy, abb. St Augustine's, Canterbury[4] and John, bp. Wells (Richter no. 47);

[1] Ernost was commemorated in Christ Church on 15 July: Le Neve/Greenway, p. 75.

[2] 3 Jan. 1081: *Historia Dunelmensis Ecclesiae* iv, in *Symeonis Monachi Opera*, ed. T. Arnold (R.S., 1882), i. 119. William's profession to Archbishop Thomas does not survive.

[3] Cf. Orderic, *Hist. Eccles.* iv. 96, 110.

[4] Woodruff, op. cit. (p. 186, n. 5 above), p. 61.

Acta Lanfranci	*Letters*	*Other documents*
		revolt at St Augustine's, Canterbury[1]
19. Aug. 1088–May 1089	Nil	Lanfranc's obit[2]

revolt at St Augustine's;[1] interregnum in Christ Church; consecration of Anselm, 4 Dec. 1093

[1] The only detailed account of the revolt against Abbot Guy, who was imposed on St Augustine's by Lanfranc and Odo of Bayeux: A.L., pp. 290–2.
[2] Gibson, pp. 227–9.

INDEX OF RECIPIENTS

INDEX OF INCIPITS

GENERAL INDEX

Bold numbers refer to **Letters,** normal type to pages.

Entries in text and translation are indexed with both page numbers. Names are given under the form used in the translation; persons before 1500 are indexed by first name, those after 1500 by surname. Counties follow the pre-1974 boundaries.

L. = Lanfranc. var. = variant

INDEX OF MANUSCRIPTS

INDEX OF QUOTATIONS AND ALLUSIONS

A. THE BIBLE

B. CLASSICAL, PATRISTIC, AND MEDIEVAL SOURCES